The Wandering Fictions of George Borrow

A Literature on the Move 1840–1940

Andrew D. Radford

EDINBURGH
University Press

Edinburgh University Press is one of the leading university presses in the UK. We publish academic books and journals in our selected subject areas across the humanities and social sciences, combining cutting-edge scholarship with high editorial and production values to produce academic works of lasting importance. For more information visit our website: edinburghuniversitypress.com

Edinburgh University Press Ltd
13 Infirmary Street
Edinburgh EH1 1LT

First published in hardback by Edinburgh University Press 2025

Typeset in 11/12.5 Baskerville by
IDSUK (DataConnection) Ltd, and
printed and bound by CPI Group (UK) Ltd,
Croydon, CR0 4YY

A CIP record for this book is available from the British Library

ISBN 978 1 3995 4642 3 (hardback)
ISBN 978 1 3995 4643 0 (paperback)
ISBN 978 1 3995 4644 7 (webready PDF)
ISBN 978 1 3995 4645 4 (epub)

Contents

Figures

Acknowledgements

'There are many Borrows in English literature,' according to critic Lafcadio Hearn, 'but there is only one Borrow worth remembering.' I had managed to finish an English Literature undergraduate degree without studying any of Borrow's works. Much later, while researching a very different topic, on successful expeditions to Mount Everest, I read Sir John Hunt in the 1954 *National Geographic*. He did remember. Enduring a day's rest at nearly 26,000 feet, Hunt 'settled down for the afternoon with George Borrow's book *Wild Wales*'. Getting from that reference to here has been a long road. I have been helped on my trek by many friends, colleagues and students. First, a warm thanks to the George Borrow Trust (Charity Number 1114630) for providing the financial support which made the publication of my 2023 critical edition of George Borrow's *Lavengro* possible. I owe a major debt of gratitude to David Storie and Dr Clive Wilkins-Jones, who are responsible for all matters relating to the Borrow Trust in the UK and overseas. Preparing that *Lavengro* text at the National Library of Scotland – a hugely enjoyable experience – laid the groundwork for arguments developed in this monograph about the fluctuating, open-ended relation between place and person.

I am grateful for this chance to publish a study of Borrow with Edinburgh University Press. I have had the good fortune to work with the Press on a few projects over the years. The eagle-eyed Fiona Conn, Emily Sharp and Elizabeth Fraser have all been there to steer me through the book production process. The anonymous reviewers who assessed my draft chapters helped me sharpen the close readings in numerous ways. For their astute questions, and for lending me a sympathetic ear, I am grateful to audience members at the various events where I have spoken about this project. I presented a first sketch of my *Wild Wales* chapter at a symposium on long nineteenth-century travelogues at Aberystwyth University in 2019. Those in attendance supplied excellent pointers on the structure and choreography of my monograph. I was able to make the final push to complete this book thanks to a sabbatical in 2024/5. In that time John Wedgwood Clarke, Ian Duncan, Gillian Fenwick, Faye Hammill, Vassiliki Kolocotroni, Nigel Leask, Anthony Leyland, Rob Maslen and Briony Wickes generously suggested leads, tips and helpful directions. An appreciative thank you as well to Helen Southworth, an expert on modernist magazines and cultures, who helped me navigate the contents of *The Tramp* journal. Roger Ebbatson's 2005 book *An Imaginary England* stretched my thinking on myths of home/land and sparked what would become the seed of my chapter on *Lavengro* and *The Romany Rye*. At a time when I was struggling to theorise Borrow's rambling narrative design in *Wild Wales*, Rhian Williams scrutinised and annotated an unwieldy typescript.

Finally, it is a pleasure to acknowledge the artist Djovan, whose Borrovian artwork 'Silhouette of person walking on forest road in dark woodland' is featured on my book cover. I hope it brings Djovan's striking computer art to a wider audience.

CHAPTER 1

INTRODUCTION: A BLAST FROM THE PAST

SNOBBISH BORROVIAN running after
GIPSY KINGS and ESPADAS
bowing the knee to
wild Mother Nature,
her feminine contours,
Unimaginative insult to
MAN.[1]

Amid the devilment and frantic *BLAST*-ing of the years 1837 to 1900 by Wyndham Lewis and his 'blood-thirsty Vorticists'[2] is a sketch of what might seem nowadays a quaint cultural phenomenon or type: the 'snobbish Borrovian'. According to the *OED*, 'Borrovian' (n. & adj.) entered the English language around 1888, the same year as the formal establishment of the Gypsy Lore Society and its quarterly journal.[3] A 'Borrovian' is a dedicated admirer or imitator of George Borrow (1803–1881), a novelist, translator, and colporteur for the British and Foreign Bible Society. Robert Thurston Hopkins, in *George Borrow, Lord of the Open Road* (1922), hailed 'Borrovians' as disciples of the noble Order of 'the Free Foot'. Invoking Augustine Birrell's earlier conception of 'the born Borrovian'[4] from *Res Judicatae: Papers and Essays* (1892), Hopkins extolled – like E. V. Lucas's *The Open Road* (1905) and Hilaire

1. Wyndham Lewis, ed., *Blast: Review of the Great English Vortex* (London: John Lane, 1914), 19.
2. Augustus John, *Chiaroscuro: Fragments of Autobiography* (New York: Pellegrini & Cudahy, 1952), 83.
3. On the early membership of the Gypsy Lore Society see Angus Fraser, 'A Rum Lot', in *100 Years of Gypsy Studies*, Publications of the Gypsy Lore Society, 5, ed. Matt Salo (Cheverly, MD, 1990), 1–14.
4. See Augustine Birrell, 'George Borrow', *Res Judicatae: Papers and Essays* (London: Elliot Stock, 1896), 120.

Belloc's *The Footpath Way* (1911) – the untold benefits of tramping 'on the highway':

> Borrovians are born not made. To be truly sensible of all Borrow's charm, one must be born with the unfettered will and daring joy of the gipsy – one must possess the untrammelled joyousness of the Free Foot. [. . .] There is nothing like a good walk for taking the foolishness out of one! Facing the wind god on the highway the walker knows the wild joy of living; teeth set, muscles clean and taut, the brain clearing as the rich blood bounds along its scarlet arteries.[5]

Borrow, an indefatigable walker, made it his vocation to record the language, costume, and usages of Romani and other Traveller communities, especially in the Iberian Peninsula, as recounted in his 1843 best-seller *The Bible in Spain*. Strictly speaking, the young Lewis of *BLAST No. 1* is not fulminating against Borrow the intrepid author-explorer. The cosmopolitan localities (Brittany, the Pyrenees) and bizarrely comic events recounted in Lewis's technically flamboyant early prose sketches – some, like 'A Spanish Household', published in his friend Douglas Goldring's short-lived 'open air magazine' *The Tramp* (1910–11) – *borrow* from his literary ancestor's sportive blend of travel memoir, shaggy dog tale, *choses vues*, and picaresque romp.[6] In *BLAST 1*, Lewis aims his satirical salvoes elsewhere. He targets Edwardian faddists who subscribed or contributed to monthly magazines such as *The Idler.* For these Borrovians, 'gypsy kings' were blithe romantic rogues with kraal-shaped blanket-tents and garishly decorated carts, not the familiar sight of dishevelled, footsore, and famished outsiders harried from town to town by uncaring law enforcement.[7] Lewis implies that the typical Borrovian's engagement with their literary idol's generically wayward and intellectually adventurous texts extended no further than Borrow's supposed adoration of a 'Mother Nature' whose 'wild' contours had been tamed, diluted, and domesticated for mass consumption.

The chief snob or high priest of this Borrovian sect, for whom 'gypsies' personified, an unsullied 'England of heath and common and windy sheep down',[8] was portraitist Augustus John. This 'rising star

5. R. Thurston Hopkins, *George Borrow, Lord of the Open Road* (London: Jarrolds, 1922), 18–19.
6. See Ian Duncan, 'Towards a Modernist Poetic: Wyndham Lewis's Early Fiction', in *Wyndham Lewis: Letteratura/Pittura*, ed. Giovanno Cianci (Palermo, 1982), 78–9.
7. See James Mortimer, 'The Cult of the Vagabond', *The Idler* 33:70 (July 1908): 425–31.
8. Kenneth Grahame, 'A Bohemian in Exile', *St James's Gazette* (27 September 1890). See Grahame, *Pagan Papers*, sixth ed. (London: John Lane, 1898), 137–8.

of British painting at the turn of the new century' met Lewis in 1903 and described the latter, not altogether warmly, as playing 'the part of an incarnate Loki' and 'sowing discord with it'.[9] Gazing back into the 'very dark cavern' of his past in *Rude Assignment* (1950), Lewis claimed that John's fixation on Romani mores, stirred by a selective (or inattentive) reading of Borrow, had shaped an ostentatiously hobohemian artistic brand: 'Following in the footsteps of Borrow, he was one of those people who always set out to do the thing that "is not done", according to the British canon.'[10] It was probably John who first introduced Lewis to Borrow's major prose narratives, such as *The Zincali* (1841), *The Bible in Spain*, *Lavengro* (1851), *The Romany Rye* (1857), and *Wild Wales* (1862).[11] John was a committed enough Borrovian to acquire the rudiments of 'the Romani tongue' – so injecting *billet-doux* to his many mistresses with a piquant rhetorical savour. In an essay-cum-hatchet job on his mentor for *BLAST No. 2* (War Number, July 1915), Lewis took umbrage at 'Mr. John's stage-gypsies emptying their properties over his severe and often splendid' gift as a painter, etcher, and draughtsman. The charismatically dashing John, with his 'barbaric chevelure', was now, Lewis grumbled, a fusty 'institution like Madame Tussaud's', a melodramatic holdover from a fin de siècle when decadent poseurs like Oscar Wilde and Aubrey Beardsley ruled the popular scene. In Lewis's lament, John had betrayed his unparalleled formal precocity. Rejecting the graft and craft required to transform graphic and painterly style, John was instead churning out works of lucrative but stodgy traditionalism: 'Rembrandtesque drawings of brown stumpy people, followed by his tribes after tribes of archaic and romantic Gitanos and Gitanas'.[12] *BLAST*-era Lewis evokes the 'Borrovian snob' John as an unrepentantly raffish performer of gypsy alterity whose exotic subject matter thrilled 'to the bone' the 'delicate and charming gentlemen and ladies of England' – wealthy dabblers seeking vestiges of 'wild life' beyond the doorstep of their Belgravia townhouses.[13] Accepting John's apology for his fuming public reaction

9. David Cottington, *Radical Art and the Formation of the Avant-Garde* (New Haven and London: Yale University Press, 2019), esp. Chapter 8; John, *Chiaroscuro*, 73.
10. Wyndham Lewis, *Rude Assignment: A Narrative of my Career Up-To-Date* (London: Hutchinson & Co., 1951), 118–19. On John's 'immoderate enthusiasm for gypsies', see Bernard Lafourcade's edition of Wyndham Lewis, *The Complete Wild Body* (Santa Barbara: Black Sparrow Press, 1982), 256.
11. See Peter Carter, 'Lewis, Borrow, John and the Gitanos: a Note on a Misunderstanding', *Wyndham Lewis Annual* (1998): 27–8.
12. See Lisa Tickner, *Modern Life and Modern Subjects: British Art in the Early Twentieth Century* (New Haven and London: Yale University Press, 2000), 49–65.
13. Wyndham Lewis, 'History of the Largest Independent Society in England', *BLAST No. 2 (War Number)* (London: John Lane, 1915), 80.

to the piece in *BLAST No. 2*, Lewis deprecated the painter's now 'boring Borrovian cult of the Gitane'.[14] In short, it was Borrow's misfortune that his once talismanic name and oeuvre, by the start of World War I, had become, at least for Lewis's Futurist-Vorticist confrères, enmeshed with the stale gypsophilia of London's more moneyed social and artistic cenacles, little better than *BLAST*-ed cultural relics and whiskered worthies like 'Codliver Oil' and 'Edward Elgar'.

The Road not Taken

This is the first full-length enquiry into Borrow's prose works and his modern(ist) afterlives when legion Borrovians, 'snobbish' or otherwise, reassessed or recreated the most enticing aspects of his goliardic travels. Such recovery work is vital. One of the roles of literary criticism is, in my view, to ascertain why culturally consequential texts that were once runaway bestsellers – Borrow's publisher John Murray brought out five editions of *The Bible in Spain* between December 1842 and July 1843 – become sidelined, mere footnotes in the Victorian canon.[15] Over a century later, the *TLS* reported a 'general reluctance among commentators to devote an entire book' to Borrow's peripateticating – to adopt the transitive verb coined by Robert Southey.[16] Such a 'book' – advocating that we give more serious thought to the anatomy and resonances of Borrow's literary language – has yet to be published. 'It is not easy to say why one should, or should not, read any writer,' critic George M. Hyde once mused. 'But maybe it is harder to answer such a question in the case of a writer who has been dropped from publishers' lists and university syllabuses so completely as Borrow has'.[17] Over the years a handful of high-profile campaigners such as A. S. Byatt have proposed that a reconsideration of Borrow's 'extraordinary' oeuvre might 'change some of our current ideas about the hierarchy of English writers'.[18] However, Ian Duncan's view is sobering, and difficult to quarrel with: 'Today

14. Wyndham Lewis, *The Letters of Wyndham Lewis*, ed. W. K. Rose (London: Methuen & Co., 1962), 70.
15. See Monika Mazurek, 'George Borrow: The Scholar, The Gipsy, The Priest', in *Victorian Fiction Beyond the Canon* (London: Palgrave, 2016), 84.
16. S. Norman, 'Vagabond and Polyglot', *Times Literary Supplement* (19 September 1958): 530; Robert Southey, *The Collected Letters of Robert Southey: Parts One-Six*, Lynda Pratt, Tim Fulford, and Ian Packer, gen. eds (Romantic Circles Electronic Edition, 2009–17), https://romantic.circles.org/editions/southey_letters, 1087
17. George M. Hyde, 'Why (Not) Read George Borrow?', *Kyoto Women's University Journal* (2002): 29.
18. A. S. Byatt, 'The Scholar Gypsy', *The Times* (2 December 1982): 10.

few Victorian scholars' at international academic conferences, symposia and seminars 'even bother to mention Borrow', who retains a modest circle of followers but comparatively few diligent readers.[19] The current state of the research field makes Thomas Seccombe's cheerful 1912 forecast – 'it would not be surprising if by 2100 A.D.' Borrow had 'become a star of the first magnitude' – seem Panglossian.[20] Seccombe made this prediction when it was admitted 'by all men of taste' that Borrow was 'a deathless British author'.[21]

Although the Lavengro Press was established in 2014 to promote and publish for sale material associated with the prolific Borrow, Anglo-American university presses have been slow to commission new critical editions of his major fiction and travelogues. The only option is for students to obtain second-hand copies of the so-called 'definitive' editions released at the turn of the twentieth century by John Murray. That Borrow has trudged along in near anonymity is especially dispiriting given that his 1850s texts document, with amazing vigour, a nomadic feeling of displacement. His sensitivity to subaltern voices at risk of occlusion by hegemonic modernity is a forerunner (or forewalker) of Richard Jefferies's *Wild Life in a Southern County* (1879), Edward Thomas's 'meanders' through *The Heart of England* (1909), R. Hippisley Cox's *The Green Roads of England* (1914), and, some decades later, Walter Starkie's *The Road to Santiago* (1957). By going off-grid in tread, parlance, and thought, inspecting 'the region' as a 'living palimpsest' with its own special atmosphere, these authors variously measure a vibrant sense of localism against the centralising policies of a progressively administered nation-state.[22] This writing model, as Kerri Andrews and Tim Fulford observe, has 'exploded in popularity', from 'the phenomenal success' of Robert Macfarlane's *The Wild Places* (2007) to Hugh Thompson's *The Green Road into the Trees* (2012), which records Thompson's long-distance trek across England from Chesil Bank in Dorset to Holme-next-the-Sea in Norfolk.[23] Alongside such works we find accessible cultural histories like Rebecca Solnit's *Wanderlust* (2001), Joseph Amato's *On Foot* (2004), Geoff Nicholson's *Walking* (2008), and

19. Ian Duncan, 'Wild England: George Borrow's Nomadology', *Victorian Studies* 41:3 (Spring 1998): 381–403. See also Michael Wharton, 'Reassessment: George Borrow', *Spectator* (25 July 1981): 247–8.
20. Thomas Seccombe, 'Encore Borrow', *Bookman* 42:247 (April 1912): 27–30.
21. C. K. S., 'A Literary Letter', *The Sphere* (20 February 1904): 182; [Augustine Birrell], 'George Borrow and His Works', *Quarterly Review* 189 (January/April 1899): 475, 491.
22. Lionel Johnson, *The Art of Thomas Hardy* (London: Elkin Mathews and John Lane, 1894), 98.
23. See Kerri Andrews and Tim Fulford, 'Introduction', *Romanticism* 27:1 (2021): 1–3.

Eluned Summers-Bremner's *Astray* (2023). These pundits remind us of Lawrence Buell's call, in *The Environmental Imagination* (1996), that proponents of ecocriticism and archipelagic studies focus more on literary amblers and their techniques of pedestrian composition. The walking text, Buell proposes, is a crucial 'form of environmental interaction', even a 'single subgenre'.[24] By appraising the long saga of human migrations, religious pilgrimages, military marches, leisurely bucolic strolls, and urban *flânerie*, these secondary critics sharpen our insight into Borrow's depiction of the embodied act of peripatetic travel alongside his Romani comrades in *Lavengro*.

My project recognises, among other things, Borrow's impact on verbal, visual, and performative representations of 'gypsy kings' between 1840 and 1940, when, as David Cressy remarks, 'more was written in English' about the Romani than 'in any previous period of history'.[25] However, I am more preoccupied with those significant particularities of authorial craft that led critic Lafcadio Hearn to maintain that Borrow had injected into English literature 'a new element – a new quality of romantic narration. None of his books are, in the strict sense of the word, either novels or romances: they are all romantic narrative of things really felt and seen.'[26] Such a quality led to Borrow's inclusion in once seminal anthologies such as Herbert Read's *English Prose Style* (1928) and Kenneth and Miriam Allott's *The Pelican Book of Victorian Prose 1830–1880*. Read's volume includes a lengthy extract from Borrow's *Bible in Spain*. Comically, Read says nothing about *why* this passage is an eye-catching 'example of narrative prose' in terms of its clause patterns, lexis, intonation, and rhythm. The Allotts choose the 'King of the Vipers' section from *Lavengro*, yet they are hardly more forthcoming about how Borrow achieves his rhetorical effects when recounting his rugged treks. In their 'Introduction', the Allotts seem to baulk at the idea of furnishing a critically responsible appraisal of Borrow's vignettes or his reliance on tropes of uncanny doubling that Tanya Krzywinska and Ruth Heholt address in *Gothic Kernow: Cornwall as Strange Fiction* (2022). Instead, the Allotts provide largely unsubstantiated impressions of one who prospered 'marginally' among 'authors

24. Lawrence Buell, *The Environmental Imagination: Thoreau, Nature Writing, and American Culture* (Cambridge, MA: Harvard University Press, 1996), 220.

25. David Cressy, *Gypsies: An English History* (Oxford: Oxford University Press, 2018), 121.

26. Lafcadio Hearn, *Some Strange English Literary Figures of the Eighteenth and Nineteenth Centuries* (1927; rpt. Freeport, New York: Books for Libraries, 1965), 72.

of predilection for small groups of enthusiasts'.[27] This perfunctory treatment prompts us to ask: given his peculiar fusion of travel notebook, *bildungsroman*, satire, sociological impressionism, and, in spite of his obvious relish for circumstantial detail, a mystical text voicing an extrasensory dimension to reality, is it better to parse Borrow as one who 'transcends the norm', in Walter Benjamin's terms? '[I]t has been rightly said,' Benjamin writes, 'that all great works found a genre or dissolve one – that they are, in other words, special cases.'[28] Secondary scholarship on Borrow's status as a 'special case' – how his storytelling resists easy classification by wandering across disciplinary and formal-stylistic borders – remains thin at best. However, it is undeniable that huge strides have been made in enriching our grasp of the Romani traditions that he recorded. Deborah Epstein Nord's close readings of Borrow's drifter-heroes (1998, 2006), Lou Charnon-Deutsch's *The Spanish Gypsy* (2004), Cressy's *Gypsies: An English History* (2020), Jodie Matthews's *The Gypsy Woman* (2020), Alistair Robinson's *Vagrancy in the Victorian Age* (2021), and Luke Lewin Davies's *The Tramp in British Literature, 1850–1950* (2021) are among the most astute literary and cultural analyses.

What these otherwise shrewdly angled articles and monographs lack is an in-depth investigation of the context, origins, and development of Borrow's aesthetic enterprise. I show that his textual idiosyncrasies extend across and between genres, and further into the transitional gaps between the fields of literary geographies and life-writing. Is this the reason why a self-proclaimed firebrand and countercultural gadfly like *BLAST*-era Wyndham Lewis, who had little patience with Borrovian peacocks like Augustus John, nevertheless affirmed Borrow as a 'great writer' in 'The Code of a Herdsman', a fictional manifesto published in the 1917 *Little Review*?[29] On one level, Lewis, the restive cosmopolite, may have identified with his literary antecedent's inability to feel completely 'at home' with himself. That sense of being foreign to one's own self is a potent nursemaid for an experimental narrative messiness – an aspect that poet-critic Lionel Johnson divined at the close of the nineteenth century. It is part of Borrow's radical novelty,

27. See Herbert Read, *English Prose Style* (London: G. Bell and Sons, 1928), 128; *The Pelican Book of English Prose: Volume V Victorian Prose 1830–1880*, Kenneth and Miriam Allott, eds (Harmondsworth, Middlesex: Penguin, 1956), xix, 183–7.
28. Walter Benjamin, 'The Image of Proust', *Illuminations*, trans. Harry Zohn (New York: Schocken Books, 2007), 201.
29. Wyndham Lewis, 'The Code of a Herdsman', *The Essential Wyndham Lewis*, ed. Julian Symons (London, 1972), 34.

Johnson averred, that you 'will hardly make up your mind whether' the author of *Lavengro* 'is most Rousseau, or Luther, or Defoe'.[30] To Arthur Conan Doyle, in *Through the Magic Door* (1907), Borrow's 1850s fiction seemed sui generis: 'Whence came this huge elfin creature, George Borrow? Where did he get' those 'strange mental gifts which place him by himself in literature?'[31] Critic Ottmar Ette is responsive to such daringly original, 'border-crossing' cultural producers with 'no fixed abode', who are beyond 'clear-cut national, continental, and territorial' frontiers, moving 'through and over the until now valid' markers of 'national-literary', 'genre-historical, or cultural kinds'.[32] What fed the young Lewis's imagination – and this applied variously to other vanguard modernists like Virginia and Leonard Woolf, D. H. Lawrence, and Ford Madox Ford – was Borrow's energetic irreverence and strategic non-alignment regarding established canons of literary taste. His key texts persistently refuse to be read as slick, cohesive, and seamless cultural artefacts; his narrators often cleave to the pose of the 'snapper-up of unconsidered trifles of information'.[33] It is no surprise then that Borrow emerges in the letters and book reviews of these modernist enthusiasts as a 'cult author'. Seeking to determine the parameters of this notoriously slippery label, Thomas Reed Whissen helps us grasp the initial critical reception of Borrow's *Lavengro* and *The Romany Rye*:

> Regardless of plot or setting, characters or time periods, symbols or themes, all cult books have elements of romantic hope and longing as well as romantic disillusion and melancholy. They dream of a different, usually better, world – or they warn against the direction they see the world heading. Entertainment, amusement, diversion, distraction – these are not their goals. They expect, they invite, they demand response. For this reason, they usually have few neutral readers. One either rejects them as trivial or boring or falls under their spell and becomes a cult follower.[34]

For the myriad fin de siècle and modernist avant-gardists who fell under Borrow's 'spell', the journeys, both local and global, on foot and

30. Lionel Johnson, 'O Rare George Borrow!', *Post Liminium: Essays and Critical Papers by Lionel Johnson*, ed. Thomas Whittemore (New York: Mitchell Kennerley, 1912), 204.
31. Arthur Conan Doyle, *Through the Magic Door* (New York: The McClure Company, 1908), 95.
32. Ottmar Ette, *Literature on the Move: Space and Dynamics of Bordercrossing Writings in Europe and America*, trans. Katharina Vester (Amsterdam: Brill, 2003), 13–14.
33. [Anon.], 'Borrow and Pugilism', *The Clarion* (Friday 2 May 1902): 6.
34. Thomas Reed Whissen, *Classic Cult Fiction: A Companion to Popular Cult Literature* (London: Bloomsbury, 1992), 10.

horseback (through the Iberian Peninsula in his 1840s travelogues; the British Isles in *Lavengro*, *The Romany Rye*, and *Wild Wales*) reflect a sly sense of comic rhythm and subversive handling of linguistic codes that some mid-Victorian journalists either struggled to construe or disavowed as 'trivial or boring'. The 1851 *Athenaeum* deplored *Lavengro* as a prolix 'portfolio of sketches', marred by closing chapters that vouchsafe little in the way of satisfying denouement.[35] If *Lavengro* ended in flimsy, unresolved fashion for the *Athenaeum*, then its sequel, *The Romany Rye*, perhaps in riposte to these same undiscerning 'pseudo-critics' (*RR* 353), closes with a verbose and scathing 'Appendix'. This series of sermons, with its keynote of affronted dignity, pushes mimetic-realist form in a startlingly new direction. *BLAST*-era Lewis may have enjoyed Borrow's excoriating contempt for his journalistic enemies in the addenda. Herbert Jenkins, however, writing around the same time in his *Life of George Borrow* (1912), was unsure as to where his subject was leading us with this parade of crotchety unpredictability. Borrow's fluster and bluster regarding the falsehoods and entitled arrogance of 'public detractors' signalled for Jenkins as much a psychic as a stylistic breakdown. *Lavengro* and *The Romany Rye*, he avers, 'go to pieces, that is as an autobiography'.[36] For Lewis, the most 'attractive' facet of Borrow's art – one which merited celebratory appreciation – was precisely this habit of making things fall apart, embracing tonal disjointedness and a sense of enriching complication. Borrow displaces narrative interest or value to a subsidiary place, handles the exigencies of linear plotting as a secondary or even trifling concern, so enabling a more richly coloured depiction of other cultural objects, energies, and interactions. *Lavengro*'s wilfully perverse and splintered structure – telling it slant – may have felt to Lewis like a foretaste of aesthetic modernism.

Virginia Woolf's early published reactions to *Lavengro* and *The Bible in Spain* for the *TLS* develop these notions. Mid-Victorian print media outlets, Woolf reminds us, frequently extolled, enforced, or relied upon specific types of critical judgement: deficiency or exorbitance regarding *correct* modes of realist-mimetic representation. However, *Lavengro* scrambles the narrative stock-in-trade by which, say, a George Eliot novel usually strives to enfold us into its imaginative cosmos. Borrow's reflections on consciousness, perception, and composition are implacably off-kilter; he makes us see things 'through the quick glancing eyes of an erratic observer', to employ Woolf's terms regarding one of

35. [Anon.], 'Reviews: *Lavengro*', *The Athenaeum* 1215 (8 February 1851): 159–60.
36. Herbert Jenkins, *The Life of George Borrow* (London: John Murray, 1912), 67.

Borrow's literary models, Laurence Sterne.[37] This makes the reading experience challenging to classify. Should Borrow 'go into the section devoted to philosophers', G. K. Chesterton mused in *The Victorian Age in Literature* (1913), 'or the section devoted to novelists, or the section devoted to liars? nobody else has ever known, even if he did'.[38] Through such questioning, we lose our sense of direction only to find ourselves anew. Borrow's 'life story as constant movement in exile', with its syntactical ruptures and anomalies, impels a different sort of movement, cherishing process over product.[39] Putative bittiness of design – or what Bonamy Dobrée termed, in 1949, 'the ribbon-development formlessness of the picaresque'[40] – paradoxically leads to coherence, the figure in the carpet. To glimpse this pattern, we must take a crucial interactive role in making Borrow's texts resonate, by following his narrators' conversational, indirect, and haphazard route. By 'spreading an atmosphere of mystery without realism', according to Geoffrey Grigson, Borrow effects surprising *departures* from the hegemonic dictates by which mid-Victorian 'three-decker' mimetic fiction holds multiple viewpoints and modes together.[41] Borrow emerges here as a stylist of ungarnished gruffness, 'in perpetual revolt against his age', whose fascination with ontological flexibility chimes with his treatment of genre as a locus of embarkment, not a zone of comfort or habitation.[42] This formally nimble approach reflects the shapeshifting ('always acting a part') and 'wandering, unsettled life' that contemporary middlebrow pundits ascribed to stigmatised ethnic groups like the Spanish Romani.[43] Such groups, in Borrow's estimation, made it their business to discount barriers, flout respectabilities, and trouble the very categories and places contemporary lawmakers (as well as literary gatekeepers and opinion formers) specified as secure, controlled, and patrolled. Just as the Romani skirted around legal sanctions and occupational

37. Virginia Woolf, 'Phases of Fiction', *The Collected Essays of Virginia Woolf*, Vol. 2, ed. Andrew McNeillie (London: Hogarth Press, 1966), 92–3.
38. G. K. Chesterton, *The Victorian Age in Literature* (London: Williams and Norgate, 1913), 151. See also Roy Kerridge, 'George Borrow, Chesterton, and the Gipsies', *The Chesterton Review* 9:4 (November 1983): 334–8.
39. Philip Davis, *The Victorians: The Oxford English Literary History. Volume 8, 1830–1880* (Oxford: Oxford University Press, 2002), 430.
40. Bonamy Dobrée, 'The Adventurous Victorian', *The Spectator* (25 February 1949): 262.
41. Geoffrey Grigson, *The Shell Country Alphabet: From Apple Trees to Stone Circles, How to Understand the British Countryside* (London: Michael Joseph, 1966), 63.
42. See Walter Starkie, 'Introduction' to George Borrow, *The Romany Rye* (London: Cresset Press, 1949), xii.
43. [Anon.], 'Borrow's Account of the Gipsies of Spain', *British and Foreign Review* 13:26 (April 1842): 371–2.

designations to survive, even thrive in a hostile physical environment, then and now, so Borrow's texts rarely linger long enough in one easily marketed niche – a source of no little bemusement to his ally and publisher John Murray III. This is why critical concepts such as the 'hybrid', the 'heterogenous', and the 'protean' reverberate through subsequent chapters. Like Borrow's rambling narrators, readers must occupy the role of wayfarers, where the movement between poles is depicted as at least as energising as the localities visited. Borrow encourages us to seize opportunities for granular analysis which his quixotic, even contrarian stance on generic 'laws' calls forth.

To probe this generic and tonal shiftiness further, I address three published reactions to Borrow from across the mid-nineteenth and early twentieth centuries. Each response is a significant moment in the critical perception and reception of Borrow's oeuvre. The first example, from the April 1842 *British and Foreign Review*, remarks with bewildered curiosity Borrow's arrival on the literary stage with the publication of *The Zincali: An Account of the Gypsies of Spain* (1841). *The Zincali* is in several respects a blueprint, or 'test run' for the more wide-ranging chronicle of his Iberian mis/adventures in *The Bible in Spain*. What is striking about the review is how its judgement on *The Zincali* is couched in terms that are repeated and refined in British middlebrow periodicals of the next decade, as pundits grapple with Borrow's peculiar gestures of authorial self-placement in *Lavengro* and *The Romany Rye*. The 'plot' or central concern of *The Zincali*, as with his subsequent published texts, is the production, fusion, or disruption of writerly norms, procedures, and subjectivities (the memoirist, the gentleman-traveller, the picaro, the polyglot and wiseacre). The *British and Foreign Review*, lacking a precise descriptive vocabulary by which to register this stylistic sleight of hand, resorts instead to what would become a lazy mischaracterisation of the author Borrow: the largely unschooled eccentric, whose habit of mind is synthetic not analytic, producing books that are lamentably diffuse, fitful, angular, and marred by 'broken fragments and tidbits of knowledge, linguistic, geographical, literary or philological'. This reproach would linger into critical writings of the next century. The 1922 *New York Times* construed Borrow as a literary naïf who 'did not know how to fashion a novel'.[44] A young T. S. Eliot, including *Lavengro* and *The Bible in Spain* in his 1916 'Syllabus for a Tutorial Class in Modern English Literature' for the University of London, addressed the '[u]nique

44. Herbert S. Gorman, 'George Borrow, Friend of Tinkers and Gypsies', *New York Times* (23 December 1923): 15.

position of George Borrow in literature. His eccentric personality. The novel of gypsy life. His relation to the "picaresque novel". Unevenness of composition.'[45]

My second example, an essay on 'Country Books' by the founding editor of the *Dictionary of National Biography*, Leslie Stephen, appeared initially in the December 1880 *Cornhill Magazine*, a year before Borrow's death.[46] This essay, the first of Stephen's 'Rambles among Books' series, canvasses Borrow's literary career when the latter's days of riding 'the wave of a popular success' were long gone.[47] The lengthy section of 'Country Books' dedicated to Borrow is tinged with a lyrical feeling that, as James Hooper averred in 1896, 'the bulk even of reading men know little of this very original' writer who left behind notes that cast 'vivid light upon one of the most obscure and, withal, one of the strangest careers' of the nineteenth century.[48] Stephen's survey was to prove hugely influential to later fin de siècle novelists and socialist campaigners who sought an ecologically attuned rural existence beyond what Edward Carpenter dubbed 'the lace-curtain dispensation of suburban life'.[49]

My third key text in the reception of Borrow's art, from the weekly newspaper *The Nation and Athenaeum*, is by Leonard Woolf, published only a few years after Wyndham Lewis's *BLAST*-ing of Augustus John and Edwardian gypsophilia.[50] The occasion for Woolf's compellingly succinct review was the recent appearance of the monumental, sixteen-volume 'Norwich Edition of George Borrow' (1923–4) – the 'first and only edition' of his writings 'that aspired to completeness'.[51] Although

45. T. S. Eliot, 'Syllabus for a Tutorial Class in Modern English Literature' (London: University of London Press, 1916). Reprinted in Eliot, *The Complete Prose of T. S. Eliot: The Critical Edition, Vol. 1: 1905–1918*, Jewel Spears Brooker and Ronald Schuchard, eds (Baltimore: Johns Hopkins University Press and Faber & Faber, 2014), 478–9.
46. Leslie Stephen, 'Rambles among Books. No. 1 – Country Books', *Cornhill Magazine* 42:252 (December 1880): 662–79. As Gillian Fenwick shows, there is credible evidence to suggest that Stephen met Borrow once. See Fenwick, 'George Borrow and Leslie Stephen: An Encounter', *George Borrow Bulletin* 3 (Spring 1992): 13–16.
47. Clement Shorter, *George Borrow and his Circle* (London: Hodder and Stoughton, 1913), 133.
48. James Hooper, 'George Borrow', *National Review* 26:155 (January 1896): 670.
49. Edward Carpenter, 'Simplification of Life', *England's Ideal and Other Papers on Social Subjects* (London: Swan Sonnenschein, Lowrey, 1887), 79–99.
50. Leonard Woolf, 'The World of Books: George Borrow', *The Nation and the Athenaeum* 35:8 (24 May 1924): 262.
51. Michael Collie and Angus Fraser, *George Borrow: A Bibliographical Study* (Winchester: St Paul's Bibliographies, 1984), 70. In the Woolfs' library are copies of *The Bible in Spain*, *Celebrated Trials and Remarkable Cases*, *The Romany Rye*, and *Wild Wales*. Most are signed by Leonard, not Virginia. See Gillian Fenwick, 'An Annotated Checklist of References to Borrow in Virginia Woolf's Writings', *George Borrow Bulletin* 4 (Autumn 1992): 13–17.

Leonard Woolf's memoirs evoke Leslie Stephen as 'one of those bearded and beautiful Victorian old gentlemen of exquisite gentility', his review of the 'Norwich Edition' takes issue with Stephen's focus on Borrow as a romanticised 'friend of jockeys, of Gypsies, and of pugilists'.[52] Woolf's intensely consuming engagement with *Lavengro* and *The Romany Rye* is grounded in respect for Borrow as a versatile and 'highly conscious' prose stylist. Woolf concludes his review by targeting Stephen's regrettable habit of 'moralizing' about Borrow's ostensibly 'odd' personality in the 'Country Books' essay – a bias that blinds Stephen to the mechanisms and processes by which Borrow attains his literary effects.

The Smell of the Field and Tent is on his Pages

Appraising the 'history of literary criticism', in *The Spirit of Romance* (1910), Ezra Pound saw 'largely the history of a vain struggle to find a terminology which will define something'.[53] This 'struggle' was played out in the pages of the 1842 *British and Foreign Review*, as it tackled Borrow's *The Zincali*. In the early paragraphs, 'Mr. Borrow' is portrayed as a creature of unpondered spontaneity, indulging in random, scattershot effusions rather than polished discursive strategies. His 'volumes' embody 'the cream of his mind, the first run of the grapes before the screw of the press has been applied'. This ostensibly untutored approach sets Borrow apart from earlier printed travel narratives on the region; for example, *Letters Written During a Short Residence in Spain and Portugal* (1797) by the self-described 'peripatetic philosopher' Robert Southey, published after a four-month excursion to the Iberian Peninsula, or later accounts by James Murphy, Richard Croker, William Morgan Kinsey, William Beckford, and Lord Carnarvon, of which Borrow may have been aware or even owned and read.

> Mr. Borrow, in spite of his name and subject, is a very original author, which is something nowadays, when men, women and children all write, and all very much like one another. He is the legitimate father of his own book; he has neither kidnapped nor disfigured the offspring of other people's brains; the smell of the field and tent is on his pages, not that of a folio-garnished laboratory, where new books are manufactured out of old materials.

52. Leonard Woolf, *Sowing: An Autobiography of the Years 1880 to 1904* (New York: Harcourt, Brace & Co., 1974), 196; Edward Thomas, *George Borrow: The Man and His Books* (London: Chapman & Hall, 1913), 40.
53. Ezra Pound, *The Spirit of Romance* (New York: New Directions, 1968), 13.

> He has never been initiated into that mystery; his works, like those of all clever but self-taught artists [. . .] show that he has never had a regular master.[54]

This reviewer argues that 'Mr. Borrow' is, at the very least, an appealingly untheoretical, in-the-field amateur ethnographer whose distinctive contribution to the act and culture of travel sidesteps that noticeable uniformity of description, commentary, and judgement which mars some rival volumes devoted to Spain and Portugal in the 1830s, when 'all sorts and conditions' of our 'Britannic Majesty's subjects' were engaged on 'one common pursuit of perpetual motion'.[55] Borrow's 'rough notes, dotted down on the spot with the coarsest lead-pencil' lend sketches of geographically and culturally marginal terrain – one that was beyond the Grand Tour itineraries – a fierce gusto. Yet this energy in seeking out the singular incident does not mask the less pleasing symptoms of an 'irregular natural style', one that betrays the autodidact in urgent need of a 'master'. Presumably, this 'master' will teach the tyro the value of craftsmanlike skill, tonal consistency, and exact research vigorously pursued. In *The Zincali*, the reviewer continues,

> Mr. Borrow suits his style to his theme. His desultory chapters stroll from subject to subject, defying the critic as his vagrant heroes do the constable [. . .] Mr. Borrow, finding his capacious pockets were getting too full and too heavy for his locomotive propensities, has turned out the heterogenous items without giving himself the trouble to arrange them [. . .] No defendant can be permitted to take advantage of his own *lâches*. If he comes into court a claimant for the honours and profits of literature, he must observe the rules of the tribunal.[56]

This extract is replete with tropes of frowned-upon, outlawed, or illicit literary procedures. This is why 'Mr. Borrow' is positioned as a bad actor or 'defendant' here: he is charged with disorderly authorial conduct – a reckless indifference, even resistance to sober aesthetic constraints and watchwords. So, what sort of *Account* is *The Zincali*, the reviewer wonders? If a contribution to the publishing of travel literature, why is 'Mr. Borrow' reluctant to address his sense impressions of foreign localities in searching detail? If a more sympathetic

54. [Anon.], 'Borrow's Account of the Gipsies of Spain', *British and Foreign Review* 13:26 (April 1842): 367–415 [367].
55. T. Morgan, 'Travelling Troubles', *New Monthly Magazine* 5 (October 1819): 337–8.
56. [Anon.], 'Borrow's Account of the Gipsies of Spain', 367.

ethnographic overview of 'gypsy' tribes, why is the reading rhythm so jumpy, disorienting, and erratic? The narrative supplies scant coverage of the topic in any crisp historical manner. 'Mr. Borrow' will not sift and compare source documents or supply a context of the cultural temperature of a Spain roiled by Carlist strife. What we get instead is a '[heaping] up' of 'facts and effects, without caring to resolve them to their original causes'. For this reviewer then, *The Zincali* is, on a formal-stylistic level, a medley of little instances of teasing flamboyance, non-conformity to, or transgression of polite aesthetic criteria. By oscillating between standpoints and tones it disqualifies itself from 'the honours and profits of literature'. What are ultimately dismissed as '*lâches*' – being remiss, profligate, or dilatory – are here the oddities of a loose-limbed verbal performance. *The Zincali* emerges from this piece as a deliberate act of defiance, offering an alternative blueprint for the travelogue through the texture of the written word. As later chapters will reveal, this construction of the wayfarer as a maverick rule-breaker will become central to the fin de siècle reactions to Borrow as a cult author.

Leslie Stephen and Borrow's Wandering Eye

Among the first nineteenth-century professional journalists to give more favourable scrutiny to Borrow's 'locomotive propensities' was Leslie Stephen (1832–1904). In the closing section of 'Country Books', Stephen addresses the movements and modulations of Borrow's 'temper of mind'. Like the *British and Foreign Review* just cited, Stephen gauges Borrow's 'originality' as a prose stylist. The stylistic 'rule-breaking', deprecated in the 1842 piece, becomes for Stephen more intriguing than a symptom of heedless or callow composition. That Stephen relishes Borrow's creative undertaking is perhaps unsurprising given that his literary precursor was, in many respects, the unofficial patron saint of Stephen's London-based 'Sunday Tramps'. This group was among the first organized – and arguably most socially exclusive – 'rambling clubs', founded by Stephen in November 1879. The novelist and poet George Meredith, himself a self-avowed Borrovian, acted as a 'convivial host' and cultural guru to what he termed a 'noble body of scholarly and cheerful pedestrians'.[57] Stephen's informal walking coterie for upper-crust metropolitan professionals – primarily lawyers, clinicians, and published authors – furnished 'common ground' for socially

57. [Anon.], 'Literature – Sir Leslie Stephen', *The Academy* 1801 (10 November 1906): 463–4.

conservative Tories and a more forward-thinking, unconventional liberal cognoscenti.[58] Stephen's essay lauds the verdant localities documented in Borrow's books – sites that inspired his tramping confrères to trace old rights of way in and around the Home Counties:

> To mention gipsies is to think of George Borrow; and I always wonder that the author of the *Bible in Spain* and *Lavengro* is not more popular. Certainly, I have found no more delightful guide to the charming nooks and corners of rural England. I would give a good deal to identify that remarkable dingle in which he met so singular a collection of characters. [. . .]
>
> Borrow is a 'humourist' [. . .] He lives in a world of his own—a queer world with laws peculiar to itself, and yet one which has all manner of odd and unexpected points of contact with the prosaic world of daily experience.[59]

In what seems like an echo of the *British and Foreign Review*, Stephen renders 'George Borrow' as an author who simultaneously invokes and infringes textual 'laws'. However, while *The Bible in Spain* and *Lavengro* move beyond the commonly determined bounds of mid-Victorian literary modes, they still reveal, Stephen argues, 'odd and unexpected points of contact with the prosaic world of daily experience'. What Stephen finds especially 'odd' about Borrow in this essay is how every facet of the traveller's biography and narrative practice engenders a baffling paradox. Aged twenty, Borrow had breezily announced to family and friends that his life goal was to reside in London, 'write plays, poetry', 'abuse religion and get myself prosecuted'.[60] So why would a self-avowed religious sceptic and controversialist undertake, as he explains in the Preface to *The Zincali*, 'the arduous and unthankful task of distributing' cheap vernacular translations of the Protestant New Testament in a Roman Catholic Spain? In his *Letters to the British and Foreign Bible Society*, covering this era of political and military strife, Borrow frequently voices pleasure at being 'employed usefully to the Deity, to man, and myself'.[61] Stephen marvels at one whose professional role as colporteur for an evangelical organisation seems totally at variance with his intoxicating vignettes of life's underwash

58. See Harvey Taylor, *A Claim on the Countryside* (Edinburgh: Edinburgh University Press, 1997), 61.
59. Stephen's 'Country Books' essay was reprinted in *Hours in a Library*, new edition with additions, 3 vols (London: Smith, Elder, & Co., 1892), III, 198–206.
60. William I. Knapp, *Life, Writings, and Correspondence of George Borrow* (London: Murray, 1899), II, 261.
61. George Borrow, *Letters of George Borrow to the British and Foreign Bible Society* (London, 1911), 15–16.

in *The Zincali* and *The Bible in Spain*, travelogues that read at times like John Bunyan trying his hand at a full-blooded picaresque romance. What Stephen dubs the 'queer world' portrayed in these texts implies that Borrow's true vocation is as panegyrist of a shady secular milieu frequented by mendicants, professional brigands, and brawlers.[62] In Stephen's lexis it is difficult not to hear his daughter Virginia's terms as she announced her creative aspirations in 1922: 'My only interest as a writer lies' in 'some queer individuality', a trait she detects in 'Borrow' and 'FitzGerald's Letters'.[63]

Stephen's identification of Borrow as a 'humourist' here is vital, as it aligns *Lavengro* with eighteenth-century authors and narrative frameworks. In an essay on 'Sterne', Stephen designates a 'humourist' as one who relishes playing on the edge of things tabooed or transgressive; giving full vent to personal quirks and outlandish fancies because 'the tragic and the comic elements of life present themselves to his mind in new and unexpected combinations'. Sterne, Cervantes, Rabelais, Swift, Defoe – all literary heroes to Borrow – 'explode empty pretences by the touch of a vigorous originality [. . .] As soon as the humourist begins to be more pungent [. . .] good quiet people who do not like to be shocked begin to draw back'.[64] There is a hint here of Dietrich Bonhoeffer's recent conception of *hilaritas* – 'defiance of the world and popular opinion', 'a high-spirited self-confidence' – which captures Borrow's narrative idiom, one that drew the disapproval of the *British and Foreign Review* in the previous section.[65] Borrow's 'pungent' wit as a 'humourist' is so 'peculiar' to Stephen's mind that the Iberian travelogues, for example, could not have been penned by any of Borrow's eighteenth-century literary lodestars, either in style or substance. As great a mystery was why *The Bible in Spain* – a favourite of Stephen's and a text that made Borrow, according to Elizabeth Barrett Browning, a cultural 'lion' in the 1840s – got relegated to the musty corners of regional libraries fifty years later.[66] Was this unmerited neglect, Stephen poses, the heavy price the 'humourist' Borrow paid for that refractory temperament noted by the *British and Foreign Review*? Borrow

62. John Telford, 'George Borrow, and his books', *The Wesleyan-Methodist Magazine* (August 1889): 587.
63. Virginia Woolf, *The Diary of Virginia Woolf, Volume 2: 1920–24*, Annie Olivier Bell, ed., assisted by Andrew McNeillie (Harmondsworth: Penguin, 1981), 168.
64. Leslie Stephen, 'Sterne', *Hours in a Library*, Volume III (London: Smith, Elder & Co., 1909), 140–1.
65. Dietrich Bonhoeffer, *Letters and Papers from Prison* (London: SCM Press, 2002), 73–77.
66. Elizabeth Barrett Browning, *Elizabeth Barrett to Miss Mitford: The Unpublished Letters of Elizabeth Barrett Browning to Mary Russell Mitford*, ed. Betty Miller (London: John Murray, 1954), 182.

had lived, as critic George Saintsbury remarked, through the entire period from the Battle of Waterloo to the Second Anglo-Afghan War – an epoch that saw the emergence and in some cases the death of literary luminaries William Wordsworth, Charles Dickens, George Eliot, William Thackeray, and Thomas Carlyle.[67] Borrow proclaimed, in *The Bible in Spain*, that intelligent and appreciative 'curiosity' was the 'leading feature' of his disposition (*BIS* III: 41). However, the volumes by Borrow that Stephen claims to cherish the most in 'Country Books' evince little 'curiosity' either about these geopolitical convulsions or the commercial fortunes of now widely taught authors. Wordsworth's *The Prelude* and *The Excursion* feature in *The Romany Rye* only to be belittled as soporific texts, whose bland descriptions of 'harebells and daffodils' would never offend Mrs Grundy (*RR* XXII: 145). In an era marked by Greenwich Mean Time, the din of steam engines, and the frenetic pace of imperial expansion, Borrow furnished, to Stephen at least, a singular view of a pedestrianism with one foot firmly in a serene Regency past.

Stephen's notion that the 'humourist' Borrow was immersed in a 'queer world with laws peculiar to itself' does not only refer to his subject's 'passion for strange wanderings in the queerest of company'. Stephen also targets how Borrow's specific patterns of walking, talking, and witnessing destabilise the 'laws' of narrative decorum, better to represent nomadic tribes that were denounced as congenital 'lawbreakers', refuseniks, and mischief-makers. This recalls 'the tribunal/court' imagery in the 1842 *British and Foreign Review* piece. By calling Borrow's literary self-construction 'peculiar', Stephen may have had in mind Borrow's own Preface to *The Zincali*. Here his narrator concedes that the 'greater part' of *The Zincali* 'has been written under *very peculiar circumstances*, such as are not in general deemed at all favourable for literary composition' (my emphasis). What appears an apology to readers expecting a cogent survey of Romani language and lore – Borrow pleads 'a want of leisure to amend' his 'rude', 'unconnected pages' – is instead a bold declaration of intent. He queries, deflects, or imperfectly reconstructs dominant habits of narrative perspective. What we discern here then, in Stephen's appraisal, is Borrow's 'art of placing us' at his 'own point of view'; 'not the man who compounds oddities, but the man who is an oddity; the slave, *not the master*, of his own eccentricities' (my emphasis). At first blush, Stephen appears to endorse the conclusion of the *British and Foreign Review* – a 'self-taught' Borrow lacking a 'regular master'.[68] However, Stephen

67. See George Saintsbury, 'Borrow', in *The Collected Essays and Papers of George Saintsbury 1875–1920* (London: J. M. Dent, 1923), II, 53–4.
68. [Anon.], 'Borrow's *Account of the Gipsies of Spain*', *British and Foreign Review* 13:26 (April 1842): 367–415 [367].

makes a different point about Borrow's observational powers. His narrators are less exercised by the mastering, pseudo-dispassionate, and neutral gaze of the would-be scientist: a standpoint that allowed intrepid gentleman-travellers to depict exotic phenomena as stable objects, structured according to coherent schema. Rather, Stephen offers us a 'Borrow' as the prototype for what we term nowadays the 'autoethnographic subject'. This figure privileges 'fancies dictated by his idiosyncrasy as if they corresponded to obvious and generally recognised realities'. Yet the 'order' of Borrow's 'ideas' are far from identical with mundane actuality; rather they are 'determined by odd, arbitrary freaks of purely personal association'. *The Zincali* subordinates overly neat conceptual constructions of knowledge ('order of things') to transient and capricious impressions of the Iberian Peninsula.[69] By situating us at their 'own point of view', Borrow's narrators stress – and celebrate – their 'odd' habits of mind as the key to unlocking foreign cultural behaviours, artefacts, and experiences.

Stephen's 'Country Books' – this is its principal virtue – accentuates that 'strange twist' in Borrow's 'mental vision' not 'shared' by other learned philologists and art connoisseurs like Richard Ford who ventured into Spain before the advent of Thomas Cook and the Sleeping Car Company. Stephen pinpoints how the lyrical and thematic texture of Borrow's work is fashioned by, and revises, ideas of the narrative subject as delimited by visual frameworks; for example, the omniscient eye of 'classic' mimetic-realism, the positivist scrutiny of scientific naturalism, each tethering optical impressions to specific narrative tools or habits. Stephen's concept of Borrow's 'strange twist' recalls one of the most memorable tableaux in Part II of *The Zincali* – an episode that is, significantly, about the seeing (and seen) subject:

> I spoke of the power of God [. . .]. I subsequently produced a manuscript book, from which I read a portion of Scripture, and the Lord's Prayer and Apostles' Creed, in Rommany. When I had concluded I looked around me.
>
> The features of the assembly were *twisted*, and the eyes of all turned upon me with a frightful squint; not an individual present but squinted, – the genteel Pépa, the good-humoured Chicharona, the Casdamí, etc. etc. [. . .] Such are Gypsies. [my emphasis][70]

69. George Borrow, *The Zincali: An Account of the Gypsies of Spain* (London: John Murray, 1841), 1.
70. George Borrow, *The Zincali* (London: John Murray, 1841), 361–2. See also Ann M. Ridler, 'George Eliot and George Borrow – A Note on *Middlemarch*', *George Eliot – George Henry Lewes Newsletter* 5 (1984): 3–4.

In Stephen's estimation, the 'squint' Borrow's narrator associates with his motley 'congregation' becomes a facet of Borrow's oblique, sceptical, wandering eye. This is visuality that exceeds mere optical perception. Borrow's anecdote, which Stephen affectionately recalls in 'Country Books', is not an isolated and droll 'twist' in an otherwise dry antiquarian treatise on Spain's nomadic clans. The moment is an essential part of what might be termed – to use a now obsolete phrasal adjective – the humourist Borrow's 'squint-minded' (perverse, fickle, variable) narrative strategies. His approach reveals and examines tensions between sight and vision, the ocular and the oracular, drab scenes of ethnographic taxonomy and bizarre flickers of hallucinatory reverie. It is no surprise to find Borrow's narrator claiming that 'it is in the eye more than in any other feature' that Romani figures 'differ from other human beings': 'Its peculiarity consists chiefly in a strange staring expression, which to be understood must be seen, and in a thin glaze, which steals over it when in repose, and seems to emit phosphoric light.'[71] *The Zincali* is replete with analogous episodes that, instead of vaguely invoking optics, foreground Borrow's wandering eye as a mode that imbues the observing (and observed) outsider with a new metaphorical and philosophical resonance.[72] This is why, Stephen concludes, your 'respectable compiler of handbooks might travel for years in the same districts all unconscious that passing vagabonds were so fertile in romance'.[73]

Leonard Woolf the Good Borrovian

Leslie Stephen's 'Country Books' went on to secure a notable place in the history of Borrow criticism, as attested by Humphrey S. Milford's *Borrow. Selections. With Essays by Richard Ford, Leslie Stephen & George Saintsbury* (1924). It was partly due to Stephen's advocacy that Borrow's texts became, in Milford's valuation, both a fruitful site of historical inquiry and a source of creative inspiration: 'no longer merely tasted by the curious few, but enjoyed by an increasingly large number of ordinary readers'.[74]

71. George Borrow, *The Zincali: An Account of the Gypsies of Spain* (London: John Murray, 1841), 354.
72. In Chapter VIII, Borrow's narrator interviews 'a very remarkable female, [who] was called La Tuérta, from the circumstance of her having but one eye'. See George Borrow, *The Zincali: An Account of the Gypsies of Spain* (London: John Murray, 1841), 234.
73. Leslie Stephen, 'Country Books', *Hours in a Library*, new edition with additions, 3 vols (London: Smith, Elder, & Co., 1892), III, 200.
74. Humphrey S. Milford, 'Introduction', *Borrow. Selections. With Essays by Richard Ford, Leslie Stephen & George Saintsbury* (Oxford: Clarendon Press, 1924), 5–10.

That same year, in the May *Nation and Athenaeum* magazine, Leonard Woolf reviewed the recently published 'Norwich Edition' of Borrow's complete works.[75] Woolf considers himself at the outset 'a good Borrovian'. There are, he opines, 'very few books in the world [*Lavengro* and *The Romany Rye*] which I read for the first time with greater enjoyment or which I can open at any moment with the certainty of refinding the old pleasure'. His review implies the intricate relationship of inheritance and contestation, deep affinity and firm resistance that he and his partner Virginia experienced with her father's voluminous critical output. Though vastly different in tone from Wyndham Lewis's abrasive critique of his gypsophile mentor Augustus John, Leonard Woolf's piece also remarks how the author of *Lavengro* has become 'almost a cult and the Borrovian almost more exasperating than the Tolstoyan'. Selecting key phrases from the 'Country Books' essay, Woolf challenges and complicates Stephen's neo-pastoralist survey. Woolf signifies that Stephen's self-designated role as a mediator of intellectual heritage hampers those 'good Borrovians' like himself who seek new ways in which to make *The Bible in Spain* and *Lavengro* appear credible and culturally relevant to a twentieth-century audience. Stephen's 'Country Books' essay casts a gloomy shadow here – obscuring rather than highlighting the foundations, brick, and mortar of Borrow's craft:

> The history of Borrow's reputation has been a strange one. *The Bible in Spain*, when it was first published [. . .] was an immediate success. *Lavengro*, published in 1851, was comparatively a failure. [. . .] Borrow seems to have written his best work precisely at the moment when people were unable to appreciate it. [. . .] It would be interesting to attempt to trace the causes which led people to feel so differently about *Lavengro* in 1860 and 1870 from what they did in 1895. I think a good deal is to be explained by the fact that from 1850 to 1900 (and perhaps beyond it) people were such inveterate moralizers. They would not allow themselves merely to enjoy Borrow, and the last thing which they thought about was his writing. Even Leslie Stephen [. . .], though he thoroughly enjoyed Borrow, almost apologizes for doing so, and seems to find the main point of *Lavengro* in the fact that it makes 'the social outcast the true centre of society'. 'The oddity' of the book, he tells us, 'repels many readers.' There is not a word about Borrow

75. On Leonard Woolf's 'love of Borrow', see his article 'Coming to London – II', *London Magazine* 2:10 (October 1955): 49–54; Leonard Woolf, 'The World of Books: George Borrow', *Nation and Athenaeum* 35:8 (24 May 1924): 262.

> as a writer, not a hint that he was a first-class writer, a master of vigorous English prose, a great character-drawer, and a real humourist. Nor does he say anything about Borrow's amazing skill in writing dialogue.

That Stephen is one of the 'inveterate moralizers' links with Woolf's later charge in a prefatory note to Virginia's posthumously published essay 'Hours in a Library' – echoing the title of one of her father's most popular volumes – that an overly censorious 'Victorian' outlook had warped Stephen's critical sensitivities. Unwilling or unable to relinquish the realm of moral stricture, Stephen's 'literary judgment' of authors like Sterne provided, in Leonard's opinion, little on the technical minutiae of writerly style.[76] Woolf also has in mind here W. M. Thackeray's 1853 lecture series *The English Humourists of the Eighteenth Century*, which damns Sterne's creative enterprise based largely on scurrilous biographical chitchat. Stephen's essay on Sterne printed in *Hours in a Library* strikes a note of admiring approval when referring to Thackeray's view of an ethically reprehensible Sterne: the 'judgment pronounced upon Sterne by Thackeray [. . .] seems to me to be substantially unimpeachable'.[77]

What is striking about this extract is that while Woolf impugns Stephen's account, both men designate Borrow as a 'humourist'. However, for Woolf, Stephen's reliance on that term merely repeats the critical error of those print media outlets like the 1842 *British and Foreign Review* that failed to register the aesthetic tools that Borrow exploited to liberate himself from standardised frameworks of narrative pacing, 'dialogue', and 'character-drawing'. Woolf argues that an 'air of spontaneity' has 'misled many people', including Stephen, into 'thinking that Borrow was one of those "natural geniuses" who produce their effects by a series of perpetually lucky flukes'. Stephen's conclusion that 'Borrow did not "appreciate his own singularity"' is, to Woolf, a grave interpretive error, since he was 'really a highly conscious artist', orchestrating his rhetorical effects with a compelling sureness of touch. By paying attention to the masonry of Borrow's authorial methods (his 'amazing skill' at the level of semantics, phonology, syntax, graphology) – as opposed to speculative psychologising about the supposedly 'odd' man – we elude, Woolf contends, the shackles of 'Victorian' recreational reading habits tainted by class prejudice. This is precisely the negative trait that *Lavengro* and the Appendix to *The Romany Rye* variously lambast. As critic Steve Ellis concludes, the Woolfs manufacture what appears to us nowadays as a

76. Leonard Woolf, 'Note', *Hours in a Library* (New York: Harcourt, Brace and Company, 1957), 7–9.
77. Leslie Stephen, 'Sterne', *Hours in a Library*, 133–4.

monolithic and stereotyped image of Stephen's Victorianism, 'and with it that of the modern' to justify their notion of literary history and Borrow's overlooked but pivotal position within it.[78]

My next chapter discusses a text that features prominently in both Stephen's 'Country Books' and Leonard Woolf's pithy riposte: *The Bible in Spain*, published by John Murray in 1843. Looking to capitalise on the positive critical scrutiny *The Zincali* garnered, at least from fellow Hispanophiles like his ally Richard Ford, Borrow felt that his next project must distinguish itself from Murray's already ambitious roster of expeditionary travel literature, which by the later nineteenth century would include A. H. Layard's account of Nineveh, David Livingstone's African adventures, Heinrich Schliemann's excavations at Troy, and Isabella Bird's solo journeys. Thanks in part to critics like Jeffrey Robinson, Anne D. Wallace, and Robin Jarvis, walking literature and narratives of organised tourism are now the focus of a burgeoning bibliography of academic monographs, conference papers, and peer-reviewed articles spanning a broad historical range.[79] However, *The Bible in Spain* receives disappointingly meagre scholarly attention. This is a missed opportunity because Borrow's years as a footslogging colporteur for the British and Foreign Bible Society overlapped with the rapidly evolving institutions, infrastructures, and practices of domestic and foreign tourism. The narrator's self-proclaimed 'genius' for learning Spanish dialects in *The Bible in Spain* chimed with a wider ethnographic fascination with folklore survivals, etymology, and the largely unvisited corners of Southern Europe that were so enticing to pluckier British, French, and Scandinavian trekkers at mid-century. By the time John Murray published *The Bible in Spain*, Romani was gaining wider recognition as a 'genuine' language, and the identification of its Sanskrit origins had ousted the reductive notion that it was merely a confected register calculated to rebuff meddlesome Gorgio ('non-gypsy') interlopers. I argue that what makes *The Bible in Spain* so effective is due in large measure to those formal-stylistic qualities that Leonard Woolf lauds in his review. Indeed, what struck Elizabeth Barrett Browning was the spirited insouciance with which Borrow's narrator casts aside 'the conventional' asceticism of 'a pattern missionary' to exploit the aesthetic

78. Steve Ellis, *Virginia Woolf and the Victorians* (Cambridge: Cambridge University Press, 2004), 6–7.

79. Jeffrey Robinson, *The Walk: Notes on a Romantic Image* (Norman, OK: University of Oklahoma Press, 1989); Anne D. Wallace, *Walking, Literature, and English Culture: The Origins and Uses of Peripatetic in the Nineteenth Century* (Oxford: Oxford University Press, 1993); and Robin Jarvis, *Romantic Writing and Pedestrian Travel* (London: Macmillan, 1997).

and ideological resources of picaresque romance.[80] By measuring *The Bible in Spain* against other seminal mid-century travelogues – David Urquhart's *The Pillars of Hercules* (1850) and Richard Ford's massive *Handbook for Travellers in Spain* (1845) – I show Borrow's inventiveness in 're-visioning' this genre and its protocols of topographical and scientific representation.

Chapter Three scrutinises the long-delayed follow-up to *The Bible in Spain* – *Lavengro* (1851) and *The Romany Rye* (1857). Instead of depicting the perilous ravines of the Iberian Peninsula, this sprawling two-part mock memoir charts the seemingly unglamorous bucolic hinterlands of 'home'. *Lavengro* reveals a burgeoning antiquarian fascination with fast-disappearing rural festivities, vocations, and superstitions at a time when 'folk-lore' (1846) and 'folk-song' (1847) were newly minted terms. This aspect of *Lavengro* made an indelible impression on W. E. Henley and William Morris.[81] The latter's essay on 'The Lesser Arts' (1877) posits that in the ostensibly 'unromantic, uneventful-looking land' of Borrow's England we uncover a storehouse of native customs, plus 'the works of our fathers yet alive amidst the very nature they were wrought into, and of which they are so completely a part'.[82]

Borrow's 1850s texts also invite comparison with Henry Mayhew's *London Labour and the London Poor*, published in three volumes the same year as *Lavengro*. Like Mayhew, Borrow charts an 'undiscovered' British 'country' as well as its destitute, renegade, and nomadic populations.[83] Borrow's conceptual 'map' of a pre-industrial island nation, inhabited by ostlers, innkeepers, broomstick menders, and stage coachmen, is as patchy and threadbare as the 'houseless wanderers' (*LSGP* XVIII: 79) he pursues through meadow, heath, and spinney. This is what separates *Lavengro* and *The Romany Rye* from other seminal Victorian domestic ethnographies, such as Mayhew's tome or William Booth's *In Darkest London and the Way Out* (1890), which portray an inner-city underclass 'of whom the public had less knowledge than the most distant tribes of the earth'.[84] Mayhew's 'cyclopaedia' of the 'great Metropolis', unlike Borrow's meandering account of rustic edgelands, is more inclined –

80. Elizabeth Barrett Browning, *Elizabeth Barrett to Miss Mitford: The Unpublished Letters of Elizabeth Barrett Browning to Mary Russell Mitford*, ed. Betty Miller (London: John Murray, 1954), 189–90.
81. See W. E. Henley, 'Borrow', *Views and Reviews: Essays in Appreciation – Literature* (New York: Charles Scribner's Sons, 1890), 133.
82. G. D. H. Cole, ed., *William Morris* (Bloomsbury: Nonesuch Press, 1934), 507.
83. See Henry Mayhew, *London Labour and the London Poor: A Selected Edition*, ed. and intro. Robert Douglas-Fairhurst (Oxford: World's Classics, 2010), 9.
84. Henry Mayhew, *London Labour and the London Poor*, i, xv, 3.

out of sheer necessity given its size – to reshape statistical surveys and slivers of first-hand disclosure from pickpockets and dock workers until they fit the forms of a cogent narrative anchored in sober deductive techniques. While Mayhew tries 'to deal with' his interviewees like a 'natural philosopher or a chemist',[85] Borrow's narrator follows an *unscientific* and 'erratic course', in defiance of the strictures of regulated programmes of 'college study' (*LSGP* XVIII: 79). Dramatising this 'erratic course' involves a reinvigoration of picaresque tropes and tactics already woven into the discursive fabric of *The Bible in Spain*.

Unlike some genre purists who treat the picaresque as a closed corpus restricted to early modern peninsular literature published roughly between 1554 and 1668 – the trinity of the anonymous 'Lazarillo de Tormes' (*BIS* L: 692), Alemán's *Guzmán de Alfarache* (1599–1604), and Quevedo's *Buscón* (1626) – *Lavengro* and *The Romany Rye* celebrate what we, as readers and writers, can *do* with this literary mode nowadays, especially its themes and tropes of episodic mobility and outsidership. Borrow blends and improvises around three key ingredients in his 1850s texts: a first-person retrospective; a jaundiced treatment of the '*fine gentry*' (*LSGP* II: 14); and a trickster-hero, a 'stranger inside the status quo', as percipient as he is resilient.[86] *Lavengro* and *The Romany Rye* depict those countercultural groups who will not accept that their place in a venal 'body politic' is fixed forever by the uncongenial circumstances of their parentage or schooling.[87] Since its emergence, however, as critic Ulrich Wicks contends, 'romances of roguery' have been difficult to resolve structurally and generically – as too were Borrow's texts (and protagonists) in the estimation of the 1851 *Christian Examiner*, which chided Borrow for his 'amphibious' narrator and stubbornly idiosyncratic plotting.[88] Borrow's reimagining of the picaro in his 1850s fiction disappointed and confounded middlebrow journalists in roughly equal measure. Pundits found little formal coherence in *Lavengro*, judging it instead as, at best, an assemblage of interlinked sketches, and at worst, a perversely 'planless' and outdated undertaking.[89] The people and subcultures Borrow delineates – prize-fighters, fairground

85. Quoted in Henry Mayhew, *London Labour and the London Poor*, x.
86. Luigi Gussago, *Picaresque Fiction Today: The Trickster in Contemporary Anglophone and Italian Literature* (Leiden: Brill, 2016), 276.
87. See J. A. Garrido Ardila, eds, *The Picaresque Novel in Western Literature: From the Sixteenth Century to the Neopicaresque* (Cambridge: Cambridge University Press, 2015).
88. [Anon.], 'Reviews: *Lavengro*', *Christian Examiner* (Boston) 50 (1851): 504–5.
89. See Herbert S. Gorman, 'George Borrow, Friend of Tinkers and Gypsies', *New York Times Book Review* (23 December 1923): 15; Bernard Groom, *A Literary History of England* (New York, 1929), 345.

cheapjacks, footpads, evangelical Methodists, coaching inns, cottage ingles – is one that had barely lingered into the more technologically advanced 1850s Britain adumbrated in his next published volume, *Wild Wales: Its People, Language and Scenery* (1862). This narrative, whose persistent popularity is borne out by the availability of myriad cheap paperback editions, is the focus of my fourth chapter.

On cursory inspection, *Wild Wales*, an account of a domestic tour, is Borrow's most formally conventional text. The Cambrophile author, in propria persona, gives us access to his private self and undistorted opinions regarding the Celtic language family along with biographical musings on the most consequential Welsh bards. As the speed of movement quickened exponentially in the 1850s (*The Romany Rye*'s 'fiery iron vehicles'), *Wild Wales* indulges the fantasy of the continuing dominance, even romance, of the solitary rambler. Borrow invests the Cambrian trek with specific cultural virtues and rewards. By eschewing main roads for muddy mountain paths that were impassable except on foot, he affirms a precious exercise that fosters sociability and a more nuanced evaluation of a region's terrain and usages. This was the assumption of early twentieth-century admirers of *Wild Wales* such as Edmund Kemper Broadus, who apostrophised Borrow in a 1919 poem as 'Thou Celtic Fielding'.[90] While Borrow's narrator might well have been cheered by this allusion to the esteemed 'author of *Amelia*' (*BIS* I: 6), Broadus's appellation implies that *Wild Wales* simply buttresses Matthew Arnold's seminal 1860s stereotypes of a whimsical and impractical 'Celtic' temperament. The years between Charlotte Guest's translation of *The Mabinogian* (published between 1836 and 1849) and *Wild Wales* saw a marked increase in public discussion about so-called 'Celtic' lore on the fringes of the Atlantic archipelago. Arnold's *Celtic* and *Irish Essays* furnish a crucial reference point in my chapter. Although Borrow's unpublished notebooks and letters supply few clues as to whether these two authors crossed paths professionally, they both shared, in George M. Hyde's words, 'some common' cultural concerns regarding Romani and Celtic history, 'and charted their ambitious (but utterly different) "criticisms of life" with the aid of a Romani paradigm drawn from the same source in the seventeenth century'.[91] Arnold, in a bohemian flourish that seems to signal his defence of minority voices, mentions his 'semi-Celtic origin' to his sister Lucy in 1859, as

90. Edmund Kemper Broadus, 'Lavengro', *The Review* 1 (1919): 14.
91. See George M. Hyde, 'Scholars, Gypsies, Poets and Priests: George Borrow, Matthew Arnold, and the romance of the margins', *Kyoto Women's University Literature Bulletin* (March 2003): 40.

well as his mother's 'Cornish ancestry'.[92] However, *Wild Wales* exposes Arnold's ethno-linguistic conception of the 'Celt' as a 'decorative accessory to British identity, simultaneously womanish and childish', locked into an essential but utterly subservient relationship with the monoglot Anglo-Saxon.[93]

My close reading of *Wild Wales* demonstrates that, as with his earlier autobiographical texts, Borrow's literary self-construction exploits a vital distance between the implied author and the bluff narrator. This permits us critically to inspect the polyglot speaker's pose as an expert translator of 'Celtic' mores as well as the varied geographical localities through which he passes. Borrow's distancing narrative strategy has become key to texts like *In Patagonia* (1977) by the nomadism-obsessed 'Bruce Chatwin', W. G. Sebald's *The Rings of Saturn* (1995), or the less technically and conceptually bold *Notes from a Small Island* (1995), at whose centre is the affable 'Bill Bryson' – a droll but partial version of the actual bestselling journalist-author. What is nowadays a familiar aspect of postmodern travelogues proved deeply problematic, even irksome, to contemporary critics of *Wild Wales*. The April 1863 *Archaeologia Cambrensis*, whose reviews sat alongside learned excavation reports and historical essays on the minutiae of Welsh toponymy, heraldry, and folklore, deplored Borrow's seeming indifference to chronological and factual accuracy.[94] Neither a reliable engagement with the antiquarian research of late eighteenth and early nineteenth-century scholars like Edward Williams and William Owen Pughe, nor a lifelong walker's 'picturesque account of the country', it was, the *Cambrensis* concluded, 'a sort of record kept by the author, of his sayings and doings'.[95] *Wild Wales*, in the eyes of the *Eclectic Review* that same year, 'belonged rather to the romance genus: it is almost of the novel kind, although it purports to refer to Wales'.[96] 'A sort of record', 'almost', 'purports': the hedging lexis in both published appraisals reflects the difficulty of construing what is an intricately stratified text – a medley or *layering* of political and

92. On Arnold's 'great penchant for the Celtic races', voiced on his return from a summer holiday in Wales – an excursion that supplied inspiration for his Oxford lectures later reworked for publication – see Mary Jean Corbett, *Allegories of Union in Irish and English Writing, 1790–1870: Politics, History and the Family from Edgeworth to Arnold* (Cambridge: Cambridge University Press, 2004), 156–7.
93. Murray Pittock, *Celtic Identity and the British Image* (Manchester: Manchester University Press, 1999), 65, 119–20.
94. For more on this, see Clive Wilkins-Jones, 'The Making of George Borrow's "The Welsh And Their Literature"', *George Borrow: The Unveiling of the Veiled Period and other Papers* (Oxford: Lavengro Press, 2016), 51.
95. [Anon.], 'Reviews: *Wild Wales*', *Archaeologia Cambrensis* 9:34 (April 1863): 174–6.
96. [Anon.], 'IV: *Wild Wales*', *The Eclectic Review* 4 (January 1863): 64.

religious analysis, comedy of manners, quotidian roadside dialogues, liverish social critique, and 'antiquarian lore' (*WW* XVIII: 114). For Angus Wilson, the profound 'puzzle' at the heart of this textual medley is whether Borrow depicts 'reasonably faithfully' the Welsh and Irish 'people he had met, or whether he was creating pegs on which to hang' Celtic 'characteristics as he perceived them', or 'wanted them to be perceived'.[97]

Chapter Five gauges the surprising 'afterlife' of George Borrow. In the years immediately following his death in the early 1880s, even some enthusiasts did not realise that the literary figure Arthur Conan Doyle portrayed as a 'huge elfin creature' had passed away. A remarkable resurgence of scholarly and popular interest in Borrow's 'strange mental gifts' can be traced at the fin de siècle. A year after Borrow's death, George R. Sims's melodramatic play *The Romany Rye* – based on his novel *Rogues and Vagabonds* – was first produced in London. Thanks in part to Sims's depiction of gypsy mores, a new generation of readers started to appreciate Borrow as 'a cross between Carlyle and Sir Richard Burton, with a touch of the Brontës'.[98] In his 1896 'Introduction' to the 'Macmillan Illustrated Standard Novel' edition of *Lavengro*, Augustine Birrell noted, in what strikes us as a double-edged compliment: Borrow 'has after his fitful hour come into his own, and there abides securely. Borrow's books,—carelessly written, impatient, petulant, in parts repellent,—have been found so full of the elixir of life' that we forget journalistic bickering as to whether they are 'true-autobiography or romance'.[99] By the time Edward Thomas published *A Literary Pilgrim in England* (1917), which construes *Lavengro* and *The Romany Rye* as conserving 'a memory of inland England, refined by dream, modified by *romance*' (my emphasis), the term 'romance' had acquired a quasi-magical inflection.[100] This tone imbues the *Blackwood's Magazine* reappraisal of Borrow's 1850s texts as 'the best romance of the road that English letters may boast'.[101] What these critics share, in their varied reactions to Borrow's aesthetic bequest, is a grasp of picaresque romance as a dynamic mode, one uniquely tailored to portray

97. Angus Fraser, 'Borrow's Political Views (Part 3): Ireland', *George Borrow Bulletin* 18 (1999): 18.
98. See Augustus Ralli, 'George Borrow', *Fortnightly Review* 98:586 (October 1915): 711–24.
99. Augustine Birrell, 'Introduction', *Lavengro: The Scholar, The Gypsy, The Priest* (London: Macmillan & Co., 1896), i.
100. Edward Thomas, *A Literary Pilgrim in England* (New York: Dodd, Mead, and Co.,1917), 246.
101. [Anon.], 'George Borrow', *Blackwood's Magazine* 191 (March 1912): 418–20.

'houseless' subjects, many resorting to trickery born of desperation, who haunt the edges of polite metropolitan society. In *Lavengro* and *The Romany Rye*, these are often Romani thimbleriggers, horsebreakers, recently dispossessed peasants, and unpropertied artisans, scorned by the ruling elite as shiftless, ignoble, or crooked: figures beset by the interminable demands of the body and destined to become the modern wage slave. What Borrow crystallises – this may explain his magnetic appeal to D. H. Lawrence, Ford Madox Ford, and Walter Starkie – is a nomadic protagonist's recalcitrant resistance to the discipline of daily labour. The wayfarer's circuitous route – a moral fable of capital whose suffocating stress on efficiency prompts Borrow to limn other ways of being – is what Edwardian devotees, 'bowing the knee' to Wyndham Lewis's 'wild Mother Nature',[102] affirm in their own cultural production.

102. Wyndham Lewis, ed., *Blast: Review of the Great English Vortex* (London: John Lane, 1914), 19.

CHAPTER 2

THE BIBLE IN SPAIN: AN UNLIKELY VICTORIAN BESTSELLER

Rethinking the Travelogue

> Conceive a vigorous man, of about thirty years of age, standing six feet two in his stocking soles, who, from boyhood, has been engaged in all manner of adventures in every country of Europe; [. . .] an adept in the use of his weapons; gifted with great personal and mental intrepidity, and by no means destitute of modest assurance; conceive him, familiar with the lowest haunts of vice, as it is seen in mendicant and gypsy life; a horse sorcerer and whisperer; speaking fluently every European language, and pattering every slang, lingua and lingo, of Frank, Jew, and Gypsy; capable of adapting himself to every variety of circumstance [. . . and] personating all kinds of men.[1]

In February 1843, *Tait's Edinburgh Magazine* found itself in possession of a singular new volume, one that catapulted its author into the principal ranks of Britain's most charismatic explorer-writers. It was the launch title for illustrious publisher John Murray's 'Colonial and Home Library' (1843–9), a series of original works, affordable reprints, and translations that would become associated with Charles Darwin's *Journal of Researches* on board HMS *Beagle* (1845).[2] In this extract, *Tait's* evokes a text whose rhetorical panache was belied by a drably descriptive cover, implying the 'commonplace' notebook of 'a sectarian' –

1. [Anon.], 'Borrow's *Bible in Spain*', *Tait's Edinburgh Magazine* 10:110 (February 1843): 75–84.
2. On John Murray, see Anne E. Peale, 'Works of travel in a publishing empire: John Murray III and domestic markets for the far away, circa 1860–1892' (unpublished PhD: University of Edinburgh, 2017).

The Bible in Spain.[3] What struck *Tait's* most forcibly was the author's elaborate self-fashioning, grounded in discursive strategies that suggested an epitome of extrovert virility, not the muted recording instrument of a factual travel narrative. Elizabeth Barrett Browning described this authorial persona as 'a Dare-all' – imposing, attention-seeking, dextrous in the acts and practices of mimicry, role-playing, and illusion.[4] He 'mystifies everybody, but nobody mystifies him', *Fraser's Magazine* agreed. 'The Jews take him for a Jew; the gypsies for a gypsy [. . .] No wonder that so many simple people thought him uncanny.'[5] *The Bible in Spain* also 'personates' and 'borrows' from popular literary modes not often found in the more serious type of expeditionary travel memoir with which the House of Murray was then linked.[6] Between 1768, the date of the House of Murray's founding, and the release of *The Bible in Spain*, the family firm had published well over 300 titles of geographical exploration, many marketed as supplying unmatched access to exotic, non-European territories.[7] That Washington Irving hailed Murray as the 'Prince of Booksellers' reflected how the firm, as official publisher to the Royal Geographical Society and the British Admiralty, had cemented a reputation for crafting lavishly illustrated volumes for an elite clientele with refined tastes and deep pockets. However, based on *Tait's* summary quoted at the beginning of the chapter, the protagonist 'George Borrow' seems to have stepped out of a swashbuckling romp, or a racy page-turner replete with vivid scenic details, penned by one of Sir Walter Scott's acolytes, such as Harrison Ainsworth. Indeed, for Scott, 'with Spain' the very 'idea of

3. [Anon.], '*The Bible in Spain*', *New Monthly Magazine* 67:265 (January 1843): 140–2. George Borrow, *The Bible in Spain; or, The Journeys, Adventures, and Imprisonments of an Englishman, in an Attempt to Circulate the Scriptures in the Peninsula* (London: John Murray, 1843). Hereafter referred to in text as *BIS*.
4. Elizabeth Barrett Browning, *Elizabeth Barrett to Miss Mitford: The Unpublished Letters of Elizabeth Barrett Browning to Mary Russell Mitford*, ed. Betty Miller (London: John Murray, 1954), 189–90.
5. [William Stirling], '*Lavengro* – "The Master of Words" ', *Fraser's Magazine* 43:255 (March 1851): 272–83. See also [F. G. O.], 'George Borrow', *The Academy* 2072 (20 January 1912): 88–9.
6. See William Zachs, *The First John Murray and the Late Eighteenth-Century London Book Trade* (Oxford: Oxford University Press, 1998). For a full bibliography of Murray's handbooks see W. B. C. Lister, *A Bibliography of Murray's Handbooks for Travellers* (Dereham: Dereham Books, 1993); Innes M. Keighren, Charles W. J. Withers, and Bill Bell, *Travels into Print: Exploration, Writing, and Publishing with John Murray, 1773–1859* (Chicago and London: University of Chicago Press, 2015).
7. See Gráinne Goodwin and Gordon Johnston, 'Guidebook Publishing in the Nineteenth Century: John Murray's Handbooks for Travellers', *Studies in Travel Writing* 17:1 (2013): 43–61.

Romance was particularly connected; and the associations which are formed upon perusing the immortal work of Cervantes, induce us for a long time to believe that the country of Don Quixote must be the very cradle of romantic fiction'.[8]

The truth, as *Tait's* acknowledged, was rather less 'romantic'. The author of *The Bible in Spain* was a dogged and snappish emissary of the British and Foreign Bible Society (BFBS) who spent the years 1836 to 1840 in the Iberian Peninsula when Carlist upheaval was precipitously unstitching the country's already fragile socioeconomic fabric. The BFBS, formed in 1804 as a byproduct of the late eighteenth-century Protestant evangelical revival, was an ecumenical and international mission governed from London.[9] Borrow was tasked by his employers with translating and disseminating sections of the Gospel of Saint Luke into Caló (Spanish Romani) and Basque.[10] This was a risky and onerous commission in a country with relatively poor infrastructure, where bellicose military and clerical authorities, viewing Borrow and his valet as 'evil guests in the house' of Spain, frequently menaced them with threats of detention, torture, and execution (*BIS* XXI: 289). If William Baxter's *The Tagus and the Tiber* (1852) can be credited, then the Iberian Peninsula must have seemed to *Tait's* a political backwater. Baxter portrays a geographical 'laughingstock' to 'civilised British' wayfarers who had witnessed elsewhere seismic advances in the speed, method, and convenience of cutting-edge transportation, including the expanding usage of steam for locomotive power. 'Canals, steamers, and railroads! What am I writing about? Roads must first be made by Portugal before such works can be thought of.' While 'express trains' hurry 'from Berlin to Vienna', there is, Baxter complained, 'not a carriage-road between Lisbon and Oporto, nor in any province of the kingdom'.[11]

Like Baxter's text, *The Bible in Spain* depicts the Iberian Peninsula as a loose confederation of enclaves or minor kingdoms, where attempts at interprovincial dialogue are foiled by an execrable road system and the mountain ranges that crisscross the country. A prolonged and bitter civil war over the succession to the throne, along with nationalist strife involving the Basque regions, compounded Spain's isolation from international affairs, rendering it the mere 'Shade' of a once 'mighty

8. Sir Walter Scott, 'Essay on Romance', *The Collected Works of Sir Walter Scott*, IV, 342.
9. On the BFBS, see Leslie Howsam, *Cheap Bibles: Nineteenth-Century Publishing and the British and Foreign Bible Society* (Cambridge: Cambridge University Press, 1991).
10. See Monica Mazurek, *The Unknown Relatives: The Catholic as the Other in the Victorian Novel* (London: Routledge, 2017), 37.
11. See William Edward Baxter, *The Tagus and the Tiber; or Notes of Travel in Portugal, Spain and Italy, in 1850–1*, 2 vols (London: Richard Bentley, 1852), I, 26–32.

Name'.[12] While Borrow's 'England' was aggressively enlarging its empire to encompass three-fifths of the world's surface, Spain and Portugal, as etiolated martial, diplomatic, and imperial forces, barely held sway over their Central and South American colonies.[13] For Borrow's bible-selling narrator, the peninsula, politically factious and largely untouched by trappings of commercial tourism, where 'caste and idolatrous superstition' shackled 'the mind with fetters of triple brass', was an ideal arena in which to telegraph his stoic, even heroic credentials.[14] He savours the tradeless, solitary hamlets and unfrequented highways, and keeps one step ahead of his many civic and clerical pursuers.[15] The bodily and affective strains of crossing undomesticated 'wastes', the vulnerability and exposure of sleeping under the open sky, signifies not only the narrator's credibility, but a 'virtue' that trumps the missionary efforts of 'others who wrought good service in the Gospel cause' (*BIS* 'Preface': iii). As the narrator claims, with typical (Christian?) immodesty: 'I have been [. . .] surprised that I experienced' no ill-treatment from the denizens of village posadas and decrepit Romani safe houses, and 'am inclined to believe that the utter fearlessness which I displayed, trusting in the protection of the Almighty', may have been the reason (*BIS* III: 20).

Although Borrow's correspondence with his BFBS employers signifies an enlightened and bracingly borderless thinker, interested in construing Spanish customs on their own terms, the narrator says much more about the sacred right of freedom of conscience that he tries to 'personify' and promulgate. You never forget, in the words of the *Manchester Guardian* nearly a century later, that this narrator 'is a true-blue Briton'. His love of peripatetic adventure on dangerous pack-tracks is equalled by a desire to make 'a home for "Church-of-Englandism" in a nation of Popish idolators'.[16] *The Bible in Spain* was published the year before Gregory XVI issued a bull excoriating evangelical nonconformist missionary societies such as the BFBS as 'Heralds of Infidelity and Heresy' in Western Europe. Borrow's text appeared at a time when many British Anglicans were still brooding over the implications of the Roman Catholic Relief Act of 1829, as well as urgent questions raised

12. Art VI, 'Ford's *Hand-Book for Travellers in Spain*', *The North British Review* 4:7 (November 1845): 149.
13. See Ann M. Ridler, *George Borrow as a Linguist: Images and Contexts* (Warborough: George Borrow Society, 1996), Ch. 7.
14. [Anon.], 'Borrow's *Bible in Spain*', *Tait's Edinburgh Magazine* 10:111 (March 1843): 161.
15. Art. III, '*The Bible in Spain*', *Eclectic Review* 13 (February 1843): 188.
16. C. H. H., 'New Books: George Borrow', *The Manchester Guardian* (1 July 1924): 7

by the high ritualism of the Oxford Movement.[17] *Tait's* and other early reviewers of *The Bible in Spain* throw into relief a decade of religious ferment and unease, which culminated in the reestablishment of Catholic hierarchy in England (1850), partly to better oversee, as Borrow's *Wild Wales* notes, the influx of destitute Irish Catholics after the Famine. *The Bible in Spain* is not shy of furnishing politically charged, even incendiary snapshots of Roman Catholic mores and history. What snared the attention of *Tait's* was the unbuttoned, rollicking prose style in which those views were couched. The volume's power to snag the attention of new reading constituencies was such that Borrow, according to his first major biographer, William I. Knapp, 'woke up one morning and found himself suddenly grown famous', eagerly perused by William Gladstone and eulogised by Sir Robert Peel in Parliament.[18] *The Bible in Spain* became a vogue of 1843, enjoyed, as the *Athenaeum* proclaimed a decade later, 'in the corner of a travelling carriage', or 'in the great chair by the library fire, when the snow and frost, and fog-bound Englishman seeks escape from spleen and distemperature by sunning his imagination in the south'.[19] In short, the text created a sensation, and 'nearly fourteen thousand copies were circulated within twelve months of the date of its publication, and five thousand in the following year'.[20]

Scripting a More Intrepid Self

> How the rage for scribbling tempts people at the present day to write about lands and nations of which they know nothing, or worse than nothing. (*BIS* XLIII: 598).

> These crudities of hasty travellers, to be gobbled up indeed during a few days' residence at an inn, form a sorry qualification for decisions on the manners of a nation.[21]

The Bible in Spain, given its focus on the trials, mishaps, and discomforts of foreign highways, can be productively measured against a

17. Owen Chadwick, *The Spirit of the Oxford Movement: Tractarian Essays* (Cambridge: Cambridge University Press, 1990).
18. William Ireland Knapp, *The Life, Writings and Correspondence of George Borrow*, 2 vols (London: John Murray, 1899), I: 398; James Hooper, 'George Borrow', *National Review* 26:155 (January 1896): 684; also [Anon.], '*Lavengro* et al.', *The Saturday Review* 104:2710 (5 October 1907): 426.
19. See [Anon], 'Our Library Table', *Athenaeum* (8 October 1853): 1192–3.
20. [Anon.], 'Most Respectable Borrow: Centenary Celebration in Norwich', *The Observer* (6 July 1913): 14.
21. Art. I [Richard Ford], 'Excursions in the Mountains of Ronda and Granada', *Quarterly Review* 63:126 (March 1839): 317.

cluster of widely reviewed travel texts, all published around or just after the appearance of Borrow's volume. These titles, variously suspicious of 'scribbling' wayfarers who make merely 'passing visits, almost flying ones' to view casually and judge in haste,[22] contributed to an evolving anti-tourist discourse – Scottish diplomat David Urquhart's *The Spirit of the East* (1838) and *The Pillars of Hercules; or, A Narrative of Travels in Spain and Morocco* (1848); Alexander Kinglake's *Eothen; or Traces of Travel brought home from the East* (1844); and *A Handbook for Travellers in Spain* (1845) – by arguably the most discerning of mid-century British Hispanists, Borrow's friend the High Tory grandee Richard Ford.[23] Ford, like Borrow, was especially vexed by those *Handbooks* 'larded with a conventional idea of Spanish life, which is handed down from one to the other, until, like an imaginary portrait, the false copy passes for a true original'.[24]

At the core of *The Bible in Spain* and other anti-tourist texts is a conception of roving masculinity marked by unflagging pedestrianism, and a resolve to assert the primacy of in-the-field attainments during an epoch of colonial expansion.[25] Journeying south and east, these narrators hymn 'braced nerves' and 'freedom from care' in archaic, comfortless, or politically unstable hinterlands.[26] Borrow's persona loses no opportunity to chaff those timorous touring parties and would-be 'scribblers' who were gripped with vertigo at the very thought of straying beyond the Pyrenees unchaperoned. We are made to feel that the excavation of a solitary pilgrim-narrator's temperament – his highly subjective reactions to the post-Napoleonic settlement, the trends and institutions of mass travel – is at least as important as the discovery of the 'lands and nations' they delineate (*BIS* XLIII: 598). This robust narratorial presence is impatient with, even disaffected by the hectic 'tempo' – the swift intensification of mobility on a worldwide scale – and the dizzying 'flood of impressions' that were linked with Nietzsche's descriptive category of urban-centred capitalist modernity in *The Will to Power.*[27]

22. [Anon.], 'The Spirit of the East', *New Monthly Magazine* 56:223 (July 1830): 426–7. See also [Anon.], 'Urquhart's Spirit of the East', *Tait's Edinburgh Magazine* 6:67 (July 1839): 475–6.
23. For a subtle analysis of this cultural production, see Roslyn Jolly, 'Mindfulness in early Victorian travel writing', *Victorian Sustainability in Literature and Culture* (London: Routledge, 2018), 85–104.
24. Art. I [Richard Ford], 'Excursions in the Mountains of Ronda and Granada', *Quarterly Review* 63:126 (March 1839): 317.
25. On how this authorial persona extends and complicates conventional notions of Romantic travel, see Barbara Korte, *English Travel Writing from Pilgrimages to Postcolonial Explorations* (London: Macmillan, 2000), 53.
26. Art. I [Richard Ford], 'Excursions in the Mountains of Ronda and Granada', *Quarterly Review* 63:126 (March 1839): 311.
27. Friedrich Nietzsche, *The Will to Power*, ed. Walter Kaufmann (London: Vintage, 1968), 47.

Borrow, Ford, and Urquhart validate 'shuffling off the frets and factitious wants of the thick-pent, artificial city' – preferring instead a return to the native.[28] Urquhart explains in his introduction to *The Pillars of Hercules*: 'I have not described, as a stranger would, a different manner of life; but endeavoured, *as a native*, to explain matters from which we might derive benefits in health, comfort, happiness' from 'their old experience' (my emphasis).[29] Showing boundless curiosity – and in Borrow's case boisterous egotism – these figures crave not momentary distraction but profound immersion, attained by long residence in the nation-states described, venues largely untainted by those mechanical contrivances and metropolitan fripperies which signify a coarsening materialism.[30] Richard Ford's text, the most celebrated of the *Handbooks* that John Murray III started in 1836, drolly enumerates the facets of advanced British culture that affluent pilgrims of pleasure will not encounter once they reach the golden sands of Spain: 'Those who expect to find well-garnished arsenals, libraries, restaurants, [. . .] railroads, tunnels, suspension-bridges, steam-engines, omnibuses' and 'pale-ale breweries' had 'better stay at home'.[31] Ford, like Borrow, distances himself from a growing number of middle-class women empowered by a rapidly evolving recreational travel industry.[32] The 1845 *Blackwood's Edinburgh Magazine* did not recommend Spain as a 'desirable travelling ground for those adventurous English dames' looking to escape peer pressure and the unrelieved mediocrity of home-making duties for a stronger sense of international fellowship. Such figures, *Blackwood's* argued, are becoming increasingly common on organised tours, 'journeying by coachfuls in France, Germany, and other peaceable lands, unsquired and unescorted save by their waiting-maids'.[33]

Borrow, Ford, Kinglake, and Urquhart variously repudiate both the '*prestissimo*' of technological modernity as well as the 'picturesque' vistas accessed through systems that made overseas travel easier, safer, and more affordable for organised tours. By contrast, these male authors, anxious to sanctify specific and exacting travel practices against the backdrop of commercial tourism, limn the corporeal and spiritual

28. Art. I [Richard Ford], 'Excursions in the Mountains of Ronda and Granada', *Quarterly Review* 63:126 (March 1839): 311.
29. David Urquhart, *The Pillars of Hercules; or, A Narrative of Travels in Spain and Morocco in 1848*, 2 vols (London: Richard Bentley, 1850), I, iv–v.
30. [Anon.], 'Ford's Handbook for Spain', *Saturday Review* 65:1703 (16 June 1888): 732.
31. Ford, *Handbook*, I, 118–19.
32. See W. Mackintosh, '"Ticketed Through": The Commodification of Travel in the Nineteenth Century', *Journal of the Early Republic* 32:1 (2012): 61–89.
33. [Anon.], 'Spain As It Is', *Blackwood's Edinburgh Magazine* 57:352 (February 1845): 181–94.

balm of a more ruminative, 'slower time'. Borrow's narrator, unlike his literary precursor Robert Southey, who was not entirely galvanised by the prospect of 'sleeping with the mules' prior to his own Iberian excursion in 1795, craves arduous conditions for their own sake.[34] In *The Bible in Spain*, such difficulties signify a making of space to cultivate, and enhance, the perceptual capabilities of the maverick, doughty, and nomadic self. This is, at root, a critique of the crude potency of steam and railway technology which aimed to tame, even conquer, largely unspoiled foreign expanses – thus hampering cherished processes of 'acute observation' *in situ*.[35] It is telling that Borrow's narrator, like Ford and Urquhart, craves self-realisation by endorsing and adopting conspicuously rickety, retro, and old-fashioned locomotion – by cart, donkeys, or footslogging – so mocking the lightning tourists whose goal was to reach their final destination with the utmost despatch. *The Bible in Spain*'s emphasis on the necessity of a 'horse or a mule' in craggy and unforgiving terrain is at first reminiscent of Urquhart's delineation of the practical 'Hardships' of 'Eastern Travel' in *The Spirit of the East* (1838), which charts his decade in the Levant. Regarding horseback riding, Urquhart concedes that this 'mode of travelling' involves 'exposure, and fatigue'. It is effortful and 'not a recreation suited to all men', and is 'trying even to those who are vigorous and indifferent to luxuries and comforts'. However, he affirms the cleansing discomfort of this embodied practice: 'there is none of that languor and feverishness that so generally result from travelling on wheels'.[36] Similarly, Ford's *Handbook* lovingly dwells upon Spanish wanderings 'out of the beaten track' on foot or horseback to inspect pre-Christian shrines. Unguided meandering – crossing a new frontier at a deliberate pace – furnishes something at least as enticing as the promise of arrival. For Borrow and Ford, this is the aesthetic and affective recompense of continuously shifting perspectives through a time-crusted kingdom, whose interior is a '*terra incognita* to naturalists, geologists, and every other branch of *ist* and *ologist*'.[37] The theatrical shunning of a transport revolution in its stages of vehicular travel is revealing about their shared attitude towards the feminising temptations and the destination-focused routes of coach or train. By lauding instead the physical rigours of itinerancy

34. Robert Southey, *The Collected Letters of Robert Southey: Parts One-Six*, Lynda Pratt, Tim Fulford, and Ian Packer, gen. eds (Romantic Circles Electronic Edition, 2009–17), https://romantic.circles.org/editions/southey_letters, 154
35. [Anon.], '*The Spirit of the East*', *Monthly Magazine* 26:153 (September 1838): 322–3.
36. David Urquhart, *The Spirit of the East* (London: Constable, 1838), 7–8.
37. Ford, *Handbook*, 77.

and equestrianism – evident in depictions of the rough bridleways of Estremoz (*BIS* VII: 87), the 'huge rocks' near Caldas, 'standing by themselves on the plain', as if 'Titans had been playing at bowls' (*BIS* XXVIII: 394) – Borrow's narrator relishes an elating intimacy with unfenced wilderness and what may happen while passing through it. In Ford's view, this is 'the *ancient, primitive,* and once universal mode of travelling in Europe' (my emphasis).[38]

The Bible in Spain's myriad paeans to footslogging and manly skills of equestrianism articulate a particularly intense corporeal and affective relationship with rugged Iberian localities. This is a conscious ploy to augment the culture, traditions, and tropes of physically draining, as opposed to the frivolous travel Borrow associated with Thomas Cook's 1854 slogan: 'To remain stationary in these times of change, when all the world is on the move, would be a crime. Hurrah for the Trip – the cheap, cheap Trip.'[39] In Borrow, trekking is a vital existential occasion that replaces the 'Trip' or package tour; it is a chance to reflect upon whether improving transportation networks in the rest of Western Europe were nudging civilised culture in the correct direction. His narrator strives self-consciously to present his own toils in parched localities as evidence of experiences unavailable to the cossetted BFBS mandarins to whom he regularly reports:

> After proceeding about a league and a half, a blast came booming from the north, rolling before it immense clouds of dust; happily it did not blow in our faces, or it would have been difficult to proceed, so great was its violence. We had left the road in order to take advantage of one of those short cuts, which, though passable for a horse or a mule, are far too rough to permit any species of carriage to travel along them. We were in the midst of sands, brushwood, and huge pieces of rock, which thickly studded the ground. These are the stones which form the *sierras* of Spain and Portugal; those singular mountains which rise in naked horridness, like the ribs of some mighty carcass from which the flesh has been torn. Many of these stones, or rocks, grew out of the earth, and many lay on its surface unattached [. . .] Whilst toiling along these wild wastes, I observed, a little way to my left, a pile of stones of rather a singular appearance, and rode up to it. It was a Druidical altar, and the most perfect and beautiful one of the kind which I had ever seen. (*BIS* VII: 82–3)

38. Ford, *Handbook*, 77.
39. Thomas Cook, quoted in Piers Brendon, *Thomas Cook: 150 Years of Popular Tourism* (London: Secker & Warburg, 1991), 65.

In Chapter VII, the narrator's journey is conceived as a travelling back in time, through an eerie twilight zone of gloomy solitudes, where the 'Romish religion' is no better than a weird benighted 'cult', heathenism in masquerade, 'distant both mentally and geographically' from sober Protestant, Anglo-Saxon orthodoxies.[40] This extract also foreshadows passages in *Lavengro* and *The Romany Rye*, in which the protagonist excavates imaginatively that which lingers beneath the crust of Christendom, the material vestiges of a deeper history in 'grave-hills', 'barrows and great walls of earth' on Salisbury Plain (*LSGP* IX: 321). In *The Bible in Spain*, the narrator underlines more the sheer physical challenge ('blast', 'violence'), via martial figurations of struggle; pitching oneself against the unforeseeable, where one's very life may be felt to be at stake. He also implies the mingled fear and fascination of traversing 'wild wastes' to view an immense 'Druidical altar' among the mountains near Estremoz, where the ground has stones sharp enough to 'cut through' his boots and wound his feet (*BIS* VII: 91). The stern 'singular mountains which rise in naked horridness, like the ribs of some mighty carcass from which the flesh has been torn' signifies the kind of grisly primal sacrifice that might once have been enacted on such altars. Borrow's imagery also suggests more recent spates of casual brutality, linked with 'those portentous beings who astounded the Old World and filled the New with horror and blood – Alba and Philip, Cortez and Pizarro' (*BIS* XXX: 429). On these trackless and silent mountains, Rome, supposedly 'in full possession of unquestioned power, guarded by the sword of the State and the fire of the Inquisition',[41] has no sway.

Urquhart's travel memoirs articulate a species of soothing 'excursion' that triggers 'absorbed repose' – 'not vacancy, but a calm communing with nature'.[42] While Borrow's narrator reveals that specific somatic, perceptual, and spiritual experiences are only available to the hardiest walkers and horsemen, his portrait of the '*sierras* of Spain and Portugal' resists Urquhart's tendency to romanticise the hazards of immersive trekking. This is the case when barely visible trails across treeless moors plus adverse weather conditions make navigation tricky even for self-declared fitness enthusiasts. Near Astorga (Chapter XXII: 318), traversing flinty tracks in choking heat and with his tongue cleaving to his 'palate with thirst', Borrow's narrator watches as numberless flies settle down on his horses and sting them 'almost to madness' – as do the 'bloodthirsty insects' later around Galicia (XXVIII: 395).

40. See Monika Mazurek, *The Unknown Relatives*, 99–101.
41. [Anon.], '*The Bible in Spain*', *The Edinburgh Review* 77:155 (February 1843): 106.
42. Urquhart, *The Spirit*, 8, 108, 12.

A Curious Pair: Borrow and Ford

> I have made acquaintance with an extraordinary fellow, *George Borrow*, who went out to Spain to convert the *gipsies*.[43]

> Ford is certainly a most astonishing fellow; he quite flabbergasts me – handbooks, reviews, and I hear that he has just been writing a *Life of Velasquez* for the *Penny Cyclopedia*![44]

The Bible in Spain's narrator is arguably closest in outlook – though not in the depth of his pockets – to Richard Ford, a patrician of independent means. Both authors elevate character-forming battles with untamed nature over a passive scrutiny of picturesque vistas that are belittled as a holdover from the Regency's vacuous gentry culture. Borrow, in a piece drafted for Murray's *Quarterly Review* but never published, argues that Ford's *Handbook* was one of the most distinguished texts ever written about Spain. The 'book before us', he declared, is 'the splendid result of the toil, travel, genius, and learning of one man and that man an Englishman'.[45] Both men – *los curiosos impertinentes*, to use Hispanist Ian Robertson's coinage[46] – exploit techniques and vocabularies of appraisal that resonated with an audience long used to construing the Iberian Peninsula through the distorting prism of *espagnolisme*, according to which regional topographies and everyday habits were imbued with a mystique and grace they did not always possess.[47] Sometimes matching Borrow's narrator in his most rasping and truculent moods, Ford deems Catalonia to be 'no place for the man of pleasure, taste or literature'; he travesties and exoticises Spanish Catholics, whom he divides 'only into two classes – bigoted Romanists or infidels: there is no *via media*'. Ford and Borrow's narrator share a great deal more than they realise with 'the Andalucian' depicted in the *Handbook*: 'the greatest boaster; he brags chiefly of his courage [. . .] He ends in believing his own lie, and hence is always pleased with himself, with whom he is on the best of terms'.[48]

43. Richard Ford to Henry Unwin Addington, 14 January 1841. See Ford, *Letters*, 179.
44. Samuel Smiles, *A Publisher and his Friends: Memoir and Correspondence of the Late John Murray*, 2 vols (London: John Murray, 1891), 344–5.
45. See Ian Robertson, *Richard Ford, 1796–1858. Hispanophile, Connoisseur and Critic* (Norwich: Michael Russell, 2004), 128.
46. Loosely translated as 'irritatingly/annoyingly curious'.
47. See Diego Saglia, *Poetic Castles in Spain: British Romanticism and Figurations of Iberia* (Amsterdam/Atlanta: Rodopi, 2000), 35.
48. [Richard Ford], *Handbook for Travellers in Spain and Readers at Home. Describing the Country and Cities, the Natives and Their Manners; The Antiquities, Religion, Legends, Fine Arts, Literature, Sports, and Gastronomy, Past and Present: with Notices on Spanish History*, 2 vols (London: John Murray, 1845), 1168, 214.

Published in the summer of 1845, Ford's *Handbook* is a hefty opus. In its original format – closely printed, in double columns, running to over 1000 pages, with a fifty-page index – it is very different from Murray's modest Gilpinesque guides designed for knapsacks and satchels. Notwithstanding its high price, 1389 copies of Ford's tome were sold in just over 'three months'.[49] Ford recounts his experiences of residing in and roaming around the country between 1830 and 1833. After the 1845 edition appeared he was hailed by many print media outlets as 'the greatest living English authority on Spain'.[50] So seminal was the *Handbook* that subsequent British sojourners, like the Shakespearean scholar William George Clarke, prefaced his *Gazpacho: Or, Summer Months in Spain* (1853) with a witty apology to the redoubtable 'Mr. Ford'. Clarke granted that his own low-key foray was doomed to join 'a hundred other little books – *Tours, Ramblings, Loiterings, Danglings*, and what not'. This was no exaggeration. Clarke's bookshelves may well have been creaking under the weight of material published by cheerful excursionists armed with notepads and compasses that proliferated during the 1840s. Clarke sought to add gloss to his own slim 'production' by filching textual 'ingredients' from Ford's amply stocked 'pantry': 'When one takes as a companion an author so racy and vigorous, one cannot but appropriate and "assimilate" his thoughts' and thereafter, unwittingly 'reproduce some of them as original'. In a sly allusion to Borrow's Iberian escapades, Clarke states that he visited Spain 'with no definite purpose – such as circulating the Scriptures', and his 'journey was deplorably void of misadventure'.[51] Given the fulsome journalistic reaction to the *Handbook*, it was perhaps imprudent of David Urquhart to use the fifth chapter of *The Pillars of Hercules* to castigate Ford and his 'chum' Borrow as vainglorious and verbose 'charlatans'. After chiding 'Mr. Borrow' as a purveyor of 'lies' who had slandered those biddable Spanish peasants who showed him such kindness on his route, Urquhart directed his fire at the *Handbook*:

> To Mr. Ford's book, however disagreeable the task, I had intended to devote a special chapter; but understanding that the two volumes are, in the second edition, reduced to one, I must infer that the author has anticipated my conclusion – that the work might be made valuable by cutting out the slang, ribaldry, opinions, and false quotations.[52]

49. See *The Letters of Richard Ford, 1797*–1858, ed. Rowland E. Prothero (London: John Murray, 1905), 201. See also Shorter, *Borrow and his Circle*, 227.
50. See Shorter, *Borrow and his Circle*, 227.
51. William George Clarke, *Gazpacho: Or, Summer Months in Spain* (London: John W. Parker, 1853), vi.
52. Urquhart, *The Pillars of Hercules*, 74–5.

Riled by Urquhart's blunt 'conclusion', Ford employed his semi-regular slot in the *Quarterly Review* to defend his own – and Borrow's – standing as intrepid and honourable 'men of the pen'.[53] Urquhart's intemperate verdict had no discernible effect on Ford's critical and commercial fortunes: thirty years later, the *Handbook* was still judged 'a treasure beyond price' and 'one of those rare books of the world' by the *Saturday Review*. It is, however, difficult to imagine a text more unlike the brisk and measured Baedekers that would become popular at the turn of the twentieth century.[54] Ford's *Handbook* supplies a Burtonesque farrago of personal bias (noted by Urquhart's *Pillars*), local history, art scholarship, lessons on lingo and deportment. So adept is he at 'embossing and embroidering' the data he shares of his Iberian trials that he makes rival titles from this period, such as S. E. Widdrington's *Spain and the Spaniards in 1843*, sound inexpressibly 'dull', in *The Athenaeum*'s verdict.[55]

Ford's displays of intimidating expertise in the *Handbook* can be measured against the literary mosaic of Borrow's *Bible in Spain*.[56] In a letter to John Murray, Ford expressed 'great delight' in the 'wild Missionary' Borrovian persona whose erratic cadence (hammering away like '*Punch*') exceeded even his rhetorical pugnacity. On the 'absurdities of Spanish Jacks-in-office',

> Borrow spares none of them. I see he hits right and left, and floors his man whenever he meets him. I am pleased with his honest sincerity of purpose and his graphic abrupt style. It is like an old Spanish ballad, leaping *in medias res*, going from incident to incident, bang, bang, bang, hops, steps, and jumps like a cracker, and leaving off like one, when you wish he would give you another touch [. . .] He really sometimes puts me in mind of Gil Blas; but he has not the sneer of the Frenchman, nor does he gild the bad. He has a touch of Bunyan.[57]

Ford extols Borrow's mercurial swagger, especially his skill in absorbing, and suddenly switching between, imagery from established and recently minted writing trends or modes – lyric verse, logbooks, letters, ethnographic transcripts, Gothic melodrama, commonplace books, captivity

53. [Richard Ford], 'Urquhart's *Pillars of Hercules*', *Quarterly Review* 86:172 (March 1850): 415–37.
54. [Anon.], 'Ford's Handbook for Spain', *Saturday Review* 65:1703 (16 June 1888): 732.
55. [Anon.], '*Gazpacho; or, Summer Months in Spain*', *The Athenaeum* 1179 (1 June 1850): 577–8.
56. [Art V.], 'Borrow's *Bible in Spain*', *Quarterly Review* 71:141 (December 1842): 172.
57. See *The Letters of Richard Ford, 1797–1858*, ed. Rowland E. Prothero (London: John Murray, 1905), 181. Ford's review of *The Bible in Spain* was featured in the *Edinburgh Review* 77 (February 1843): 105–38.

narratives, tales of seafaring derring-do ('The Storm' section of Chapter XV).[58] Here is an example of what critic Jean Roudaut calls the 'stratified' travel text, constituted of diverse 'layers of voices, vocabulary'.[59] Startling juxtapositions and tonal gearshifts – from impassioned gravity to weird farce – occur between and within individual chapters of *The Bible in Spain*. Ford's droll reaction to the irregular, jolting prose rhythms ('bang, hops, steps, and jumps') captures how the restrained, homely, and colloquial cadence of Borrow's travel sections, liberally sprinkled with Romani jargon, morphs into the ornate rhetoric of his sermonising moods, showing a speaker immersed in the lexicon and timbre of the King James Bible ('make of a barren and thirsty wilderness a green and smiling corn-field'). This is what avowed 'Borrow fan' Sherwood Anderson later described as unconventional 'flamboyancy and gusto'.[60] The extravagant apostrophes and proselytising 'gusto' frequently segue into the sentimental melancholy of reminiscence, or unsettling Gothic word-painting: for example, the brief meeting with the 'maniac', a 'miserable object in rags', 'gibbering and mowing' in the wind-beaten watchtower of Chapter VII (*BIS*: 92). As in this episode, Borrow's nerveless narrator enters those tribal enclaves, hidden among 'remote and mountainous parts of Spain' (*BIS* XIX: 268), where even the brash, formidably combative Richard Ford fears to tread.

Borrow's 'abrupt style' in *The Bible in Spain* both reflects and performs his thematic content. Like the distinct Spanish provinces, each of which in earlier periods comprised an independent kingdom with its own dialect, mores, and costume, Borrow's chapters are (barely) held together by a common filament of religion. Borrow reshapes the 'book of travels' in his own obstreperous image, by melding Ford's antiquarian relish for Spanish architecture, political history, and village customs, with a spiritual autobiography and romance tropes – a textual hybrid at whose centre is 'a hotch-potch of the jockey tramper, philologist, and missionary'.[61]

With Richard Ford's 'magisterial' text in mind, the *Saturday Review* remarked of Murray's *Handbooks* in 1858 that 'it is well that this universal Guide, if not infallible, is so thoroughly excellent and trustworthy as

58. See David Howarth, *The Invention of Spain: Cultural Relations between Britain and Spain, 1770–1870* (Manchester: Manchester University Press, 2007).
59. Quoted in Jan Borm, 'Defining Travel: On the Travel Book, Travel Writing and Terminology', *Perspectives on Travel Writing*, Glenn Hooper and Tim Youngs, eds (London: Routledge, 2004), 20.
60. Sherwood Anderson, *Letters of Sherwood Anderson*, ed. Howard Mumford Jones (Boston: Little, Brown and Co., 1953), 431.
61. Art IV, '*The Bible in Spain*', *The Edinburgh Review* 77:155 (February 1843): 105.

it is. We owe a debt of gratitude to the famous red series, for it has revolutionized the whole department of letters to which it belongs.'[62] Apart from the *British Magazine*, which hailed Borrow's 'air of candour in all he says',[63] most 1840s middlebrow reviewers were unsure as to whether *The Bible in Spain* presented us with such a dependable cicerone. The main 'epistemic problem raised by exploration and travel and its written reports is that of trust', critic Innes Keighren argues. 'How could the testimony' of '"geographically privileged persons"' be gauged as to its 'reliability by audiences elsewhere?'[64] Did *The Bible in Spain* precisely render actual personalities and phenomena from Borrow's recent past? Or does the narrator strike myriad novel poses in print, both fanciful and subversive, resulting in a 'very odd', even rumbustious travel performance?[65] Querying Borrow's professional self-placement, the 1843 *Monthly Magazine* remarked that '*Punch* would caricature him in the character of Harlequin propagating the Gospel in foreign parts'.[66] The lexis here hints at a wiseacre figure, who 'knows so many things' about Iberian usages, public spectacles, communal festivities, 'and tells them so well'.[67] Telling things 'well' is not the same as telling them frankly, however. For John Murray, veracity and exactitude regarding topographical description were central pillars of its brand identity that it worked tirelessly to maintain in its growing roster of *Handbooks*. Ford's opus embodied the 'gold standard' in terms of furnishing salient inside information gleaned on the spot. *The Bible in Spain* by contrast implies a more complex blend of 'unvarnished truth' and 'romantic wildness'.[68] 'It is no easy task', the 1843 *Gentleman's Magazine* confessed, 'to know how to give a view of such a production as this'.[69] This sentiment was shared to some degree by one of Borrow's most consequential British readers in the 1840s, a figure who enjoyed a long and close association with the House of Murray.

62. See [Anon.], 'Recent Guidebooks', *Saturday Review* (1 October 1859): 398–9.
63. [Anon.], 'Notices and Reviews: *The Bible in Spain*. By George Borrow', *British Magazine* 23 (March 1843): 315.
64. Keighren et al., *Travels into Print: Exploration, Writing, and Publishing with John Murray, 1773–1859*, 72–3.
65. [Anon.], '*The Bible in Spain*. By George Borrow', *The Athenaeum* 790 (December 17, 1842): 1080.
66. [Anon.], 'Miscellaneous Notices: *The Bible in Spain*. By George Borrow', *Monthly Magazine* (February 1843): 170–1.
67. [Anon.], 'Notices and Reviews: *The Bible in Spain*. By George Borrow', *British Magazine* 23 (March 1843): 434.
68. See Ryan Ross, '"There, in the fastness of Rural England": Vaughan Williams, folk song and George Borrow's *Lavengro*', *Musical Times* 156:1933 (Winter 2015): 43–56.
69. [Anon.], '*The Bible in Spain*. By George Borrow, Esq. 3 vols', *Gentleman's Magazine* (June 1843): 563–78.

Speaking the Gospel Truth?

> MR. GEORGE BORROW'S WORK ON SPAIN
>
> [Borrow] should, after all Portuguese, Spanish, and Gypsy words, insert the English of them in Italics, and between brackets.
>
> [. . .] passages are left unfinished, in order to produce an air of mystery. This is taking an unwarrantable liberty with the reader. A Novel writer, or even a writer of Travels, may pretend to be ignorant of things in order to keep them back; but they have no right to conceal what they admit they know. I would recommend that these gaps be filled up.
>
> [. . .] This is just one of those books the interest of which would be augmented by the readers knowing something about the writer. I would strongly recommend, therefore, that Mr. Borrow should prefix to his narrative a few pages of preface, telling us very concisely his birth, parentage, and education, [. . .] especially his connection with the Bible Society.[70]

Towards the end of 1841, John Murray consulted one of its principal reviewers of manuscripts on biography, military memoir, and expeditionary travel – Henry Milton, brother of the prolific Frances Milton Trollope and uncle to novelist Anthony.[71] Among the most trusted and well-rewarded of the firm's network of literary advisors and expert witnesses, Milton was tasked with gauging two-thirds of *The Bible in Spain*, along with correspondence that Borrow had sent from the Iberian Peninsula to BFBS officials in London. A hesitant John Murray II had given the manuscript of Borrow's previous volume, *The Zincali*, to Richard Ford.[72] Alert to the text's commercial clout – indeed it would create 'a great sensation far and wide' – Ford had urged acceptance.[73] Murray subsequently produced *The Zincali* in an edition of 750 copies. So impressed was Ford that he depicted the aspirant author Borrow as someone with serious literary and ethnographic credentials, indeed a valuable property who will go on to lay numerous 'golden eggs' for

70. William I. Knapp, *Life, Writings, and Correspondence of George Borrow*, 2 vols (London: John Murray, 1899), I, 383–5.
71. On Milton see Angus Fraser, 'A Publishing House and Its Readers, 1841–1880: The Murrays and the Miltons', *The Papers of the Bibliographical Society of America* 90:1 (March 1996): 4–47.
72. Clement K. Shorter's *The Life of George Borrow* (London: Hodder and Stoughton, 1913), 248–59, offers a lively though not entirely accurate overview of Ford's correspondence and friendship with Borrow.
73. See Richard Ford, *The Letters of Richard Ford, 1797–1858*, ed. Rowland E. Prothero (London: John Murray, 1905), 179–80. Ford also wrote an article on *The Zincali* (*British and Foreign Review* XXVI: 367).

Murray: 'secure him in your coop, and beware how any poacher coaxes him with "raisins" or reasons out of the Albemarle preserves'.[74] Milton, however, had reservations about what he felt was the puzzling, piecemeal design and emotive register of Borrow's sophomore effort. His request that Borrow furnish uninitiated readers with English translations of foreign vocabularies and a straightforwardly autobiographical paratext implies Milton was measuring *The Bible in Spain* against more soberly structured and 'trustworthy' eighteenth-century portrayals of Spain and Portugal, linked with the assiduous fact-gathering of Joseph Baretti, Richard Twiss, Henry Swinburne, and Joseph Townsend. Milton's detailed account reminds us of the potential 'makeovers', revisions, and redactions that travel texts underwent before publication at the House of Murray, thus complicating the recognised professional categories of author, in-house editor, publisher's pundit-reader, compositor, and book capitalist. That there were retainers not named on Murray's title pages who could yet soften or standardise the verbal fabric of *The Bible in Spain* – an extra-authorial hand threatening the integrity of his final cut – irked Borrow since he was the source and seat of expressive meaning.[75] Wary of the 'literary assistance' proffered by different agents within and attached to Murray – effectively an in-house regime of regulatory measures – Borrow ignored the bulk of Milton's feedback.

In what can be viewed as a riposte to Milton's commentary, the Preface to *The Bible in Spain* defends a distinctive aesthetic. The bullish tone contrasts with the Preface to *The Zincali*. Like Captain C. R. Scott in *Excursions in the Mountains of Ronda and Granada* (1839), who self-identifies as a 'mere scribbler of notes and journals',[76] Borrow's *Zincali* exploits the familiar topos of the *excusatio propter infirmitatem* – a 'modest' author's confession of *rhetorical* deficiency, nonprofessional or accidental authorship ('the style rude and unpolished'). In *The Bible in Spain*, however, Borrow proclaims that he is 'no tourist' or amateur scribbler 'of books of travels'. His Preface alludes to rival titles published 'about Spain' already. He may have had in mind Robert Southey's take on Romantic pedestrian poetics in his self-reflective *Letters Written During a Short Residence in Spain and Portugal* (1797), or 1830s texts by William

74. Ford to Murray, *A Publisher and his Friends: Memoir and Correspondence of John Murray*, 343–4.
75. See P. Meusburger, D. N. Livingstone and H. Jöns, eds, *Geographies of Science: Knowledge and Space* (Dordrecht: Springer Science, 2010).
76. Captain C. Rochfort Scott, *Excursions in the Mountains of Ronda and Granada, with characteristic sketches of the inhabitants of the south of Spain*, 2 vols (London: Henry Colburn, 1838), II, 34–5.

Beckford, Sir Arthur de Capell Brooke, George Dennis, and Sir James Alexander, which manifest the persistence of Southey's travel habits as a keen observer of Iberian lore.[77] Such volumes on the subject, Borrow implies, had portrayed broadly analogous marching routes, meetings, and scenic features. This superficial homogenisation of Iberian excursions throws the originality of his *Bible in Spain* into sharper relief. His 'remarkable errand' to the peninsula, characterised by improvisational feats of wayfaring, necessitates an equally remarkable (and flexible) textual mode to capture it, unadorned, direct, and responsive to new reference points and geopolitical realities in the aftermath of the Peninsular War. Borrow's Preface validates a deeply personal chronicle unlike the ostensibly conventionalised, instructional format linked with the brochures that Murray released over the next decade, such as Edward Whiteley's *Hints to Travellers in Portugal* (1852).[78] Against the backdrop of a fiercely competitive market and burgeoning readership, Borrow posits 'that the present [volume] is the only one in existence which treats of missionary labour in that country' (*BIS*: vi).

For Milton, however, Borrow's declaration of intent proved problematic. Milton had difficulty accepting certain claims of topographical correctness because *The Bible in Spain* merges the fictional embellishments of 'A Novel writer' and the more detached, evidence-based methodology by which a 'writer of Travels' pinpoints, articulates, and rebuts ethnographic data in print. This difficulty was compounded by how *The Bible in Spain* wilfully subverts the familiar attitudes, patterns, and tropes of Romantic-era travel notebooks: chronological, sequential entries that depict and compare various modes of conveyance, places of accommodation, rules of hospitality, and the geographical attractions of the itinerary. The issue that Milton most deplored – Borrow's gap-strewn narrative in which he seems to take mischievous pleasure in proffering dubious information – was a key part of *The Bible in Spain*'s charm to a highly literate consumer market. Milton's discomfort was not with travel writing per se; it is, after all, 'the most kinetic of writerly forms', a chronicle of escape and empowerment which is 'always on

77. William Morgan Kinsey, *Portugal Illustrated: in a series of letters* (London: Treuttel, 1828); Sir Arthur de Capell Brooke, *Sketches in Spain and Morocco* (London: Henry Colburn and Richard Bentley, 1831); Charles Rochfort Scott, *Excursions in the Mountains of Ronda and Granada* (London: Henry Colburn, 1838); George Dennis, *A Summer in Andalucia* (London: Richard Bentley, 1839); Sir James Edward Alexander, *Sketches in Portugal, during the Civil War of 1834. With observations on the present state and future prospects of Portugal* (London: James Cochrane and Co., 1835).
78. [Edward Whiteley], *Hints to Travellers in Portugal* (London: John Murray, 1852).

the move or contemplating movement'.[79] The domain of the travelogue seemed to Milton as pleasingly vast as the zones through which intrepid Britons had wandered. He relished the diversity of the texts Murray sent him during the 1840s, ranging from reminiscences of former infantrymen who had moulded 'their swords into steel pens',[80] scientific explorers' journals, visits to sites of patriotic pilgrimage like Waterloo, and *rites de passage* in accounts of the continental Grand Tour. Milton's critical struggles with *The Bible in Spain* stemmed from what Ryan Ross has recently dubbed Borrow's 'quirky hybrid' structure and elliptical tone: 'No one seems sure where and to what degree' the text is rendering 'actual people and events or merely spinning' invented scenarios – a tactic that connotes an irrepressible metafictional roguishness.[81] *The Bible in Spain*'s doctored autobiographical musings and wittily staged verbal skirmishes – some echoing classic setups from eighteenth-century European picaresque romance – supply a conceptual test for poststructuralists concerned with that 'precarious never-never-land between' what the author 'claimed as true and what we can accept as proven'.[82] If *The Bible in Spain* did not qualify as a credible fund of knowledge both about the traveller's temper and the Iberian regions surveyed, if it showed such cavalier unconcern for prescribed modes of fieldwork, lacking clarity of mission and motivation, then what sort of text was Milton reviewing?

The Borrovian narrator's apparent unwillingness to play a 'disinterested' eyewitness or arbiter of factual and rhetorical coherence was for Milton an 'unwarrantable liberty' (as aesthetic lack, law-breaking, infringement). Here we recall the *British and Foreign Review*'s reaction to *The Zincali*, featured in my introduction: if Borrow 'comes into court a claimant for the honours and profits of literature, he must observe the rules of the tribunal'. Milton's remarks are also reminiscent of Robert Southey's essay 'On the Accounts of England by Foreign Travellers'. Southey discusses that '*improper license of speech* wherein travellers and story-tellers are apt to indulge' (my emphasis).[83] However, in Ross's recent reappraisal, this 'liberty' or 'license' is a panorama of stylistic

79. Elizabeth Edwards, '"A Kind of Geological Novel": Wales and Travel Writing, 1783–1819', *Romanticism* 24:2 (2018): 137.
80. Art. I [Richard Ford], '*Excursions in the Mountains of Ronda and Granada*', *Quarterly Review* 63:126 (March 1839): 278.
81 Ryan Ross, '"There, in the fastness of Rural England": Vaughan Williams, Folk Song and George Borrow's *Lavengro*', *Musical Times* 156:1933 (Winter 2015): 43–56.
82. W. J. Keith, 'Borrow and Biography', *University of Toronto Quarterly* 53:2 (Winter 1983/4): 213.
83. Robert Southey, *Essays Moral and Political*, 2 vols (London: John Murray, 1832), I, 261.

opportunity and innovation, more appealing than the contested claims of veracity. What Milton ignores is how Borrow's experiential subjectivity blends the public masks of earnest colporteur, commoditised touristic dilettante, diligent philologist, bohemian rover, and blowhard whose impatience with constricting social norms generates a feeling for cultural relativism. The creative autonomy Borrow asserts in his Preface to *The Bible in Spain* prepares us for his obsession with drifters, mendicants, ne'er-do-wells, and Romani clans that epitomise *liberty* of profession. Behind this narrative strategy, at least for Christopher Wordsworth reviewing two biographies of Borrow in 1982, was an incurable trickster whose unique way of looking, love of mischief, 'humbug', and catchpenny page-turners overwhelms any responsibility to sprinkle the text with 'pious' missionary platitudes:

> Borrow's work with the Bible Society in [. . .] Spain, although thorough and courageous, elevated humbug to a fine art as he seized his chance to soak up strange tongues and wild surroundings without giving a tinker's curse for the pious point of the mission except to deliver a hefty kick on the posterior of that loathed bloodsucker the Pope.[84]

The 'liberty' to undertake hazardous travel furnishes Borrow with alternative, ludic, even enticingly transgressive models for authorial self-construction that do not require him to announce social prestige by reducing 'wild surroundings' to some sort of imperial grid. A generically hybrid project of soaking up 'strange tongues' enables him to 'elevate' his 'art' above the itineraries of serious-minded scientific observers funded by the Royal Society, well-heeled Grand Tourists, as well as souvenir-hunting excursionists toting a *Baedeker* or a *Murray* under their arm.

Unfortunately, Milton was not receptive to Borrow's technical flair. Indeed, it would prove costly for Murray when Alexander Kinglake offered *Eothen* to the firm in 1843. Milton was asked for his expert views on this manuscript. His written report has not survived, but Murray rejected the volume, writing to Kinglake: 'I for long meditated printing your book'. However, 'that wicked spirit of jesting at everything, which forms the essence of the book might I feared have raised a clutter and proved for my Colonial Library a place on the list of prohibited books'.[85] *Eothen* was a major hit when it was published by a rival firm

84. Christopher Wordsworth, 'The Quest for Borrow', *The Observer* (23 December 1982): 8.
85. See Gerald de Gaury, *Travelling Gent: The Life of Alexander Kinglake (1809–1891)* (London, 1972), 48.

in 1844 – six editions appeared in the following two years. As Angus Fraser notes, in 'Albemarle Street, where the travel genre formed such a specialism, it was particularly inopportune that the critical apparatus was not long-sighted enough' to embrace Kinglake's insouciant narratorial self – a deliberate and puckish deviation from the formal, 'dispassionate' and arid fact-gathering mode that marred some rival 1840s travelogues.[86] Borrow's 'wicked spirit' in *The Bible in Spain* contributed to a literary-historical development of the travel memoir that permitted Kinglake to devise a mode in which a blithe persona spurns any pretensions either to ethnographic insight or classical erudition. Murray was slow to recognise Kinglake's status as the charismatic 'captain of a literary revolt', though he eventually bought the copyright of *Eothen* in 1859.[87]

Central to Borrow's playful design – one which Kinglake's imitators refined in the next decade – is his pointed stress on 'rambling' (*BIS* XXII: 310). At first glance, this term reminds us of Kinglake's rival 'rambles among the wonders of Egypt' in *Eothen*'s Chapter XVIII, or Wilkie Collins's localised *Rambles beyond Railways: or, Notes in Cornwall Taken A-Foot*, published the same year as *Lavengro*, in 1851. Ford, in his 1842 correspondence with Borrow, encouraged his friend to 'Give us adventure, wild adventure' and '*rambles* in out of the way lands' (my emphasis).[88] For Borrow, 'rambling' denotes more than an unreliable lexical performance or what F. M. Wunderlich terms 'discursive walking', typified, in contrast to utilitarian 'purposive walking', by an easy-going outlook, varying pace, and with no demarcated route or destination – the goal being movement itself.[89] Borrow's rambling in Spain signals the halting, haphazard, and accumulative processes of striding, witnessing, and composing – the interplay of footprints and textual imprints. His practical and observational engagement involves highly creative 'translations' of a time-bound vista into what Ford praised as 'racy' prose in their 1842 correspondence. Ford points to something crucial in Borrow's conception of the English scholar-pilgrim abroad – an obstinate nonconformist who snubs the regimented thinking and staid rhetoric synonymous with a 'serious, puritanic education' (*BIS* V: 58). Borrow's ramble not only implies the stroll for pleasure through the largely neglected enclaves of Spain: ('Tired at last with rambling,

86. Angus Fraser, 'A Publishing House and Its Readers, 1841–1880', 29.
87. [Anon.], '*Eothen*', *Fortnightly Review*, n.s. 34 (1883): 380–1.
88. Quoted in Knapp, *Life*, I, 362.
89. F. M. Wunderlich, 'Walking and Rhythmicity: Sensing Urban Space', *Journal of Urban Design* 13:1 (2008): 125–39.

we repaired to a coffeehouse, where they regaled me with chocolate and sweetmeats' [*BIS* XXII: 310]). 'Rambling' also distils the narrator's grammar and syntax of thought, which Henry Milton was unable to parse in his report for Murray – a haptic, experimental processing of sights and sounds that opens 'paths' of self-development and 'discovery' (*BIS* XII: 131).

A pivotal aspect of Borrow's literary descriptions of ambulatory travel, 'rambling' promises – via musings that Spanish Romani is 'the mother of all the languages in the world' – though does not deliver, like later Haggardian romances, a quest for human origins. *The Bible in Spain* is a tribute to the ideologically incomplete and scrappy, where mendicancy and nomadism, in effect being 'a stranger' wherever one roams amid the 'silent and cheerless towns' (*BIS* XXII: 310), is simultaneously fraught and energising. The narrator is not a roving sensation-seeker here but a more capricious political entity who invests libertarian self-exile and 'solitude' (*BIS* XLIV: 616) on the barren plains with a singular potency. Far from the 1896 *National Review*'s conception of a suave 'walking lord of gipsy lore',[90] the narrator, prone to bouts of anxiety at scenes of 'desolation truly appalling' (*BIS* I: 11), retreats into his preferred role: the connoisseur of 'a speech spoken' by recently dispossessed peasants and Romani who seem outside the law but inside the state, his attention snagged by 'uncommon' ethno-cultural and zoological 'specimens' (*BIS* XXXIII: 487). This rambler chafes against the British homeowner's fixed ideas of territorial space or rootedness in a single, urban locality. He recalibrates 'dwelling' (*BIS* I: 4) to indicate a tumbledown structure under whose roof he takes shelter. 'Dwelling' also evokes his rhythms of reflective memory, even 'dreamy rapture' triggered by staying among the 'ruined walls' of former religious orders (*BIS* VI: 82). Therefore *The Bible in Spain* both depicts and performs a revelling in the desultory and discontinuous – a subtle interplay of 'wandering' and 'wondering' (*BIS* II: 28; XXIX: 419).

Caught in the Act

The Bible in Spain's rambling, episodic plot helps us chart a vital development from an Enlightenment gentleman amateur to a 'shiftier' post-Romantic figure, a seasoned performer whose exploits probe the nature of authenticity, individual liberty, and felt sensation. Proudly empirical and hands-on rather than theoretical, Borrow's narrator welcomes

90. James Hooper, 'George Borrow', *National Review* 26:155 (January 1896): 670–84.

the prospect of getting lost among the outlaws of labour, 'the dregs of the populace' (*BIS* XLIX: 670), to find himself afresh. He locates metaphysical solace in unsafe spaces, derelict retreats or other zones of social abandonment – a sly corrective to Murray's 1840s *Handbooks*, which map other parts of Western Europe via often lyrical descriptions of elegant Romanesque porches, vestries, and quaint village churches. Borrow's slippery narrator dons a renegade social mask, becoming what gypsiologist Charles Boner termed 'a most picturesque' and swarthy 'mass of rags'.[91] Chapter X, which portrays an officious national guard, reveals the narrator's quiet satisfaction in being mistaken for a dubious 'stranger' at the gates, even a confrère of 'gypsy fellows':

> 'Who are you?' said he, in rather rough accents; 'from whence do you come?'
>
> 'From Badajoz and Trujillo', I replied; 'why do you ask?'
>
> 'I am one of the national guard', said the man, 'and am placed here to inspect strangers. I am told that a gypsy fellow just now rode through the town [. . .] Do you come in his company?'
>
> 'Do I look a person', said I, 'likely to keep company with gypsies?'
>
> The national measured me from top to toe, and then looked me full in the face with an expression which seemed to say, 'likely enough'. In fact, my appearance was by no means calculated to prepossess people in my favour. Upon my head I wore an old Andalusian hat, which, from its condition, appeared to have been trodden underfoot; a rusty cloak, which had perhaps served half a dozen generations, enwrapped my body. My nether garments were by no means of the finest description, and, as far as could be seen, were covered with mud, with which my face was likewise plentifully bespattered, and upon my chin was a beard of a week's growth'. (*BIS* X: 135–6)

The passage nicely captures the frisson of camouflage – the mud-caked, bedraggled, and bearded narrator is literally 'swarthy'. He both invites yet withstands official inspection because of what 'enwrapped' his body. The phrasing by which he is delineated and circumscribed confounds as much as it enthrals. A 'rusty cloak' implies a type of magic mantle of invisibility, permitting the colporteur to look on while 'the national' measures him from 'top to toe'. A mishmash of sartorial stylings, scraps, and patches signals the narrator's self-hybridisation:

91. Charles Boner, *Transylvania, Its Products and Its People* (London: Longmans, Green, 1865), 30.

'Andalusian hat', travel-stained 'nether garments.' Just as there was no uniformly agreed upon orthography of 'gypsy' in the nineteenth century, so in this scene, there are no obvious criteria by which the National Guard can 'spell out', calibrate, or prosecute the narrator's ostensible 'gypsiness'. He immerses himself in his role – a 'method actor' who relishes being momentarily opaque or illegible to a self-important agent of the state. If we employ Bakhtin's lexis when describing the trickster-picaro, then Borrow's narrator becomes '"other" in this world'. Slandered by his 'betters' as social scum, disposable life, or a non-salvageable subject, Bakhtin's picaro can 'confuse', 'tease', and 'hyperbolize', and is able to 'parody others while talking', 'act life as a comedy', and 'treat others as actors', with 'the right to rip off masks'.[92] Borrow's playacting protagonist is as watchful and evasive as the Romani wanderers, starving paupers, and panhandlers with whom he consorts, for example his friend Manuel, 'a haggard, houseless, penniless man, in rags and tatters', a 'seller of lottery tickets, driver of death carts', and 'poet laureate in Gypsy songs' (*BIS* XLIX: 670). The narrator has no objection to passing 'for a Catalan' and mimicking their 'harsh' accent if it means securing refuge at a *choza* ('hut') in Chapter XXIX. Moreover, his respect for his cosmopolite ally Baron Taylor in Chapter XV brings into focus his own personal credo: Taylor's 'disposition' is 'so pliable that he finds no difficulty in accommodating himself to all kinds of company' (*BIS* XV: 221). There is a 'mystery about' Taylor, an uncanny liminality, conveying an aura of always being in character: 'who he is no one pretends to assert with downright positiveness' (*BIS* XV: 221) – a precious trait when moving through a country mired in bitter political infighting. As the narrator avers, 'I am invariably of the politics of the people at whose table I sit or beneath whose roof I sleep [. . .] by pursuing which system I have more than once escaped a bloody pillow' (*BIS* XVI: 237). What links all these moments is the narrator's extemporising verve. That the 'guard', confronted by this inscrutable because 'bespattered' entity, falls back on lazy prejudice indicates how 'gypsiness' is also a conundrum for mid-Victorian mimetic realist texts and the forms of property ownership, gendered subjectivity, and national affiliation they depict and applaud. Is it even possible to represent, realistically, these enigmatic 'strangers', without relying on ethno-cultural slurs, since the 'gypsy' is 'enwrapped' in 'half a dozen generations' worth of inexact, stigmatising, even contradictory 'layers' of meaning?

This question also reverberates through the numerous dramatic dialogues larded with the unglossed indigenous argot that Henry

92. Bakhtin, *The Dialogic Imagination*, 159–63.

Milton censured in his reader's report for Murray. Though these scenes were 'amongst the best parts of the book', Milton felt that 'in several of them the tone of the speakers, of those especially who are in humble life, is too correct and elevated, and therefore out of character'.[93] Theodore Watts-Dunton concurred, remarking in *Old Familiar Faces* (1916) that the 'bookish' locutions in these dialogues are 'the one great blemish in *all* Borrow's word-pictures of gipsy life'.[94] For Oliver Elton, in his 1920 *Survey of English Literature*, 'the speech of the gypsies, like that of jockeys and postillions, is sometimes artificially raised' above colourful cant.[95] This misconstrues Borrow's literary tactics in *The Bible in Spain*. He does not pretend to supply semi-faithful transcriptions from life like those found in texts by gypsiologists Charles Godfrey Leland or Francis Hindes Groome. Rather he devises, as in his 'interview' with La Tuérta ('The One-Eyed') from *The Zincali* (VIII: 276), complex, wittily self-reflexive playlets that parade their artifice. '[E]very writer,' Dickens proclaimed, 'though he may not adopt dramatic form writes, in effect, for the stage.'[96] Borrow explicitly uses such 'form' in these interludes to glorify a history of dramaturgy that recalls the *commedia dell'arte* as well as the conventions of unofficial cultural productions like farce, pantomime, puppet theatre, burlesque, and street pageantry. Staginess is not an artistic lapse here: in a narrative steeped in the nuances and lexis of theatricality ('curtains', 'scenes', 'comedy'), it is the very goal of Borrow's verbal performances. In the extract that follows, from Chapter X, *The Bible in Spain* conveys 'a peculiar foreignness' to show that these gypsy dialogues are elaborate 'translations' from Spanish.[97] Such a quality would be blunted if Borrow had acquiesced in Henry Milton's editorial advice ('simplifying a few of the turns of expression and introducing a few contractions – *don'ts, can'ts,* etc').[98]

> In the afternoon I was seated with the gypsy mother in the hall, the two *Callees* were absent telling fortunes about the town and neighbourhood, which was their principal occupation. 'Are you married, my London *Caloro*?' said the old woman to me. 'Are you a *ro*?'

93. Quoted in Knapp, *Life*, I, 359–60.
94. Theodore Watts-Dunton, *Old Familiar Faces* (New York: E.P. Dutton, 1916), 60.
95. Oliver Elton, *A Survey of English Literature 1820–1880* (London, 1920), I, 323.
96. Charles Dickens (29 March 1858), *The Speeches of Charles Dickens: A Complete Edition*, ed. K.J. Fielding (Hemel Hempstead: Harvester Wheatsheaf, 1988), 262.
97. John E. Tilford, Jr, 'A Note on Borrow's Bookish Dialogue', *Studies for Sturges E. Leavitt*, Thomas B. Stroup and Sterling A. Stoudemire, eds (South Atlantic Modern Language Association, 1953), 202.
98. Quoted in Knapp, *Life*, I, 359.

Myself – Wherefore do you ask, *O Dai de los Cales*?

Gypsy Mother – It is high time that the *lacha* of the *chabs* were taken from her, and that she had a *ro*. You can do no better than take her for *romi*, my London *Caloro*.

Myself. – I am a stranger in this land, O mother of the gypsies, and scarcely know how to provide for myself, much less for a *romi*.

Gypsy Mother. – She wants no one to provide for her, my London *Caloro*; she can at any time provide for herself and her *ro*. She can *hokkawar*, tell *baji*, and there are few to equal her at stealing *a pastesas*. Were she once at *Madrilati*, where they tell me you are going, she would make much treasure [. . .]

Myself. – Your plan is a plausible one, mother, or at least some people would think so; but I am, as you are aware, of another *chim*, and have no inclination to pass my life in this country. (*BIS* X: 123–4)

We recall the national guard tasked with inspecting 'strangers' (*BIS* X: 135–6) when the narrator announces, in this playlet, that he is 'a stranger in this land', from another *chim* ('kingdom'). His author-creator, however, is no stranger to 'ancient novels of Spain' (*BIS* L: 682). The repeated references to 'mother' here evoke the commercial sex worker turned crafty procuress who is greeted by assorted social pariahs as 'Mother' in the 1499 novel in dialogue, *La Celestina*, a comic progenitor of picaresque fiction. The extract just cited suggests 'gypsy mother' is at least conversant with that shadowy domain (populated by so-called 'witches', folk-healers, doulas, and abortionists) from which Celestina emerges. Borrow's playlet unfolds like a lampoon of a bourgeois courtship negotiation ('high time that the *lacha* [virginity/maidenhead] of the *chabs* were taken from her'). Unlike the passive, decorative femininities floated on the marriage market and sold off to the highest bidder, 'gypsy mother' offers the narrator a fiercely independent and roving partner (in crime and love), who is blessed with redoubtable survival skills (a *romi* or married gypsy-woman 'wants no one to provide for her'). Ultimately, 'gypsy mother' personifies a different unhoused condition, marked by flight and fugitivity, beyond the cycles of rent and debt. This is a snapshot of the unboundedness of subsisting otherwise than as a hapless wage slave. In their gleeful opposition to the logics of private property, gypsy mother and her itinerant Romani *Callees* (lasses) practice a type of underclass magic: *hokkowar* (lying, deception) and *baji* (telling fortunes to 'make much treasure').

Like the Lascars, Methodist preachers, Armenian traders, and other 'world-wanderers' that the narrator observes in *Lavengro*, gypsy mother is a 'symbolic daguerreotype'[99] – implying profound, yet largely unchronicled sociological resonances and trends in the first quarter of the nineteenth century. *The Bible in Spain* also shares with Borrow's 1850s mock memoirs a pronounced reliance on this playwriting technique – or quasi-ethnographic exercise? – of 'discoursing' with peripheral citizens who walk the errant path like gypsy mother, who is not afraid to think, speak, or act wildly (*LSGP* XVII: 106). These exchanges, into whose textual fabric are woven a wide array of italicised and untranslated idioms from Spanish Romani, Arabic, Greek, and Hebrew, supplied contemporary audiences with vivid literary figurations of the abjectly poor or homeless subject, such as the surly '*contrabandistas* of the lowest class', who earn 'a miserable livelihood by smuggling [. . .] rubbish from Portugal into Spain' (*BIS* III: 35). The fifth chapter of David Urquhart's *The Pillars of Hercules* takes a far less generous view of what he deems the distortions, quirks, and exaggerations to which the self-appointed 'English Gipsy' Borrow is prone.[100] Urquhart felt that the studied and pompous 'discoursing' with Romani matriarchs, watercarriers, local gaffers, and militiamen warranted some joshing in the introduction to *The Pillars*, which includes a satirical snippet of 'a conversation' between an unnamed 'Author' and a 'Spaniard'.[101]

In the extract, Borrow's narrator is not content merely to confirm readers' national bias or other prejudices by surveying only the gypsy mother's garb, behaviour, and habitation. His playlet gauges the expressive capacity of her lexis through a process of cross-class infiltration, scrutiny, and debate. On the one hand, these disclosures, liberally sprinkled with Caló phrases, imply philological authority, freshness, and the credibility of felt experience in contrast to what Borrow viewed as the laboured unreality of armchair anthropology, synonymous with E. B. Tylor's *Primitive Culture* (1871) later in the century. As in his 'discoursing' with his Romani 'brother' Antonio (*BIS* Chapter X), Abarbenel (*BIS* Chapter XI), the avid 'treasure-seeker' Benedict Mol (*BIS* Chapter XXVII), and the Barbary Jew (*BIS* Chapter XXVIII), Borrow's narrator craves access to the 'strange secrets' (*BIS*: vi) of exiled or immiserated groups. Such dialogues seemingly circumvent mediating data, leading directly to knowledge of otherwise reclusive or mistrustful social actors associated with the 'toilworn peasantry' (*BIS*: xiii). Such ethnographic flourishes are neither impersonal (like official statistics), nor biased (like hasty generalisation), nor overly abstruse (like conceptual paradigms).

99. Anon. [William Bodham Donne], '*Lavengro*', *Tait's Edinburgh Magazine* 18 (1851): 271.
100. Urquhart, *The Pillars of Hercules*, 72–3.
101. Urquhart, *The Pillars of Hercules*, vi–viii.

On the other hand, the conversations with Spanish Romani exhibit that delight in verbal jousting and badinage characteristic of European picaresque (the narrator admiringly alludes to 'Le Sage' in Chapter XII). In these interviews, the narrator tells us he frequently encounters chicanery. However, his own practice of formal legerdemain implies that for him the most effectual strategy when confronting double-dealing is not to expose, but rather to compound it. These playlets are then ambiguous textual events, where the field ethnographer and wily dramatist fuse. There appears to be little rationale for sudden switches from Borrow's customary method – lines of direct dialogue, marked by brisk tempo and set off by quotation marks – to this 'stagey' routine, in which a speaker, specified by name, delivers lines separated from that name by a dash. Even when the narrator confers with his valet and confidant Antonio, he resorts, on occasions, to this verbally and visually arresting playwright's mode. Are such moments meant to change the cultural conversation about, or improve the civic and institutional perception of Spain's execrated and downtrodden ethnic minorities? Or do the gypsy parochialisms add no more than 'local colour' to the text by reheating stereotypes of Romani as workshy ruffians who fake adversity to hoodwink gullible visitors into funding their criminal campaigns? That the narrator is simultaneously participant, performer, dramatist, and (voyeuristic) observer raises questions about the overlap between intimacy (learning the 'secrets' of fellow nomads like gypsy mother) and publicity (converting nonstandard vernaculars into the permanency of print).

Ultimately, these exchanges with Romani smugglers, muleteers, hucksters, and village innkeepers make comparisons with the design of Richard Ford's massive *Handbook* difficult. Such dialogues also deviate from those more measured late Victorian ethnographies of the Iberian Peninsula, many of which boasted learned appendices with grammars of Caló-Spanish, or tables comparing families of Sanskrit and Caló terminology.[102] While Ford's sprawling opus was acclaimed as the most 'distinguished Victorian guidebook to any European country',[103] *The Bible in Spain* parades its storytelling quirks by introducing dramatic 'scenes' and 'characters perhaps unprecedented' in any chronicle of religious activity (*BIS*: vi). Irreverent verve and psychological acuity are properties of the narrator's extended 'interviews' with subcultural figures like gypsy mother. Yet these playlets (or case studies?) do not coalesce into a neat, conclusive ethnographic 'message' (*LSGP* XXXIX: 239) about the supposed Indo-European provenance, history, and current social plight

102. See Charnon-Deutsch, *The Spanish Gypsy*, 134–5.
103. Howarth, *The Invention of Spain*, 125–6.

of the Spanish Romani. Instead of arriving at a reassuring 'genealogy of cultural and linguistic forms',[104] the narrator's 'discourses' – with 'dusty', 'unwashed people' of 'mixed' national origin (*LSGP*: xii) – melt into air. His conceptual map of the Iberian Peninsula becomes as makeshift and nebulous as the itinerants he meets while navigating far-separated towns, stony ravines, and vast, barren sierras. Not only do these conceptual and formal idiosyncrasies expose the intricate procedure of 'writing up' that occurs between the moment of the narrator's encounter with, say, gypsy mother and that of publication. Such highly contrived encounters leave us uncertain as to where 'a faithful narrative of what befell me' (*BIS*: vii) ends and dramatic embroidery or imposture begins, given the 'various faults and inaccuracies' to which the narrator freely admits in 'the present work' (*BIS*: iii).

Contemporary middlebrow scribes seized upon the narrator's playlet/debate with gypsy mother concerning rival traditions of courtship, cohabitation, and (un)seemly gender roles as an example of how Borrow's comically exuberant rhetorical repertoire sailed too close to the wind, at least in the eyes of his starchy BFBS employers. Borrow, conscious that his (tall?) tales of near-romantic entanglement and extreme peril should feature more evidence of 'an acceptable pilgrimage' (*BIS* XXIX: 409), threads through encounters with underclass figures a humanitarian logic to bolster his appeal to an evangelical readership at home. This gave him the air of a 'bourgeois Byron', according to critic Robert R. Meyers. Readers of the 1840s

> suddenly had upon their hands a [. . .] hero whom they could take to their hearts with no feelings of guilt. [. . .] Nonconformists could read about cutthroats, gypsies, and thieves without feeling that they were idling precious time away because the man who was recounting his perilous life among these scoundrels had, after all, gone there to distribute Bibles and to preach Protestant Christianity.[105]

The very secular, even salty verbal texture of Borrow's playlets featuring Romani 'scoundrels', the 'liberties' his narrator takes with the truth, and the apparent sidelining of questions regarding the 'best means of distributing the Gospel' (*BIS* I: 10), must have given his BFBS colleagues cause for worry. The organisation's leadership, anxious to safeguard the prestige of their missionary project as the geographic reach of British travel expanded, felt that Borrow had fallen far short of

104. Duncan, 'Nomadology', 124.
105. Robert R. Meyers, *George Borrow* (New York: Twayne, 1966), 41–4.

Richard Ford's glowing estimation of his friend as a courageous agent of religious change, who had made the circulation of the New Testament '*the* business' of his existence: 'wherever moral darkness brooded, there, the Bible in hand, he forced his way'.[106] For BFBS officials, Borrow had been too quick to cast aside the colporteur's solemn robes in pursuit of unusual, even sacrilegious, Romani curiosities.[107] *The Bible in Spain* was not the spiritual resource his employers had anticipated – nor could they promote Borrow's playlets as a 'useful' intellectual asset to diplomats or other colonial mandarins. Returning to England, having been relieved of his formal duties, Borrow faced criticism for his topographical errors and limited humanitarian exertions, especially from rival travel writers and Hispanists. Terence MacMahon Hughes's *Overland Journey to Lisbon at the Close of 1846* and S. E. Widdrington's *Spain and the Spaniards in 1843* variously commented, with no little schadenfreude, on 'the success of Mr. Borrow's expedition' to deliver Iberian peoples into a more devout, mutually respectful, and law-abiding way of life. It was 'not only a most complete and utter failure', Widdrington gloated, 'but of such a nature as entirely to defeat any future attempt of the same kind'.[108] Be that as it may, what caught the public's imagination was the bourgeois Byron's vivacity and dedication to following hazardous tracks rather than distributing tracts.

Among the initial middlebrow reviews, *The Literary Examiner* was closest to crystallising the public mood: 'we say of *The Bible in Spain* that notwithstanding its sober, grave, and truthful pretensions, it has of nothing reminded us so much as of dear, delightful *Gil Blas*'.[109] Borrow's narrator alludes to the unrivalled freshness of Alain-René Lesage's picaresque blockbuster in Chapter XII (*BIS*: 179) and he presents himself throughout as a learned student of this literary tradition. The roving protagonist of *Lavengro* and *The Romany Rye* is, like Gil, the child of humble parents and becomes a close observer of outlaws and exiles rather than a gleeful participant in criminality. In *The Bible in Spain*, San Lucar is a locality 'famous' in texts belonging to 'that class

106. Ford, quoted in Ian Robertson, *Richard Ford, 1796–1858. Hispanophile, Connoisseur and Critic* (Norwich: Michael Russell. 2004), 189.
107. Ann M. Ridler, 'Obedience and Disobedience: George Borrow's Idiosyncratic Relationship with the Bible Society', *Sowing the Word: The Cultural Impact of the British and Foreign Bible Society 1804–2004*, Stephen Batalden, Kathleen Cann, and John Dean, eds (Sheffield: Sheffield Phoenix Press, 2004), 286.
108. Samuel Edward Widdrington, *Spain and the Spaniards in 1843*, 2 vols (London: T. & W. Boone, 1844), II, 304–5. See also T. M. Hughes, *An Overland Journey to Lisbon at the Close of 1846, with a Picture of the Actual State of Spain and Portugal*, 2 vols (London: Henry Colburn, 1847).
109. [Anon.], '*The Bible in Spain*', *Literary Examiner* (17 December 1842): 804.

called Picaresque, or those devoted to the adventures of notorious scoundrels, the father of which, as also of all others of the same kind, in whatever language, is Lazarillo de Tormes' (*BIS* L: 682). The remark – 'all others of the same kind' – reminds us of Borrow's published tributes elsewhere concerning Defoe, Fielding, and Sterne. These authors variously adapted the anonymously published *Lazarillo* and Francisco de Quevedo y Villegas's *The Swindler* (1626) to retool the first-person vernacular voice associated with the earliest picaresque tales, and which Borrow refines in his travelogue, to the point where the text becomes, at least for his friend Ford, 'a spiritual *Don Quixote*, a *Gil Blas*, a *Pilgrim's Progress* into the land of contradiction'.[110]

The Bible in Spain's flourishes as 'a spiritual *Don Quixote*' reflect what the 1797 *Critical Review* labelled an 'age of peregrination'.[111] My next chapter shows that Borrow's 1850s texts *Lavengro* and *The Romany Rye* dig deeper into the aesthetic stock-in-trade of 'Picaresque' (*BIS* L: 692) – the argot, behaviours, and social ceremonies of the uprooted and unhoused – to devise a narrative that is off the regulation roads. The March 1851 number of *John Bull* addressed the blend of invention and hyperbole in what it judged a profoundly 'strange, paradoxical kind of book': 'Of adventures [*Lavengro*] contains more than a dozen novels, and yet it cannot be called a novel'.[112] Nor could it be read as an autobiography. While *The Bible in Spain* at least pretended to be a 'faithful' chronicle according to Ford, *Lavengro* and *The Romany Rye* lacked that 'substratum of fact and probability' which would nurture widespread mainstream 'acceptance', according to *The Athenaeum*.[113] So flummoxed was the *Saturday Review* that it felt obliged to proffer some guidance to 'Mr. Borrow', should he ever feel compelled to draft a sequel to *Lavengro*: 'we suggest that his continuation of *Lavengro*—if any such there are to be—would be far more interesting if they were written in the form of the *Travels of George Borrow*. Writing in his name, and confining himself to facts, he would avoid many crotchets which greatly diminish the pleasure which his later books afford us.'[114]

Among the 'crotchets' was Borrow's conception of the eponymous hero. He is neither a notorious scoundrel living by his wits, 'always one step away from the whip and the noose', nor a valiant defender of

110. [Richard Ford], '*The Bible in Spain*', *Edinburgh Review* 77:155 (February 1843): 105.
111. [Anon.], 'Travels through Germany, Switzerland, Italy, and Sicily', *Critical Review* 19 (April 1797): 361–8.
112. [Anon.], 'Literature', *John Bull* 31:1578 (8 March 1851): 8.
113. [Anon.], 'Reviews: *The Romany Rye*', *The Athenaeum* 1543 (23 May 1857): 653.
114. [Anon.], 'Reviews – *Lavengro* and *The Romany Rye*', *Saturday Review* (23 May 1857): 655.

'Protestant Christianity' (*BIS* XII: 179).[115] In *Lavengro*'s reimagining of the picaro's progress, a hack writer escapes the oppressive drudgery of producing 'copy' in London bohemia by assuming a vagrant tinker's trade in the English hinterlands. We follow a mercurial yet principled outsider, alienated from his own self, with a poet-translator's passion for arcane dialects. At first blush, *Lavengro* invites comparison with another pseudo-autobiography charting an intensely patriotic autodidact's experiences of hunger – Charles Kingsley's *Alton Locke, Tailor and Poet* published anonymously the year before Borrow's text in 1850. While Kingsley paints a portrait of a radical propagandist, *Lavengro* evokes a brooding drifter, fired more by philology than improving the living conditions of the urban proletariat. I will demonstrate that Borrow supplies an alternative 'Odyssey' here, what *The Romany Rye* terms a 'wild gypsy dream' (*RR* XII: 80). This signifies on one level a dream vision of a demographic category without overseers or masters; picaros who snub the complacent careerism frequently debunked by Rudyard Kipling's stories of imperial masculinity, such as *Plain Tales from the Hills* (1888). Borrow gambled that the 'Odyssey' recounted in *Lavengro* and *The Romany Rye* would resonate with a reading public already conversant with the picaresque tropes knitted into the imaginative fabric of Dickens's *Pickwick Papers*, the quasi-Newgate novel *Oliver Twist*, W. M. Thackeray's *Barry Lyndon*, and *Vanity Fair*. Borrow, as it turned out, misjudged the critical mood in affirming, across two volumes, the unmanacled individualism and digressive format linked with picaresque. Mid-century journalists, eager to buy fiction that vaunted their own 'settled' and prosperous domesticity, were unsympathetic to, even needled by Borrow's conviction in *Lavengro* and *The Romany Rye* that the rituals of bourgeois politesse and efficiency were fraudulent. Indeed, such systems were calculated to reduce many honest, dutiful citizens (like himself) to the level of penniless and disgruntled picaros, completely unshielded and lacking legal rights. Borrow's model of picaresque nonconformism in his 1850s fiction is responsive to the plight of those who have been compelled to abjure their languages, literature, and unique lore in the name of an 'advanced' (or amnesiac?) modernity.[116] If this makes *Lavengro* sound like tired nostalgia, then it is worth recalling the mock memoir's politically subversive edge.[117]

115. Silvia Federici, *Caliban and the Witch: Women, the Body, and Primitive Accumulation* (New York: Autonomedia, 2017), 85.
116. [Anon.], 'The Literary Examiner: *The Romany Rye* A Sequel to *Lavengro*', *The Examiner* 2573 (23 May 1857): 324–5.
117. See Chris Waters, *British Socialists and the Politics of Popular Culture, 1884–1914* (Manchester: Manchester University Press, 1990).

Borrow's merger of mimetic realism, quest romance, and ethnographic transcript illustrates the hardscrabble lives of navvies, hawkers, and handicraft tramps not to fetishise their radical alterity and 'linguistic cosmopolitanism'.[118] Instead, Borrow's narrator assumes the guise of a tinker to collect and enshrine cultural singularities that an imperialist, technocratic, and centralising agenda sought to denigrate or erase altogether.[119]

118. Nord, *Gypsies and the British Imagination*, 72.
119. Ann M. Ridler, 'Obedience and Disobedience: George Borrow's Idiosyncratic Relationship with the Bible Society', *Sowing the Word: The Cultural Impact of the British and Foreign Bible Society 1804–2004*, Stephen Batalden, Kathleen Cann, and John Dean, eds (Sheffield: Sheffield Phoenix Press, 2004), 286.

CHAPTER 3

'THE LAST GENUINE EXAMPLE OF THE PICARESQUE'?[1] *LAVENGRO* AND *THE ROMANY RYE*

Breaking the Laws of Genre

W. G. Sebald's 'The Mystery of the Red-Brown Skin', an essay included in *Campo Santo* (2006), surveys the published works of 'that tireless traveller' Bruce Chatwin:

> Just as Chatwin himself ultimately remains an enigma, one never knows how to classify his books. All that is obvious is that their structure and intentions place them in no known genre. Inspired by a kind of avidity for the undiscovered, they move along a line where the points of demarcation are those strange manifestations and objects of which one cannot say whether they are real, or whether they are among the phantasms generated in our minds from time immemorial.

This assessment says as much about Sebald's literary undertaking as it does Chatwin's abiding interest in travellers' tales of wonder, a tradition 'going back to Marco Polo where reality is constantly entering the realm of the metaphysical and miraculous'. It is also difficult to find a more elegant précis of *Lavengro* and *The Romany Rye*, texts which draw upon 'adventure stories looking back to our early childhood reading, collections of facts, dream books', and 'personal confession'.[2] The questions Sebald poses here regarding Chatwin's oeuvre – 'how to classify his books' – recalls Northrop Frye's appraisal of Borrow half a century earlier. In *The Anatomy of Criticism* (1957), Frye posits that *Lavengro* should

1. Lionel Stevenson defines *Lavengro* and *The Romany Rye* in these terms. See *The English Novel: A Panorama* (Boston: Houghton Mifflin, 1960), 293.
2. W. G. Sebald, 'The Mystery of the Red-Brown Skin: An Approach to Bruce Chatwin', *Campo Santo*, trans. Anthea Bell (New York: The Modern Library, 2006), 217.

be deemed a what-is-it, instead of a whodunit: 'Is Borrow's *Lavengro* fiction? Everyman's Library says yes; the World's Classics puts it under "Travel and Topography"'.[3]

Frye's concern with generic taxonomy has dominated the journalistic and scholarly debate surrounding *Lavengro* and *The Romany Rye* from the very start. Borrow, in what might be his first reference to *Lavengro*, wrote to his publisher John Murray on 1 December 1842: 'I hope our book [*The Bible in Spain*] will be successful. If so, I shall put another on the stocks – capital subject: early life, studies, and adventures; some account of my father.'[4] The next year, Richard Ford remarked to a correspondent that Borrow had sent him 'word that his *Life* is nearly ready, and it will run the *Bible* hull down. If he tells truth it will be a queer thing. I shall review it for the *Edinburgh*.'[5] *Lavengro, An Autobiography* was advertised in the January 1850 number of the *Quarterly Review*. *Tait's Edinburgh Magazine* enthused: 'Since the days of "Waverley Novels", no announcement of a book has excited more expectation than Mr. Murray's repeated advertisements of *Lavengro*.'[6] This notice would not have pleased the notoriously tetchy Borrow. *Lavengro*'s portrait of the artist-rambler as a callow young man, starting from the date of Borrow's birth, 1803, up to around 1826, was very different from the 'grand personages' of whom people 'have read in their novels', 'their Ivanhoes, their Marmions, and their Ladies of the Lake' (*LSGP* XCIV: 503). It is deeply ironic, the *Cornhill Review* averred in 1899, that Borrow voices an 'unaccountable' rancour against 'Sir Walter Scott', which led him to denounce the popularity of *Old Mortality* and *Waverley*. Such texts comprise, according to *The Romany Rye*'s narrator, an unblushing apology for arbitrary power, Jacobitism, and Catholicism. However, the most telling novelistic blueprint for Borrow's repackaging of picaresque – at least in the *Cornhill*'s judgement – was the Waverley novels and their portrayal of dramatic encounters among largely 'untamed' tribes.

Lavengro was not ready for release until February 1851, the year of the Hyde Park Great Exhibition, by which time Borrow had devised a new subtitle: *The Scholar, The Gypsy, The Priest*. The sheer oddity of

3. Northrop Frye, *The Anatomy of Criticism: Four Essays*, foreword by Harold Bloom (1957; Princeton and Oxford: Princeton University Press, 2000), 303. Frye argues that the 'romance-confession hybrid is found, naturally, in the autobiography of a romantic temperament, and is represented in English by the extroverted George Borrow' (312–13).
4. Quoted in Michael Collie, 'George Borrow's Joseph Sell', *Nineteenth-Century Fiction* (1982): 133–4.
5. Quoted in Shorter, 164. See also Ana Maria Suárez, 'Richard Ford. Travels in Spain 1830–1833', *British Art Journal* 15:2 (2014): 122. http://www.jstor.org/stable/43492124.
6. Anon. [William Bodham Donne], '*Lavengro*', *Tait's Edinburgh Magazine* 18 (1851): 270–6.

Borrow's professional career, as a colporteur in first Russia and then Spain would make his 'life', *Fraser's Magazine* opined, 'well worth the reading, provided always that George Borrow would have the goodness to write it'.[7] The problem for *Fraser's* was that *Lavengro* and *The Romany Rye*, in contrast to the autobiographies of, say, John Stuart Mill or even Thomas Carlyle, stage lived experience as if it is an elaborate game of hide and seek, an 'indistinguishable blend of truth and lies', 'forever hovering between Romance and Reality'.[8] This ambiguous fact-fiction relationship seemed calculated to hoodwink professional journalists by supplying something, as the *Saturday Review* wryly remarked, 'autobiographic *à faire rire*'.[9] Even the ordinarily reassuring and buoyant Ford confessed to being 'somewhat disappointed with the very *little* you have told us about *yourself*: I was in hopes to have had a full true and particular account of your marvellously varied and interesting biography'.[10] Perhaps at Murray's instigation, Borrow furnished a declaration of intent in his 1851 Preface to the First Edition of *Lavengro*:

> In the following pages I have endeavoured to describe a dream, partly of study, partly of adventure, in which will be found copious notices of books, and many descriptions of life and manners, some in a very unusual form.
>
> The scenes of action lie in the British Islands. Pray be not displeased, gentle reader, if perchance thou hast imagined that I was about to conduct thee to distant lands, and didst promise thyself much instruction and entertainment from what I might tell thee of them. (*LSGP*: vii)

This Preface suggests *Lavengro* is pitched at readers of voyages of territorial discovery who could not credit that it was feasible to publish 'anything interesting relative to travels in our own land'.[11] *Lavengro* and *The Romany Rye* ignore the far-flung imperial topographies familiar to acolytes of H. Rider Haggard's *Allan Quatermain*. Instead, Borrow recovers alternative English identities by depicting an island nation studded with disparate cultural and archaeological traces such as

7. [William Stirling], '*Lavengro* – "The Master of Words" ', *Fraser's Magazine* 43:255 (March 1851): 272–83.
8. Arthur Ransome, 'The Romany Rye', *The Bookman* 31:185 (February 1907): 229–30. [William Stirling], '*Lavengro* – "The Master of Words"', *Fraser's Magazine* 43:255 (March 1851): 272–83.
9. [Anon.], 'The "Redoubtable Borrow" ', *Saturday Review* 66:1710 (4 August 1888): 144–5.
10. Quoted in Robertson, *Richard Ford*, 306.
11. [Anon.], 'Reviews of Books', *Bury and Norwich Post and Suffolk Standard* 6299 (20 March 1900): 5.

Stonehenge (*LSGP* LX: 319). His 1850s texts restore 'wonder' – the primary article of Borrow's aesthetic credo, according to his editor, Theodore Watts-Dunton – by recording, in sharply observed detail, the flora, dimensions, and pre-Christian survivals of our shores: 'What a beautiful country is England! People run abroad [. . .] and leave their own behind unknown, unnoticed. [. . .] And then, again, what a country for adventures!' (*RR* XXX: 177).

For *The Athenaeum*, the vague prefatory reference to *Lavengro* as 'a dream, partly of study, partly of adventure', coupled with the new subtitle, was irrefutable evidence that Borrow had no more clue how to specify and promote his literary creation than contemporary print media outlets.[12] A baffled *Blackwood's Magazine* felt the adventures 'neither bear the impress of the stamp of truth, nor are they so arranged as to make the work valuable, if we consider it in the light of fiction'.[13] Borrow's switch in focus, from *The Bible in Spain*'s quickly moving parade of storms at sea, freezing sierras, and bandit-infested bridle-paths on the Iberian Peninsula to the furze and overgrown dingles of the 'British Islands', was a blow to his publisher Murray, though not a huge surprise. As Angus Fraser and Michael Collie explain, the first edition of 3000 copies of *Lavengro* lasted twenty years, and fewer than 6000 copies of *The Romany Rye* sold in Borrow's lifetime.[14]

Hail to Thee, Spirit of De Foe!

The lukewarm press and public reception of *Lavengro* reveals a wrong-headed insistence on viewing Borrow's creative project through a strictly autobiographical prism: 'various portions of the history are known to be a faithful narrative of Mr. Borrow's career'.[15] This fails to grasp what is a multifaceted ideological and stylistic medley. An early chapter of *Lavengro*, thick with apparently 'authentic' mundane detail, evokes the narrator's privations while compiling criminal biographies for an avaricious London publisher. Alongside this task, he drafts *The Life and Adventures of Joseph Sell, the Great Traveller*, a picaresque potboiler that is both a product of and a sly commentary on the hazards of aesthetic toil.

12. [Anon.], 'Review of *Lavengro*', *The Athenaeum* (8 February 1851): 159.
13. [Anon.], 'Lavengro', *The Home Journal* (New York) 15 (12 April 1851): 4.
14. See Collie and Fraser, *George Borrow: A Bibliographical Study* (Hampshire: St Paul's Bibliographies, 1984), 52. William I. Knapp, *The Life, Writings and Correspondence of George Borrow* (London: John Murray, 1899), II, 9, 17–21. Knapp's *Life* (II, 3–24) throws into relief Borrow's (sometimes fraught) relationship with his publisher and 'dear friend' John Murray III, as well as the gestation of *Lavengro*.
15. [Anon.], 'Reviews – George Borrow', *Quarterly Review* 101 (January–April 1857): 472.

No such volume exists in Borrow's oeuvre, though the name 'Joseph Sell' carries a waggish resonance: 'In Norfolk, as elsewhere, a "sell" is a word in current slang used for an imposture or a cheat.'[16] It is then that we realise why *Lavengro* and *The Romany Rye* situate Daniel Defoe, whose fiction is replete with swindlers, chancers, and canny operators, as the narrator's favourite author and creative lodestar. Defoe's influence, which Borrow's narrator proclaims with halting literariness in the opening pages ('England has better bards than either Greece or Rome, yet I could spare them easier far than De Foe') partially explains why contemporary professional journalists were so exercised by the truth-status of *Lavengro*. The *Christian Examiner*, for example, could not account for a text that was 'now running wild, as it would seem, in the most vagrant extravagance, and now settling down into honest and matter-of-fact biography'.[17]

Lavengro, instead of 'pursuing a topic' to a neat conclusion, epitomises, in George Hyde's recent estimation, a picaresque 'setting off cross-country at tangents', a haphazard movement in body and mind that 'takes greater pleasure in concatenated episodes unified by personal knowledge than in beginnings, middles, and ends'.[18] For the May 1851 *Tait's Edinburgh Magazine*, this work of detours, indiscipline, and divagations, in which Defoe emerges as a talismanic name, was hardly synonymous with a new frontier of literary communication: 'The public,' it averred, 'looking for a second Marco Polo, have been presented, instead, with a nineteenth-century De Foe.'[19] Borrow cites Defoe at least five times in *Lavengro* alone; reading *Moll Flanders* is a transformative spiritual event for specific characters like the 'apple woman' whom the narrator meets on London Bridge.[20] In Chapter III of *Lavengro* he recalls how, as a child, he first encountered *Robinson Crusoe*, which induces a moment of multiplied consciousness.[21] The flowing alliteration of liquid 'l' in 'strange thri*ll* of p*l*easure' intimates the delicious intensity of the folding of time back on itself. This is a simultaneous revisitation and recreation of the awe triggered by perusing a book 'which has exerted

16. Shorter, *George Borrow and His Circle*, 102–3. See also David Chandler, '"Born To Be a Great Traveller": Joseph Sell as Borrow's Imaginary Portrait of the Artist as a Young Man', *George Borrow: Three Fraser Memorial Lectures* (Warborough: Lavengro Press, 2014), 30–45.
17. [Anon.], 'Reviews: *Lavengro*', *Christian Examiner* (Boston) 50 (1851): 504–5.
18. Hyde, 'Why (Not) Read George Borrow?', 31.
19. [Anon.], '*Lavengro*', *Tait's Edinburgh Magazine* 18:209 (May 1851): 271.
20. See J. A. Garrido Ardila, ed., *The Picaresque Novel in Western Literature: From the Sixteenth Century to the Neopicaresque* (Cambridge: Cambridge University Press, 2015).
21. Richard Squibbs, 'Review of Garrido, ed., *The Picaresque Novel in Western Literature*', *Studies in the Novel* 47:4 (Winter 2015): 568–9.

over the minds of Englishmen an influence certainly greater than any other of modern times' (*LSGP* III: 28):

> I opened it, and as I did so another strange thrill of pleasure shot through my frame. The first object on which my eyes rested was a picture; it was exceedingly well executed, at least the scene which it represented made a vivid impression upon me, which would hardly have been the case had the artist not been faithful to nature. A wild scene it was—a heavy sea and rocky shore, with mountains in the background, above which the moon was peering. Not far from the shore, upon the water, was a boat with two figures in it, one of which stood at the bow, pointing with what I knew to be a gun at a dreadful shape in the water; fire was flashing from the muzzle of the gun, and the monster appeared to be transfixed. I almost thought I heard its cry. I remained motionless, gazing upon the picture, scarcely daring to draw my breath, lest the new and wondrous world should vanish of which I had now obtained a glimpse. (*LSGP* III: 18)

In *Lavengro*'s passages of anamnesis, concrete nouns often provide 'vivid' points of focus; verb forms are subtly altered (past to present participles 'peering', 'gazing', 'pointing'); effects appeal to eye and ear like anaphora ('I' plus verb formula), sibilance ('*s*ea', '*sh*ore'), assonance and alliteration ('*w*ild scene it *w*as', '*f*ire was *f*lashing', '*w*ondrous *w*orld'), and homeoteleuton (exceeding*ly*, hard*ly*, scarce*ly*). The ebbing and flowing between the labial ('w', 'm', 'b', 'p') and the glottal ('h') conveys the hypnotic potency of this Borrovian 'spot of time'. 'I almost thought', 'I heard', 'I remained', 'I obtained' imply the ceremonial iterations and sonorous cadence of Scripture, as if the young child suddenly 'glimpses' in *Crusoe* a holy book, a bearer of oracular insight, one belied by its 'dingy' calfskin binding. For critic Martin Armstrong, however, the narrator's remembrance of things past, the boy's 'raging curiosity' concerning 'the contents' of *Crusoe* (*LSGP* III: 17–18), arrayed in a self-consciously mannered and hypotactic style, is 'clumsy' and riddled with redundancies ('the journalese reluctance to call a spade a spade'). In the closing sentence, Armstrong asserts, 'one of the two phrases "I remained motionless" and "gazing upon the picture" might be cancelled without diminishing the impression of the child's absorption in the picture'.[22] Armstrong is also struck by what he construes as the narrator's unfortunate reliance elsewhere on formal

22. Martin Armstrong, *George Borrow* (London: Arthur Barker, 1950), 59–60.

apostrophes and periphrasis ('birds' are 'the feathered tribes' [*LSGP* LXVIII], 'horses' the 'equine race' [*LSGP* XIII]). Armstrong's objections signal that a written utterance should prioritise conceptual argument over style, which is at best ornamental, a superficial gloss, not a layered series of clues about how the child parses the objects of perception. Armstrong's chief complaint is this: the narrator's 'unwieldy' eighteenth-century diction seems ill-suited to orchestrate and convey the freshness of embodied cognition (namely the child's somatic 'thrill of pleasure'). However, the vowel and consonant patterns, far from gratuitous embroideries, cluster and cohere to mirror, as well as delineate the child's epiphany ('sc*a*rcely *da*ring to *dr*aw my br*ea*th').

The narrator's invocation of 'the spirit of De Foe!' (*LSGP* III: 19) here is not just a florid tribute to a literary predecessor who had instigated what Borrow felt was a seismic shift in the thematic, technical, and affective range of anglophone prose fiction. The allusion to the 'hunchbacked rhymer' in this episode suggests that Defoe had replaced Pope's classical learning ('bards of Greece or Rome') with a more urgent, street-savvy vernacular. Defoe's unquiet 'spirit' haunts the verbal masonry of the extract given, determining why particular pronouns and sound sequences are chosen over others to evoke how the engravings 'fascinated' the child's eye. This is neither a 'hangover from the past'[23] nor a misguided attempt to rebrand fustian locutions that Wordsworth famously critiqued in his 1800 Preface to the *Lyrical Ballads*. Rather, Borrow's narrator is at once perceiving and composing a scene that signifies an intricate economy of human attention for both the breathlessly rapt child and us. He renders the contrasts between verbal and visual texts, dramatic action ('fire was flashing'), and stasis ('motionless'), precisely graded via effects of suspension, rhythmic and grammatical parallelism, balance, and climax. Just as 'the monster appeared to be transfixed' in the tableau, so is the child *spellbound* by the accuracy with which *Crusoe*'s illustrator has concocted this 'wild scene', suggestive of elemental turbulence and mortal peril.

The calf-bound volume of Defoe, which furnishes the six-year-old boy with such delight in *Lavengro* ('new and wondrous world') is not one of those Wordsworthian 'beauteous forms'. Instead, the illustrated text belongs to a less rarefied milieu of domestic bric-a-brac that the narrator aligns with the earlier lyrical sensibility of Cowper, 'England's sweetest and most pious bard' (*LSGP* III: 15). Some contemporary reviewers construed Borrow's paeans to Cowper and Defoe as a quaint,

23. Hyde, 'Why (Not) Read George Borrow', 35.

even outdated stylistic signature. His intertextual strategies signal the opposite, however. Defoe's picaresque does more than chart a humble drifter's tribulations. Rather this literary mode epitomises a prowler or uncanny passenger within, and caustic about, a semiotic power structure which justifies market relations. Defoe's tales reverberate in some other accent, conveying a 'deep doubt at the heart of modernity, a doubt that refers to the questioning of the universal validity' of the financial scaffold that upholds 'this modernity'.[24] An instrument to think with then, especially at times of civic ferment, Defoe's picaresque crystallises for Borrow issues of representation, verisimilitude, and being 'faithful to nature' (*LSGP* III: 18) – in this case, 'faithful' to the 'history of subaltern classes', which is, as Gramsci notes, 'necessarily fragmented and episodic'.[25] So the narrator's obsession with Defoe's fictional scrappers, opportunists, and ne'er-do-wells reveals, as critic Philip Davis contends, 'a lost and alien part' of a pre-capitalist folk culture, 'and also somehow of himself'.[26] Richard Ford urged Borrow to keep the faith by elaborating this chronicle of 'the lower classes' (*LSGP* XXV: 161) – even if the text's blunt disregard for Victorian social climbers would necessarily affront sham-genteel, 'niminy-piminy' reading clusters:

> Avoid fine writing [. . .] and stick to personalities. Never fear the 'rum and rare'. Make the broth thick and slab. Never mind niminy-piminy people thinking subjects *low*: things are low in manner of handling. Draw nature in rags and poverty yet draw her truly. [. . .] I hate your silver-fork, curly-hair school; one cuckoo note is better than many commonplace conventionalities.[27]

Ford's emphasis on '*low*' here carries a complex political charge. Like 'De Foe', whose driving force of 'personality' is felt in his appeal as a first-hand witness of 'nature in rags and poverty' – a milieu captured by crime broadsides and Old English chapbooks – Borrow's foot-slogging protagonist does not recognise his roadside interlocutors as 'low'. He refuses to look and speak down to 'labourers and mechanics' (*LSGP* XXV: 161) from a well-appointed carriage. Standing alongside

24. Francisco J. Sanchez and Nicholas Spadaccini, quoted in Jorge Téllez, *The Picaresque and The Writing Life in Mexico* (Notre Dame, IN: University of Notre Dame Press, 2021), 10.
25. Antonio Gramsci, *Selections from the Prison Notebooks*, ed. and trans. Quintin Hoare and Geoffrey Nowell Smith (New York: International Publishers, 1971), 54–5.
26. Philip Davis, *The Victorians: The Oxford English Literary History. Volume 8, 1830–1880* (Oxford: Oxford University Press, 2002), 430.
27. Richard Ford to George Borrow, quoted in Knapp, I, 361. This passage is also quoted in Starkie, 'Introduction' to Borrow, *The Romany Rye* (London: Dent, 1949), xxvi.

and listening to testimony without condescension is a crucial gesture of solidarity with those for whom walking is a necessity of daily existence, not a source of bracing exercise or aesthetic diversion. By such means, *Lavengro* contests, resists, even defamiliarises the sociolects and 'conventionalities' of tourist guidebooks and novels of fine manners ('silver-fork' school).[28] For Borrow, the teleology of the mimetic, its architectonic coherence and glib stories of upward mobility, foist a bogus template upon a chaotic cosmos by implying that the arbitrary, the unjust, and the traumatic perform a weighty if not immediately discernible purpose ('it was good to be afflicted', a smug parish clergyman avows in *The Romany Rye* [XXXIV: 201]). Borrow's eponymous protagonist, by contrast, a 'wanderer the greater part' of his life (*LSGP* II: 9), registers the protean flux and evanescent value of human experience. Instead of a humanistic perception of a knowable locality, 'everything is enigmatical' (*LSGP* XXV: 159). Bakhtin's thesis in *The Dialogic Imagination* regarding 'the close link between the motif of meeting and the chronotope of the road ("the open road")' stresses how immemorial trackways are apt 'for portraying events governed by chance'. This reminds us of 'the sociohistorical heterogeneity of one's own country' given the range of events that occur along roads.[29] Building on Bakhtin's insights, Franco Moretti eloquently describes a particular symbolic topography, a 'country of roads: where strangers meet, walk together, tell each other the story of their lives'. This is, he argues, 'the great symbolic achievement of the picaresque: defining the modern nation as that space where strangers are never entirely strangers'.[30] What if, however, as in the case of Borrow's 1850s mock memoirs, the protagonist is a 'stranger' even to himself, rudderless and discomposed by his own deepest impulses, for whom the nation's 'fluid, tangled pathways' never quite unfurl 'a map of home'?[31] We see here what Roger Ebbatson discerns in the land-writing of Borrow's biographer Edward Thomas: a sense of an England that 'does not hold together' since it is 'an impossible space', a 'site of constantly renegotiated conflicts between different representations of English identity in which contrasting language and class orders struggle for precedence'.[32]

28. Richard Squibbs, 'Review of Garrido, ed., *The Picaresque Novel in Western Literature*', *Studies in the Novel* 47:4 (Winter 2015): 568–9.
29. M. M. Bakhtin, *The Dialogic Imagination*, trans. C. Emerson and M. Holquist (Austin: University of Texas Press, 1981), 98, 244–6.
30. Franco Moretti, *Atlas of the European Novel, 1800–1900* (London: Verso, 1997), 51.
31. See Ian Duncan, 'Wild England: George Borrow's Nomadology', 384–5.
32. Roger Ebbatson, *An Imaginary England: Nation, Landscape and Literature, 1840–1920* (Aldershot: Ashgate, 2005), 166–8.

This conception of England triggers in Borrow's roving narrator a 'great depression of spirits' (*RR* XXIII: 136); he registers an existential limbo or 'labyrinth' of disjointed events (*LSGP* XXV:159) among the downtrodden, the distressed, and the renegade. The quotidian lives of these 'playthings of fortune' are marked by tenuous working conditions and irregular income.[33] This focus on non-elite subjects, or in contemporary parlance, a rural precariat – 'an army of servants, grooms, postillions, shoeblacks, cooks, scullions' (*RR* XXIV: 140) – fosters a textual design of random contingency, interruption, and unsettlement where loose ends are left untied. Borrow's poetics of the provisional exposes how concepts of moral and aesthetic resolution fail to explain states of extreme need and insecurity among 'the poorer classes' (*LSGP* I: 5) who have 'nothing to subsist by' but their 'wits' (*RR* XLII: 270). The countercultural 'spirit of De Foe' operates at variance with that smooth uniformity of structure, rooted in basic processes of cause and effect, that the *Gentleman's Magazine* deemed indispensable to any novel's success as a plausible surrogate for actuality. The parabola of *Lavengro*, with its ceaseless, aimless migrations through sundry phases of civic life, plus a closing section that thwarts any hope of a cathartic outcome, was not, the *Magazine* protested, 'complete enough, nor is there enough in it', of 'definite aim and purpose to render it permanently popular'.[34] Similarly, *The Athenaeum*, upholding omniscient novelistic realism as a disciplinary skill and the model of providential deliverance with which it was associated, contended that *Lavengro* could 'scarcely be called a book at all'.[35] The eponymous protagonist 'has consorted with vagabonds, – but has learnt little from them except their slang'. For *The Athenaeum*, the text's want of 'philosophy' (*improving* moral didacticism) was of a piece with its author's pertinacious refusal to orchestrate dramatic events that unfold in a logical sequence and culminate in an emotionally satisfying payoff.[36]

In *Lavengro* and *The Romany Rye*, Defoe's 'spirit' is felt in other ways. *Moll Flanders*, for example, puts readers under pressure from the very opening sentence, via a retrospective first-person narrator, a lowborn fraudster whose episodic setbacks, humiliations, and narrow escapes on the road is enfolded in an apocryphal haze. To what extent is this

33. Tobias Smollett, 'The Life of Dr. Smollett, M.D.,' *The Miscellaneous Works of Tobias Smollett, M.D.*, 6 vols (Edinburgh: Mundell, Doig, and Stevenson, 1806), 183.
34. [Anon.], ['Mr. Urban'], 'Review of *Lavengro; the Scholar, the Gypsy, the Priest* by George Borrow', *Gentleman's Magazine* (March 1851): 293.
35. [Anon.], 'Reviews: *Lavengro* [First Notice]', *Athenaeum* 1215 (8 February 1851): 159–60.
36. [Anon.], 'Reviews: *Lavengro* [Second Notice]', *The Athenaeum* 1216 (15 February 1851): 188–9.

picara, a usurper of male privileges and mobility, in charge of their memories of exigency and privation, the arrangement and moral import of their disclosures? Similarly, *Lavengro* records what Edward Thomas terms 'life in the backward dream of memory'.[37] In this extended flashback, as *Blackwood's Magazine* noted, we are forced to confront the grievous limits of any single perspective; past and present events become smudged, 'the fact destroys the fiction, and the fiction neutralizes the fact'.[38] The narrator proceeds with an apparent biographical linearity. He openly addresses his 'gentle reader' and explains his date of birth and how he first 'saw the light' (*LSGP* I: 1). However, the 'truth' of his ethical and spiritual awakening or *enlightenment* is uncertain, as are other rhetorical scenarios in *The Romany Rye* where he entreats our indulgence. 'But to return to my own history,' he remarks in Chapter III of *Lavengro*, 'shall I state what intellectual progress I had been making up to this period? Alas! upon this point I have little to say calculated to afford either pleasure or edification' (*LSGP* III: 16). The omissions, evasions, or redactions are at least as intriguing as what survives the editorial amputations in this written 'history' of how he elevates himself above the averageness to which his 'low and plebeian origin' (*LSGP* I: 1) consigns him. And we must make a leap of faith before we credit this mischief-making narrator as one who has renounced links with that world of vice which the dominant power of market capitalism can never entirely quell. Concerning 'crime and virtue', he confesses at one stage, 'I was in doubt; I doubted that the one was blameable and the other praiseworthy' (*LSGP* XXV: 159). His first foray into this twilight zone beyond 'virtue' relates to a series of elliptical messages that he receives long before perusing the 'dingy' copy of Defoe.[39]

Through a Glass Darkly: Portrait of the Trickster as a Young Child

Lavengro charts the narrator's travels and travails as the second-born son of a Cornish recruiting officer, a 'man of excellent common sense' (*LSGP* XVIII: 110) in a newly formed regiment. He follows his father from barrack to barrack across 'Scottish crags and the heaths of Ireland' (*LSGP* XV: 94) during the Napoleonic era. For this nomadic narrator, the 'paths to knowledge' (*LSGP* III: 20) involve revelatory encounters

37. Thomas, *George Borrow: The Man and His Books*, 35.
38. [Anon.], 'Reviews: *Lavengro*', *Blackwood's Edinburgh Magazine* 69 (1851): 322–37.
39. See David Chandler, 'Borrow's *Robinson Crusoe*', *George Borrow Bulletin* 15 (Spring 1998): 7–27.

with assorted 'ruffians', horse-copers, thimbleriggers, and petty delinquents on moorland and fells (*LSGP* IX: 58). Chapter I chronicles from earliest infancy the progressive phases of his thinking, especially his seemingly magical skills as a 'devilkin', a 'sap-engro, a chap who catches snakes, and plays tricks with them' (*LSGP* II: 13). Adept at 'taming reptiles', aping other people's parlance, and acquiring obscure dialects, he eventually sets out for London hoping to become a professional poet-translator. Demoralised by years of impoverished obscurity in a soulless literary marketplace, overseen by a fluctuating oligarchy of bourgeois impresarios, he leaves the city to explore, on foot and horseback, the British edgelands. Borrow underscores the oneiric aspects of these wanderings in his 1851 Preface to *Lavengro* – 'part dream, part reality'. 'Dream', however, does not signify a self-indulgent creative ruse, one that deals indiscriminately with empirical data and fanciful invention. Rather it implies how childhood becomes 'an enchanted spot', or what critic Saidiya Hartman calls a type of 'archive', a '*dream book* for existing otherwise', for illuminating 'the possibility and the promise of the errant path' (my emphasis).[40] In this 'dream book', time flows in instances of heightened perception rather than seasonal shifts. The child's hedgerow discoveries are embellished, disillusionments elided, bizarre underclass figures suddenly materialise as if from a parallel dimension, while discrete slivers of feeling are tied and irradiated by lyrical asides. This is what prompted critic George Saintsbury to posit in his *History of Nineteenth-Century Literature* (1906) that *Lavengro* and *The Romany Rye* adjust 'the picaresque novel to *dreamland*, retaining frequent touches of solid and everyday fact'.[41]

Saintsbury's commentary is valuable. Borrow extends the scope of 'the picaresque novel' by incorporating motifs associated with the *bildungsroman*, whose tools of psychological analysis are more trenchant than those of earlier mock-autobiographies he admired, like Defoe's *Moll Flanders* or *Colonel Jack*. As George Hyde argues, the 'peculiar hesitations and tail-chasing reduplications and shifts of emphasis' in *Lavengro* 'seem to wind deeper into some unspoken personal mystery'.[42] This 'mystery' is bound up with the narrator's early experiences of 'everyday facts': 'By nature slow of speech', he cries when spoken to and 'many years elapsed before I was able to understand the nature

40. Saidiya Hartman, *Wayward Lives, Beautiful Experiments: Intimate Histories of Social Upheaval* (New York: Norton, 2019), xv, 93.
41. George Saintsbury, *A History of Nineteenth-Century Literature (1780–1895)* (London: Macmillan, 1906), 163.
42. Hyde, 'Why (Not) Read George Borrow?', 32.

of letters, or to connect them' (*LSGP* I: 7). He self-identifies as frail, 'sad and melancholy' (*LSGP* I: 6), comparing himself to a fathomless lagoon on a mountain peak, 'dark, solitary, and almost inaccessible'. Upon his perceptual faculties, we are told, 'gloomy shadows' formed, 'which, strangely modified as gusts of wind agitated the surface, occasionally assumed the shape of monsters' (*LSGP* I: 6). This echoes Book Five of Wordsworth's *Prelude*, where 'Esthwaite's Lake' emblematises the speaker's evolving poetic sensibility: as a boy 'not nine years old', he recalls the recovery of a drowned man from the depths of the lake, a 'spectre shape / of terror'.[43] In *The South Country* (1909), Borrow's biographer, Edward Thomas, also documents the 'terror that enrolled' a young Welsh boy for whom an eerie, 'endless pale road' signifies the nightmare, not the promise, of the peripatetic mode.[44] *Lavengro*'s narrator grasps from an early age what Thomas later evokes as a 'yawning pit': 'I was as a child in the habit of fleeing from society, and of sitting for hours together with my head on my breast'. Conscious of a 'peculiar heaviness within me', this 'strange sensation of fear' occasionally 'amounted to horror' (*LSGP* I: 7). Concerning this childhood dread the narrator recalls a curious episode involving a Jewish peddler. Sitting on the ground, the child draws meaningless patterns in the dust. To the amazed peddler, the narrator has 'the look of one of our people's children', a 'prophet's child' (*LSGP* I: 8). After claiming that the narrator can already read and write, the peddler flees when he discerns the traces in the sand, 'muttering something about "holy letters"' (*LSGP* I: 8). The peddler's ascription of preternatural capacities to the child seems to be confirmed when the narrator, 'not [yet] three years old', suffers a viper's bite. The wound transforms a sickly, nervous infant to one 'hale' and robust (*LSGP* II: 10). This new feeling of corporeal vitality brings with it a sharpened sense of his palpable surroundings. While sightseeing with his mother and brother in the Kentish coastal town of Hythe, the narrator discovers the ancient skull of a Danish pirate, 'a huge grim thing' that can barely be lifted.[45] The Daneman's skull, 'like the apparition of the viper in the sandy lane' (*LSGP* II: 13), represents, for the narrator at least, a crucially formative moment. He links his later command over 'brutes and reptiles' as well as old Norse dialects to this spectacle of 'confused and mouldering heaps' of bones (*LSGP* II: 12).

43. William Wordsworth, *The Prelude* (Harmondsworth, Middlesex: Penguin, 1987).
44. Edward Thomas, *The South Country* (London: J.M. Dent, 1909), 75.
45. Ford Madox Ford quotes this moment in Chapter XI of *The Cinque Ports*. See Ford Madox Hueffer [Ford Madox Ford], *The Cinque Ports: A Historical and Descriptive Record* (London and Edinburgh: Chapman, 1900), 219–20.

The narrator's gift of 'tongues' prompts the Romani community with whom he consorts in later chapters to label him a 'goblin' (*LSGP* IV: 33) because of his ability to marshal the incantatory nuances of words: 'Philosophy can explain many strange things', he observes, 'but there are some which are a far pitch above her' (*LSGP* II: 10). It is no accident that he speaks of his first exposure to *Robinson Crusoe* in terms of the numinous sensations already awakened by memories of the viper and the gigantic skull: 'something within told me that my fate was connected with the book' (*LSGP* III: 17).

That the viper seems to signal a mystical rather than a dangerous potency ('a line of golden light') is reinforced by the narrator's habit of withholding identifying labels. This is the process of perceiving with an entranced child's eye, largely unencumbered by conceptual prejudices, rather than generating an air of mystery for its own sake, as some early reviewers complained. He sketches people or cultural objects before categorizing them – signifying a desire to uncover and address tensions between names and what they represent. So the snake glides as 'a bright yellow', 'beautiful and glorious' (*LSGP* II: 9). This narrative tactic is of a piece with his reluctance elsewhere to disclose his full birth name: a tribute to earlier picaresque texts such as Mateo Alemán's *Guzmán de Alfarache* (1599–1604), in which a speaker camouflages their modest, mean, or scandalous upbringing by resorting to sobriquets, aliases, or *noms de plume*. In Defoe's *Colonel Jack*, the picaro-narrator declares that he knows little of any 'surname that belonged to me; so, I was left to call myself *Mr. Anything*, what I pleased, as fortune and better circumstances should give occasion' (my emphasis).[46] Borrow's narrator, another canny 'Mr. Anything' alert to the processes by which demographic groupings are devised, codified, and subjected to disciplinary control, prefers the title 'Lavengro' ('word-master') that the leader of a Romani clan bequeaths upon him. In the opening chapters, the narrator deliberately veils his proper name as well as his exact place in his own family. On one occasion he assumes a spectator's role, studying himself arriving home. A 'mirror' offers a topography of the traveller's body and 'sunburnt face':

> Why dost thou [mother] suddenly raise thy dark [. . .] eye from the volume with a somewhat startled glance? What noise is that in the distant street? [. . .] There is someone in the vestibule, and now the door of thy apartment opens, there is a reflection on the

46. Daniel Defoe, *Colonel Jack*, Gabriel Cervantes and Geoffrey Sill, eds (Ontario: Broadview Editions, 2015), 11.

> mirror behind thee, a travelling hat, a grey head and sunburnt face. My dearest Son! My darling Mother! (*LSGP* I: 4–5)

As readers, we do not learn the identity of this 'visitor' until the end of the passage, so we 'see' the narrator as 'a stranger' (*RR*: xxx). Readers become theatregoers: we watch as these 'actors' appear on stage, but do not know whether they are blood relations until they begin to address each other affectionately. The narrator is a 'reflection', an image seen in the glass. We must interpret Chapter 23 of *Lavengro* from a comparable standpoint. Related in the third person, the scene unfolds without any reference to proper names. Only after glimpsing the appearance of 'the youth' can we apprehend that these two individuals are, in fact, the young narrator and his tutor. These quasi-theatrical set-pieces, coupled with Borrow's strategy of opening a chapter not with already-established characters but rather with ambiguous pronouns, shadowy actor-participants, and discrete episodes, underscores the narrator's penchant for performing 'various kinds of tricks' with words (*LSGP* IV: 26). Other cloaking devices ('I have no intention of drawing a portrait of myself in childhood', 'at that time I never looked into mirrors' [*LSGP* I: 5]), uncanny doublings and substitutions proliferate across the two-part mock-memoir. The narrator's 'wonder' upon opening *Crusoe* as a child is intensified during his later engrossed strolls around London, whose shops are 'gorgeous with precious merchandise, and lighted up with lustres, the rays of which were reflected from a hundred mirrors' (*LSGP* XXXII: 198).

The narrator's self-proclaimed otherness, singularity, and love of disguise – later in *The Romany Rye* 'he wanders the country with a face grimy from occasionally mending kettles' (*RR* V: 282) – is reinforced by his father's uneasy reaction to him as a stranger in the house (Chapter XIV). '"God bless the child! I love him, I'm sure; but I must be blind not to see the difference between him and his brother. Why, he has neither my hair nor my eyes; and then his countenance! why, 'tis absolutely swarthy, God forgive me! I had almost said like that of a gypsy' (*LSGP* XIV: 87). His second son's 'swarthy' skin may irretrievably impair the child's prospects of gainful employment. The exclamation 'God forgive me!' shows the soldier's susceptibility to the rise of European nationalisms and the stereotyping (even criminalising) of itinerant minorities which results. It also suggests the narrator's mystical connection with the 'ways and manners' of demonised social and ethnic clusters (*LSGP* XIV: 88). Borrow realised through his intensive scrutiny of Defoe that picaros thrive, not just survive, by repeatedly rescripting their own lives. It only takes a deft costume change to become

'Mr. Anything'. A picaro sharpens the trained actor's gift for donning then spurning a dizzying variety of social personae and rhetorical strategies; this eclectic ingenuity of performance is about not getting trapped in any one style. As in the early childhood encounter with the Jewish peddler, Borrow's narrator is 'everlastingly posing'; he makes himself unearthly to test, trouble, even collapse, the very notion of perceptible, incontrovertible ethno-cultural attributes.[47] His mask-wearing is even more audacious given that the parents who raise him are admired by neighbours for their archetypal white-is-right, strongly Protestant, and Royalist 'rectitude'. His Cornish father has 'passed the greater part of his life in meritorious exertion in the service of his country' (XIV: 86). The narrator's brother meanwhile combines an 'Anglo-Saxon' sense of fair play with a 'Celtic' verve which contrasts with the narrator's own 'melancholy' disposition.

As if to buttress his deep affinity with ethnic others, the narrator intuits a 'poetical' quality in the commercial and social transactions of those deemed eccentrics, renegades, or beneath contempt by his bigoted father – Quakers, 'dark-faced Lascars', and 'Rabbins of the Sephardim' (*LSGP* LI: 285). The narrator's body seems marked by fugitive or persecuted 'strangers' (*LSGP* I: 7). He has 'a kind of irregularity' in his 'features' which bespeaks 'something of the Armenian look' (*LSGP* LXIX: 280). However, the narrator's 'swarthy' skin tone implies the *unpoetical* reality of being openly targeted due to supposed ethnic inferiority. This trope reminds us of the narrator's alertness to the Romani whose 'tents' are 'as tawny as their faces' (XVII: 107), evoking William Cowper's tawny-skinned gypsies, a 'vagabond tribe' garbed in fluttering rags from the 1785 poem *The Task* (l. 568). The young narrator's 'vagabond', 'irregular' credentials are enhanced by how he assumes the 'look' of Irish 'rascals', crooks, and loafers (XIV: 88). Elsewhere, he is designated as a 'devilkin!' (*LSGP* IV: 33) whose speech patterns reveal 'flowers of Irish rhetoric' (*LSGP* XII: 72).[48] All these minutiae indicate that he personifies an 'uncommon' energy and eloquence, as well as insight into the nature, causes, and consequences of Romani alterity.

The Magic of Words

> The author of [. . .] *The Romany Rye* knows the advantage of a sign which looks cabalistic and encourages a belief in the possession of

47. See Francis Hindes-Groome, 'New Books – *The Bible in Spain*', *The Bookman* 17:101 (February 1900): 145–6.
48. Walter Starkie, 'Introduction' to George Borrow, *Lavengro* (London: J. M. Dent & Sons, 1970), vii.

> strange gifts and virtues, which people who only speak and write in their plain mother-tongue cannot assume.[49]

The 1857 *Athenaeum* review of *The Romany Rye* noted how Borrow portrays the narrator's passion for, or possession by, the intoxicating 'magic of words'. It is this passion which brings him into close contact with underclass groups like Romani who regale him with songs and tales in a seemingly 'cabalistic' language beyond the 'plain mother-tongue'. The cavalcade of nonconformist, troubled, and 'reprobate' figures that the itinerant narrator meets on his trek are all aspiring, and in some cases, obsessive storytellers (*RR*: 305). Some contemporary journalists bridled at *The Romany Rye*'s demand that we assume a very active interpretive role here, hence the rhetorical challenge 'What does the reader think?' at the close of Chapter XIV. Borrow's picaresque is a frequently 'interrupted' chronicle where esoteric 'signs' function by turns as blessing or hex (*RR* XVII: 112). After his first exposure to *Crusoe*, the narrator represents his interlocutors through the lens of other 'wondrous' volumes by Defoe (*LSGP* II: 12). So, the 'old apple-woman' (*LSGP* XL: 240) on London Bridge, grieving for the loss of her criminal son, receives spiritual solace from perusing *Moll Flanders*. This 'uncouth-looking old volume' bound with 'greasy black leather', like the narrator's 'dingy' *Crusoe*, transmits the deathless 'air, style and spirit of the writer' who 'first taught' the young boy to love a literary mode which celebrated resilience and roguery for its own sake irrespective of an enforced moral standpoint.

Moll Flanders and later first-generation romantic texts allow the narrator to better grasp his own fruitless 'strivings' and 'strugglings' (*RR* VIII: 50) – as well as the profound psychological crises that beset other troubled readers on his route. He buys a copy of the Bible for the apple-woman when the illicit escapades of Moll Flanders begin to unnerve her. He relieves the suicidal dissenting Welsh preacher Peter Williams of his 'mental misery' with a citation from the 'unabashed De Foe' (*LSGP* III: 19). In Chapter XXII of *The Romany Rye*, the narrator meets a bachelor whose daily reading of Wordsworth has cured his 'malady' of insomnia (*RR* XXII: 132). Later he learns of a kindly old gentleman whose recovery from the grief caused by his fiancée's tragic death is expedited by the discipline of decoding Mandarin Chinese 'hieroglyphics' etched on porcelain trinkets (*RR* XXXII: 185). Like the narrator, this gentleman proves himself a sedulous philologist by mastering an extremely challenging language largely unaided. In myriad other micro-stories, the narrator intervenes personally, offering reassurance

49. [Anon.], 'Reviews: *The Romany Rye*', *The Athenaeum* 1543 (23 May 1857): 653.

to emotionally brittle figures who are, in different ways, suffering a long *sentence* (an interplay of il/literacy and il/legality). While he produces decisive change in other people's lives through the teachings of 'singular' volumes, some from the picaresque canon (*LSGP* XXXI: 287), he cannot rid himself of persistent and debilitating bouts of readerly muddle and misgiving. He is racked by doubts that he is 'wasting [his] time foolishly and *unprofitably*' (XXIX: 183; my emphasis) in pursuing a career as a professional translator and poet. These nervous attacks – epilepsy or melancholia? – point to the psychic cost of disappointing his Cornish father, who expects him to train in the law, a vocation that induces in the young man a 'state of torpor'. Such existential ennui is remedied by parsing 'precious relics' of Welsh, which he believes to be 'the first speech of Britain, perhaps of the world' (*LSGP* XIX: 117).

The 'dreadful fears and despondencies' (*LSGP* LVI: 307) that bedevil the narrator as he rambles across the British edgelands are indissolubly tied to problems of language acquisition, bookishness, and self-representation. The narrator's 'horror' is such that the 'lamp of reason' is 'unable to dispel' this 'eidolon' from waking perception (*LSGP* XVIII: 110). At one stage, he speculates whether his 'shattered nerves' might be a wellspring of artistic innovation, 'the mother of wisdom, and of great works: it is the dread of the horror of the night that makes the pilgrim hasten on his way' (*LSGP* XVIII: 111). However, the prospect of a creative surge seems far removed from the sporadic 'horrors' that tip the narrator into a neurasthenic collapse (*LSGP* IV: 117, 437–41). Three of the embedded tales in *Lavengro* and *The Romany Rye* evoke the essence, dimensions, and affective repercussions of this 'horror' since the term reverberates through each one. The nauseating anxiety that afflicts each character mirrors that felt by the narrator, who is a victim of his own 'peculiar mind and system of nerves' (*RR*: 302). Just as fictional messages conveyed through 'yellow and dog-eared pages' aid some characters in existential crises, so challenges of mis/translation trigger in others acute psychic 'maladies'.

The 'apple-woman' is an elderly fruit-seller with whom the narrator converses in the eighth chapter of *Lavengro*. She reads religiously (and literally) from *Moll Flanders*, a 'volume' which, according to her, instead of showing 'the terrible consequences of crime', rather confirms that there is little 'harm in stealing' (*LSGP* XXXI: 194). Like the narrator, the apple-woman believes her own lived experiences are woven into the verbal texture of someone else's literary production. She construes *Moll Flanders* not as a rousing, fanciful picaresque romance. Instead, it is indisputable evidence that her cherished son, a thief transported to Botany Bay, will eventually return to her, just as the eponymous protagonist 'came back' in Defoe's 'wondrous' text (*LSGP* III: 19). However, when she recalls the Biblical commandment 'Thou shalt not steal', having first surveyed these words in a school primer, she bewails her avid recreational reading of *Moll Flanders*. The narrator can only help the apple-woman, who assigns 'the vices and follies of her life to being able to read', by exchanging her copy of the now irredeemably sullied Defoe for a Bible (*LSGP* XLIV: 256). In a novel that many 1850s reviewers deplored as shapeless, Borrow shows here a subtle sense of design. He encourages us to measure the apple-woman's predicament against the narrator's own, whose 'peculiarly miserable circumstances' as a hack-author in London Bohemia, generating 'copy' to placate an uncouth yet capricious public, evokes Thackeray's story of Pendennis and Warrington. The depersonalising experiences of Borrow's narrator in this joyless metropolitan milieu had 'nearly killed him' and he gets 'sick of reading' (*RR*: 326).

The 'mighty preacher' Peter Williams's tale also revolves around the recondite potency of books, papers, and manuscripts. The narrator is rescued and tended by this Welshman and his wife after the Romani matriarch Mrs Herne tries to kill him with a poisoned cake (*LSGP* LXXI: 381). In relating his own 'history', the tormented Williams confesses that, as a child, he committed what he terms 'the sin against the Holy Ghost'. The result is that he suffers bouts of 'horror' and attempts suicide after reading an extract from the Welsh Bible. The unnamed sin here seems to be that of 'blasphemy' – using words in a forbidden manner, 'the remembrance of which in after life' preys upon the preacher's already strained nerves (*RR*: 305). As with the aged apple-woman, Williams's mental health struggles stem from being a literal reader. When the 'horror' of his transgression overpowers him, he peruses his father's Bible 'at random', only to find a passage condemning all those who commit his sin. The narrator saves a suicidal Williams not with the 'Good Book'. Instead, he selects a quotation 'from the life of Mary Flanders, cut-purse and prostitute, which life Lavengro had been in the habit of reading at the stall of his old friend the apple-woman, on London Bridge, who had herself been very much addicted to the perusal of it, though without any profit whatever' (*RR*: 306). The narrator contends that Williams's real sin here is appearing 'proud, fanciful, and squeamish' around 'low society' – an insight that acts as a balm to Williams's 'agonised mind' (*RR*: 306).

Like Peter Williams and the apple-woman, the unnamed 'Author' in the third embedded text longs to unburden himself of his psychic woes and 'horrors', some of which mirror the narrator's irrational habits and gestures. The obsessive-compulsive 'Author' ranks as one of the most stricken figures among the brigade of misfits, malcontents, and castaways in *Lavengro* and *The Romany Rye*. The severity of his plight is marked by the epizeuxis 'Mercy, mercy! What will become of me? I am afraid I shall go mad' (*LSGP* LXV: 343). He cannot help but touch with his finger every gewgaw he sees to stave off some dreaded eventuality or 'evil chance' (*RR*: 362). His formative years, like the narrator's own, are 'overshadowed', as he describes it, by the fear of his mother's death (*LSGP* LXV: 342). Both men also brood incessantly over questions of provenance and providence, human agency and authenticity, as well as the tangible circumstances that make narrative art possible. The 'Author', in addition to his morbid *folie de toucher*, cannot rid himself of a suspicion that everything he publishes simply repeats and reheats the findings and imagery of other, more precocious literary stylists. His anguished testimony triggers a mode of repetition. At an overnight stay at the Author's residence the guest-narrator dreams that he has become his host by 'acting over the story which I had heard before I went to bed' (*LSGP* LXVII: 351). In these disturbing dreams, the narrator imagines he had completed a book and bequeathed it 'to the world, and the world shouted; and all eyes were turned upon me, and I shrunk from the eyes of the world' (*LSGP* LXVII: 351). Are these shouts of widespread critical approbation, like those which greeted the publication of *The Bible in Spain*, giving Borrow fleeting celebrity status in literary London during the 1840s? Or does the narrator 'shrink' from an irate and vituperative crowd? Like the mysterious 'Author', whom he perceives as a kindred spirit with a 'gift of words' (*LSGP* LXV: 344), Borrow's narrator is gripped by insecurities that his published texts will be vigorously mocked as vulgar, trite, not entirely in his own voice – a painful reminder of his London hackwork assembling other people's textual scraps: the *Newgate Lives and Trials*. What seems equally probable, however, is that the narrator, given to insinuating he is undercover, hiding in plain sight, living a romance of the margins, *shrinks* from a settled, market-driven milieu. In this more professional world, an audience can read his 'book/body' by its 'cover/face' – on which his proper name is emblazoned. Borrow's narrator is acutely conscious of the risks attendant on being revealed or uncostumed in this manner. This implies a kind of legibility, visibility, or permanent public trace that can be classified as personhood or an obvious authorial brand by the 'pseudo-critics' and pettifogging bureaucrats against whom he inveighs in *The Romany Rye*'s virulently acerbic addenda.

In each of these three micro-stories, the narrator identifies and addresses the source of a 'horror'. This is crucially what separates the triad of 'crisis tales' from the narrator's own rare nervous disorder.

His is 'a dread', he concedes, 'of I know not what, and there the horror lies' (*LSGP* XVIII: 112). The affliction eludes diagnostic categories, just as *Lavengro* and *The Romany Rye* defied efforts by disgruntled middlebrow pundits to align the volumes with a recognisable literary mode: 'is this a history' of Borrow's life, 'or a romance of which he is the hero?', the 1851 *Fraser's Magazine* pondered.[50] Regarding this triad of micro-tales, the narrator seeks to exercise the control he has already displayed as a professional 'translator' (*LSGP* XLVIII: 275). In each instance, he maintains his fantasy of analytical authority, ever hopeful of uncovering a partial panacea for 'the dark feeling of mysterious dread which comes over the mind' (*LSGP* XVIII: 110). There is solace in the interpretive act, in both the knowledge of 'cabalistic' lore and the proficiency to express it. Concerning the elderly apple-woman and Peter Williams, the narrator takes pride in discerning the 'principle of woe itself, the fountain head of all sorrow co-existent with man' (*LSGP* XVIII: 110). In the case of the unhappy 'Author', however, the narrator's prescription is ignored.

It is telling that the narrator's own melancholia coincides with those occasions when he is in danger of sliding into a fixed public role, or plagued by worry that he is little better than other Gorgios [non-Romani interlopers], whom gypsy matriarch Mrs Herne chides unsparingly as 'stupid, *single-tongued* idiots' (*LSGP* XVII: 104; my emphasis). Borrow's version of the picaro suggests that one must be ready to play 'all parts', moving adroitly between linguistic registers, selecting then discarding various occupational masks (attorney's clerk, bookseller's hack, vagrant tinker, assistant ostler).[51] While the multiplication of social poses generates existential unease in *Lavengro* and *The Romany Rye*, it also signifies that a single name, 'tongue', or subject position cannot account for the recurrent and elusive felt sensations that the narrator tries to convey.[52] Without that ideological agnosticism and shiftiness, beliefs can harden into a lazy reliance on ethno-cultural stereotypes, as the narrator asserts in Chapter IX of *Lavengro*: 'A bigot and an Orangeman! Oh, yes! It is easier to apply epithets of opprobrium to people than to make yourself acquainted with their history and position' (*LSGP* IX: 60). In evoking different Irish communities, the narrator undercuts, even reverses the swift judgements of contemporary ethnography, by first portraying

50. [Anon.], '*Lavengro* – The Master of Words', *Fraser's Magazine* 43:255 (March 1851): 273.
51. [Anon.], 'A Bible-Distributor Painted by Himself: *The Romany Rye*', *The Rambler* 9 (February 1858): 135–6.
52. See Lucille Herbert, 'George Borrow and the Forms of Self-Reflection', *University of Toronto Quarterly* 40 (Winter 1971): 152–67.

the object of scrutiny before taxonomising it. Thus, his initial portrayal of the locals in Chapter IX of *Lavengro* contradicts the subsequent disobliging view of the 'rascal Irish' proffered by his chauvinistic military father, who is more concerned with defending his family's reputation as 'sturdy yeoman stock', living 'close to the land' and attending church with 'great regularity'.[53]

Navigating a Labyrinth of Language

The narrative trajectory of *Lavengro* and *The Romany Rye* – the protagonist's emergence as a learned and 'shifty' iconoclast, a free-spirited 'hero' of the road (*RR*: 311) – is punctuated by efforts to record, and decrypt, other wayfarers' tangled and tall tales. These interpolated and elaborate micro-stories (e.g. the postillion's, Jack Dale's, Murtagh's) reflexively underline the narrator's facility with a dizzying array of 'low' and 'high' linguistic procedures, from cramming 'Lilly's Latin Grammar' (*LSGP* VI: 38), compiling pulpy *Chronicles of Newgate* (*LSGP* XXXVI: 214), and producing translations with 'notes critical, historical, and explanatory'. His eclectic repertoire of textual skills cannot stop him querying the substance and legitimacy of his own erudition and lived experience, or betraying frustration at impulses he cannot classify ('a dread I know not what'), let alone control. In declaring himself 'a shrewd walker, thanks to constant practice', he deviates from 'ground firm to the tread' and gets lost in a metaphorical 'labyrinth of doubt' (*LSGP* XXV: 159). This is apparent in his early drudgeries in London Bohemia, hawking about 'unsaleable translations of Welsh and Danish bards'.[54] Through this vortex of discordant tastes and fashions, ensnared in capitalised existence, with its cycles of rent and debt, alienation and wage labour, he makes himself,

> master of the sum of human wisdom; namely that everything was enigmatical and that man is an enigma to himself; thence the cry of 'What is truth?' I had ceased to believe in the truth of that in which I had hitherto trusted, and yet could find nothing in which I could put any fixed or deliberate belief (*LSGP* XXV: 159).

Here the narrator takes up a position of extreme scepticism. In a site of calcified habit, violent rupture, and negation, 'Is not all that I see a lie', or '– a deceitful phantom? Is there a world, and earth, and sky? Berkeley's doctrine—Spinoza's doctrine! Dear reader, I had at that

53. Eileen Bigland, *In the Steps of George Borrow* (London: Rich and Cowan, 1951), 15.
54. Herbert Jenkins, *The Life of George Borrow* (London: John Murray, 1912), i.

time never read either' (*LSGP* XXV: 160). He disparages the idealist philosophy linked with Berkeley and Spinoza – where all objects are mediated by subjective perception. Nevertheless, his own toils in a figurative 'labyrinth' are triggered by these very misgivings. Despite aiming to 'master' the 'sum of human wisdom', a hidden design escapes his gaze; or worse, an absence of any absolute logic or discernible 'pattern' in this tumultuous 'world of sensations and ideas' (*LSGP* III: 17). That would explain his inability to make firm professional commitments. His is an in-between subjectivity, neither property owner nor full-time worker, to the obvious distress of his military father who thinks his second son is either fatuous or secretive. The narrator's neurasthenic 'dread' is compounded by the fact that his translational labours require him to submerge his voice to render and animate the cadences of others. But what if translation is 'at best an echo, and it must be a wonderful echo to be heard after the lapse of a thousand years' (*LSGP* XXV:160)? Rather than supplying sudden, revelatory expansions of thought, his translations leave him deflated: his textual efforts will not invest his 'name' or 'signature' with the cultural kudos and permanency he craves. He falls short of Thomas Carlyle's lofty conception of 'the *true* Literary Man, what we here call the *Hero* as Man of Letters', who is 'our most important modern person', a veritable 'Prophet' for those wishing to savour thought-adventures, 'full of splendour'.[55] Not only does the narrator fear he is slavishly aping the locutions of others: he suspects that his own artistic creations are tepid copies of the weighty sayings of those whom he regards with unqualified 'respect and veneration', like Defoe: '"There is nothing new under the sun!" exclaims the king in Jerusalem who is himself only repeating what Buddha said "thirty centuries before"' (*LSGP* XXV: 160–1). Behind every thought, the narrator implies, is the spectre of another thought, the existence of which strips all other renditions of their conceptual freshness and heft.

The narrator's disillusioning metropolitan sojourn leads him to a position in which 'the material' of his own philological and poetic experiments seems like a sad, distant 'echo' of 'an original speech' (*LSGP* XVII: 107). His research is shot through with disclaimers and contradictions that mirror, condense, and elucidate but rarely resolve the civic and philosophical ambiguities of his London routine. Little wonder then that the narrator finds his own stable personhood shaken: 'Am I not myself a dream – dreaming about translating a dream?' (*LSGP* XXXVI: 218) – a dream that proffers scant opportunities for

55. Thomas Carlyle, *On Heroes, Hero-Worship, and the Heroic in History*, ed. Henry David Gray (New York: Longmans, Green, and Co., 1906), 151–2.

self-development or self-discovery. What the increasingly frantic narrator realises is that every metropolitan institution or 'settled' profession (*RR* V: 31) is geared towards deliberately programming him; yet if he does not have a niche in a socioeconomic framework, the danger is that he might never escape this 'labyrinth' of crippling angst. As Borrow would have noted from reading European picaresque fiction such as *Lazarillo* and *Gil Blas*, dread, abjection, and precarity constantly shadow the picaro's pursuit of cultural objects, property, and professional wellbeing. Like the beleaguered nomadic wanderers in these texts, the narrator strives for eloquence within and against the grain of his different audiences: urban and rustic, dominant and resistant, endemic and exotic, settled and itinerant, all variously perplexed about the mechanisms of individual and institutional authority.[56] This partially explains why *Lavengro* and *The Romany Rye* show how the narrator's scholarly allusions – in the case presented shortly quoting the ancient bard of sub-Roman Britain 'Taliesin' – cannot completely veil his exhausted panic, even 'horror', that his self-identity is as fragile as those similarly vexed ramblers he meets, such as the guilt-ridden Welsh preacher Peter Williams:

> Peter [Williams] came running after me: 'One moment, young man, who and what are you?'
>
> 'I must answer in the words of Taliesin', said I; 'none can say with positiveness whether I be fish or flesh, least of all myself. God bless you both!'
>
> 'Take this', said Peter; and he thrust his Welsh Bible into my hand. (*LSGP* LXXX: 432)

Even the holy 'Word' of Williams's 'Welsh Bible' cannot proffer the epistemic comfort the narrator craves. This is a stark contrast to the outspoken confidence of the pilgrim-narrator in *The Bible in Spain*, whose missionary enterprise is fuelled by the affective and spiritual resonance that he discerns in the Gospels. The attempt at a genial tone in the extract just given ('God bless you both!') stresses, rather than disguises, the narrator's difficulties both with the act of achieving 'high name and celebrity' through the permanency of print (*LSGP* XVII: 107) and the process of self-construction that takes him through a spectrum of public roles. There are some benefits to this revelling in role-play: crafting new expressive modes, social scripts, and myths of citizenship. However, there is always the grave risk that manufacturing oneself through premeditated artifice ('none can say [. . .] whether

56. See C. M. Bowen, 'George Borrow', *Westminster Review* 173:3 (March 1910): 302.

I be fish or flesh') strays into the ultimate diffusion and loss of self. The unfettered liberty associated with a 'vagabond on the roads of England' (*RR* VI: 37) may devolve into a nightmare, where personhood becomes an anarchic assemblage of subject positions.

The Horror! The Horror!

The narrator's plight – 'none can say with positiveness whether I be fish or flesh' – was, for late twentieth-century admirers of *Lavengro* and *The Romany Rye*, such as Anthony Burgess, the most salient facet of the saga's formal, affective, and conceptual ambition, given its blending of epic and lyric, dream and drama. Burgess evokes the sudden visitations of 'horrors' as a 'black incubus of a kind more interesting to the exorcist than the alienist or blood-letter'.[57] Burgess's phrasing is suggestive. This 'black incubus' – or what A. S. Byatt described in 1982 as 'fits of black, nihilistic hysteria' – signals how the narrator's undiagnosed psychic ailment in *Lavengro*'s early chapters ('a dread I know not what') gradually assumes the looming somatic presence of 'the Man in Black', a mouthpiece of Popish idolatry.[58] It is the unclean spirit of Roman Catholicism that the narrator 'exorcises' from the 'body politic' in *The Romany Rye*. This is a marked shift of emphasis from *The Bible in Spain*, especially its blithe claim that British 'people are too fond of light to embrace darkness': they 'would smile at the idea of exchanging their gospel privileges for the superstitious ceremonies' of 'the church of Rome' (*BIS* XXI: 272–3). In *The Romany Rye*, the Jesuit Man in Black crows that the British are peculiarly vulnerable to his rival creed because the 'middle and upper classes' are meretricious consumers. A patrician's unabashed 'love of what is foreign', turning himself into an exotic curio or fantastic human anecdote, is evidenced by their dressing up in 'a *zamarra*' (*RR* IV: 19). This undiscriminating relish for overseas fads, customs, and manners will, the Man in Black predicts, inevitably lead to a wholehearted embrace of 'foreign' religion. The postillion's tale at the end of *Lavengro* describes this very occurrence. He informs the narrator of a baronet's family he formerly served who, while sightseeing in Italy, were manipulated by a cabal of Catholic priests, overseen, as it turns out, by the Man in Black.

57. Anthony Burgess, 'The Open Road of Language', *The Observer* (21 September 1982): 32.
58. A. S. Byatt, 'The Scholar Gypsy', *The Times* (2 December 1982): 10. See also Sally Shuttleworth's account of Borrow's 'inexplicable fear' in *Fear in the Medical and Literary Imagination, Medieval to Modern: Dreadful Passions*, Daniel McCann and Claire McKechnie-Mason, eds (London: Palgrave, 2018), 188–201; Clive Wilkins-Jones, '"Is it possible that I am under the roof of an author?": Borrow's treatment of the creative sensibility in *Lavengro*', *George Borrow Bulletin* 34 (2007): 62–71.

The family, taught to 'despise the religion of their own land', 'take up that of the foreign country in which they were' (*LSGP* XCVIII: 536).

The postillion's vivid 'witness statement' serves a crucial function in Borrow's textual design. The 'horror' that the narrator portrays in *Lavengro* as crippling despondency becomes a violently anti-Papist Anglicanism, to which *The Romany Rye* gives unbridled voice. So shrill is this note in *The Romany Rye* that the narrator's increasingly paranoid sketch of the 'cat-like and gliding' Catholic priest, operating undercover to convert the credulous in the years predating the 1829 Catholic Emancipation Act (*LSGP*: ix), invites comparison with Dostoevsky's Roman Catholic cardinal, the 'Grand Inquisitor' from *The Karamazov Brothers* (1880). The Inquisitor's dogmas and equivocations in his lengthy monologue seem to prepare the ideological ground for the emergence of atheistic Russian Communist totalitarianism.

Pointed early references to the narrator's 'black' moods and disturbing doubts in *Lavengro* are striking for how Borrow blends the grave cadences and archaic second-person pronouns of the 1611 King James Version with a note of more modern epistemological gloom reminiscent of Joseph Conrad's seafaring tales ('inscrutable', 'horror'):

> the flood-gates of horror may be cast open, and the dark stream engulf him for ever and ever! Then is it not lawful for man to exclaim, 'Better that I had never been born!' Fool, for thyself thou wast not born, but to fulfil the inscrutable decrees of thy Creator; and how dost thou know that this *dark principle* is not, after all, thy best friend; that it is not that which tempers the whole mass of thy corruption? It may be, for what thou knowest, the mother of wisdom, and of great works: it is the dread of the horror of the night that makes the pilgrim hasten on his way. (*LSGP* XVIII: 111; my emphasis)

The mature 'pilgrim' Lavengro recalls this moment when seized by a severe epileptic fit in Mumper's Dingle: 'I found my right hand grasping convulsively the three forefingers of the left'. In the Dingle he 'started up' and 'could scarcely repress the shriek which was rising to my lips. Was it possible? Yes, all too certain; *the evil one* was upon me; *the inscrutable horrors* which I had felt in my boyhood' (*LSGP* LXXXIV: 449; my emphasis). These figurations, hinting at the manic-depressive anguish that regularly prostrates him, are seeded early: the 1851 Preface to *Lavengro* depicts the Church of England jettisoning 'Popery' from the island nation 'with disgust and horror' (*LSGP*: ix). What the Anglican Church ejects is coded as a 'dark stream/dark principle', implying an inescapably alien source of 'corruption' that once thrived in the shadows before the Reformation's cleansing light. Such a 'dark principle', now embodied by the gliding Man in Black, proves seductive to the 'weak, the timid', and the snobbish, such as Parson Platitude in *Lavengro*, the son of a tanner who 'went to college an ass' and 'returned a prig' and a Tractarian convert (*LSGP* LXVII: 355).

Recent critics, like Roy Kerridge, find the literary portrayal of Borrow's atheistic priest (the 'evil one') so intemperate as to be implausible, serving at best a one-dimensional and predictable allegorical function.[59] Yet the anti-Catholic vitriol of *Lavengro* and *The Romany Rye* reflected contemporary parliamentary debates in which many self-declared 'old school' Tory MPs like Henry Drummond confounded religious liberty with the 'horrors' of papal encroachment. The 'Romish Controversy' – and questions of religious affiliation more broadly – were deeply political matters for Drummond and similarly minded parliamentarians in 1850, the year before *Lavengro* was published. The Holy See, engaged in the reestablishment of the Catholic diocesan hierarchy in England, triggered riots, and effigy-burning of the Pope, especially after the appointment of Cardinal Wiseman as Catholic Archbishop of Westminster. In the Commons of March 1851 Drummond, remarking that Wiseman's recent appointment was 'needlessly offensive' to those espousing 'a plain John-Bull love of truth', apostrophised Roman Catholics thus: 'your nunneries are prisons or brothels' in which a young lady 'may be either starved or whipped to death' – allusions which, the 1851 *English Review* averred, 'the delicacy of the present age cannot tolerate, and which of course raised a furious storm amongst his auditors'.[60]

The subtitle of *Lavengro* – *The Scholar, the Gypsy, the Priest* – is frequently construed as referring to the triad of a bookish narrator, his Romani blood brother Jasper Petulengro, and the Jesuit Man in Black as the enemy of Drummond's 'plain John-Bull love of truth'. What seems equally credible given the anti-Catholic animus in these mock memoirs is that the subtitle signifies the pilgrim-narrator's three attributes, like those of Vishnu. The narrator is erudite, a wanderer who has 'been everywhere', and a mystagogue seeking that 'sweetness' in the earth's sacraments which act as panacea for his trapped rage ('overstrained nerves'). However, the red-haired and conniving Man in Black – if we view him as the narrator's submerged self, foil, or evil twin – proclaims a corrosive cynicism that drowns out Jasper's paeans to the restorative effects of heaths and green

59. Roy Kerridge, 'George Borrow, Chesterton, and the Gipsies', *Chesterton Review* 9:4 (November 1983): 334–8.

60. [Anon.], 'XIII.-Speech of Henry Drummond, Esq., M.P, in the House of Commons, on the Second Reading of the Ecclesiastical Titles Bill', *English Review* 15:30 (June 1851): 451.

lanes. When we look through a glass darkly at the narrator, we espy on occasion the Jesuit's outlines. He is also a drifter, whose dissident world-view, barren of humour, idealism, or empathy, matches the narrator's own when he is at his lowest ebb, picking through the wreckage of his stalled professional career as a poet-translator in London. The priest's resolve to keep his birth name a secret matches that of the narrator's: '"no one in England knows it but myself, and I will not declare it, even in a dingle"' (*RR* IV: 16). The Man in Black's derision of English patricians as 'wretches', 'full of cold vice', the aspirational 'middle classes' as laughable social climbers or toadies, his snide conception of 'literary men' as 'lickspittles', shunned 'even by those who benefit by their dirty services' (*LSGP* XCIV: 503–5) could be a recitation from the narrator's furious Appendix to *The Romany Rye*. In this jeremiad, the aristocracy represent 'the dastardly great' (*RR*: 313), 'the trumpery titled' (*RR*: 314), who, bereft of 'rank, wealth and fine clothes', would be deemed 'infamous' (*RR*: 328). Elsewhere, Borrow concludes, 'there are no employments or honours in England for any but the connexions and lickspittles of the aristocracy' (10 October 1855)[61] – a feeling shared by Lavengro in his prolonged verbal jousting with the Man in Black.

What this rhetorical sparring makes clear is that the priest's argument about the historic potency of Roman Catholicism signals a threatening proximity to the narrator's philological explorations of the deep structures in tongues 'of old renown' (*LSGP* XXXI: 191). As much as the narrator strives to 'exorcise' the Man in Black, the latter is in fact the wheedling stranger within, an unwelcome intimate, a Gothic doppelgänger as well as Anthony Burgess's 'incubus'. The Man in Black contends that all 'Old World' religions flow from the same arcane fountainhead, and acquire peculiar identities over time, just as all communities 'from Calcutta to Dublin, are of the same stock and *were originally of the same language*' (*RR* I: 10; my emphasis). By projecting such a thesis onto the priest, the narrator tries to convince himself that the Man in Black's Church is little better than a heathen cult like Buddhism or Hinduism, not a discrete Christian denomination hallowed by time and consecrated by tradition. However, the Man in Black's theory of religious evolution, overlapping with the nascent science of comparative mythology that would result in Tylor's seminal *Primitive Culture* (1871) and J. G. Frazer's *The Golden Bough* (1891), rhymes with the narrator's terms when hailing the magic of venerable Welsh words. 'I cannot help observing [. . .] whilst studying this Welsh, generally supposed to be the *original language of Britain*', that this minority tongue boasts

61. Knapp, *Life*, II, 161.

linguistic 'relics, precious relics' of the 'first speech' of 'the world' (*LSGP* XIX: 117; my emphasis). The narrator's stress on 'relics' here – splinters rich in historic and affective resonance for a self-taught lexicographer – also implies, ironically, the Catholic 'holy relics' that the appalled postillion enumerates at the end of *Lavengro*. He recounts how his former patrician paymasters were exposed to 'a frightful, ugly black figure of Holy Mary' and 'a great many things which were called holy relics': 'hair and teeth' to 'cure all kinds of disorders' (*LSGP* XCVIII: 538). So the narrator's 'horror' at and repudiation of a foul 'Romish Church' with its fetish-worship is *haunted* by the Man in Black's phraseology and logic. This haunting in turn compels the narrator to repress unavoidable and disturbing ethnographic findings. If there is a single key to unlock the mysteries of all global religions and 'tongues of old renown', then surely the narrator's deeply held conviction of a *pure* Anglican faith – elevated above 'savage' rival sects such as 'Mumbo Jumbo' of 'the Barbary shore' (*RR* III: 13) – is at risk of seeming nothing more than a lonely maverick's 'deceitful dream' (*LSGP* XXXVI: 218).

Instances where the narrator is gripped by 'a fit of horror' (*LSGP* LXV: 343) are, then, inextricably meshed with his painstaking labours as an amateur philologist ('analysing strange words and names' [*RR*: 330]). His unstinting scholarly efforts seem to fold languages – 'the flowers of Irish rhetoric', 'Armenian', or 'Chinese' – into one, eroding the Word to the point where it seems arbitrary. Early in his studies of the Romani 'tongue', the narrator remarks to Jasper: 'Would it not be a rum thing if divine and devilish were originally one and the same word?' – 'God' in Romani being 'Duvel', and 'divine', 'duvelskoe' (*LSGP* XVII: 106). This episode augurs the verbal duels between the narrator and his nemesis/alter ego, the Man in Black, who posits that 'the popish religion, that of Greece and Rome, and the old Indian system were, in reality, one and the same' (*RR* III: 9). The proof, he claims, is in how the term 'Amen' is derived from an 'old Hindoo formula': 'Omani batsikhom' (*RR* III: 14). The Catholic priest's ghastly, mirthless chuckle – 'Oh, what hearty laughs our missionaries have had when comparing the eternally-sounding Eastern gibberish of Omani batsikhom' and 'the Ave Maria and Amen Jesus of our own idiotical devotees' (*RR* III: 14–15) – gives the narrator pause. Do words then, he muses, have as much to do with other words as they do with tangible, exterior givens? If so, then 'truth' becomes a matter of blind 'Faith' (*LSGP* X: 64), a quest set forth in *Isaiah* 59:10: 'Like the blind we grope along the wall, feeling our way like people without eyes'. This seems to capture the heart of darkness to which the lonely narrator-pilgrim's geographic and scholarly 'Odyssey' leads.

Put Out of One's Tale

What promises an escape from this 'labyrinth of doubt' (*LSGP* XXV: 159), exacerbated by the Man in Black's 'machinations', is glimpsed through the narrator's evolving alliance with Jasper Petulengro's clan, 'the children of Roma', *not Rome* (*RR* 303). Here is a kinship model whose ethos of community care grounded in mutuality does not entrap him in another person's rigid denominational 'pattern' or check his 'unconquerable love of independence' (*RR*: 302). Jasper vouchsafes a freewheeling alternative to the twin fates of attritional joylessness (the narrator's hand-to-mouth existence as a London hack) and diffuse role-playing. As *The Romany Rye* attests, there are always risks of being mired in what the narrator depicts as an 'ugly dream' of repetition (*RR* VI: 38). This 'dream' is 'repeated' in the very formal design of a text that charts the narrator's persistent struggles to name and nourish his own buried self, where 'the mind or soul, call it which you will, has its habitation' (*LSGP* III: 17). His pragmatic and plain-speaking father misconstrues this tendency as his second son's lamentable 'want of frankness', even a wilfully perverse need to 'cover' himself 'with mystery' so as not to be trammelled by any one cultural label (*LSGP* XXVII: 174–5). *Lavengro* and *The Romany Rye* are studded with moments where the narrator not only envelops himself 'with mystery' but seems to disappear into a 'labyrinth' of discordant cadences – an ostensibly never-ending chain of tales-within-tales. His idiosyncratic use of 'field interviews' compels the 'gentle reader' (*LSGP*: iv) to view him at a chilly distance. At other times, this figure of 'peculiar mind and system of nerves' (*RR*: 302) is camouflaged behind various textual screens, masks, or layers: the pseudonym, the nested narrative, rhetorical detours, redactions, circumlocutions, or the ethnographic 'transcript' that the 1843 *Dublin University Magazine* explored in its review of *The Zincali*.[62]

Lavengro was originally conceived as 'My Life, A Drama', a not unhelpful subtitle given significant portions of the text are carefully 'scripted' like the meta-discourses linked with Oscar Wilde's literary criticism or Théophile Gautier's 1835 epistolary novel *Mademoiselle de Maupin*. We take the seat of a spectator, viewing Borrow's textual production, with its competing or contradictory standpoints, as if it were 'sixpenny theatre' (*RR*: 332). As in Gautier's text, stylistic quandaries – how do we interpret a novelist who is also a fictional 'editor' – merge into epistemological issues: how to express, or translate, a 'life of roving

62. [Anon.], 'George Borrow, *The Gypsies in Spain*, and *The Bible in Spain*', *Dublin University Magazine* 21:122 (February 1843): 248–68.

adventure' (*RR*: 303) that is riddling, fissiparous, and plural. Jasper's warm tribute to the narrator – 'Lavengro' or wordsmith – hides the birth name he will not, or cannot, freely share with us. This is a habit already glimpsed in *The Bible in Spain*: Borrow's narrator frequently replaces the meditative intensity of unique lived experiences across the Iberian Peninsula with awkwardly inserted guidebook passages ('Here you will find the Plaza of the Inquisition'). Or he retreats into landscape word-painting of an obviously 'picturesque' stamp, using elaborate parallelisms, rhetorical questions ('who are the travellers of these districts?') and poetic inversions ('grand are its plains') to evoke the 'vastness and sublimity' of 'Old Castile' in Chapter XXI. By such means he absents himself from the vista he sketches, implying little subjective investment in the scene or the 'few solitary rustics' ambling across it (*BIS* XXI: 345). These distancing devices echo, in the narrator's mind at least, how the Romani tribes he scrutinises circumvent a political establishment, whose ordinances hamper travelling communities with petty fines for littering, trespass, poaching, lighting prohibited fires, grazing animals, and loitering near or obstructing highways.

Many of the narrator's fraught reflections in *Lavengro* as to 'whether' he 'be fish or flesh' – and those 'horrors' experienced by fellow-sufferers on the road – are rendered as vivid fragments, often marked by unexpected switches from reported to direct speech. The embedded narratives mirror facets of the narrator's disposition yet divert attention from his deepest needs, 'hopes', and sympathetic 'projects' (*LSGP* XXVII: 175). What is especially striking about these episodes is how they disclose the narrator's reliance on unceasing digression. He brings into sharp focus what it is like to be continually 'put out of one's tale' (*RR* XLI: 245) by others' animated interjections and practical advice, which sometimes fill entire chapters. For the unmoved 1857 *Leader* reviewer, this made it 'extremely difficult to discover' the 'object' of Borrow's two-part mock memoir. It is 'part of a narrative which will probably never be terminated' – a process of endless deferral.[63] While the narrator opens his account with a measured overview of his martial family's movements from one encampment to the next, he continually deviates, dithers, or dilates – invoking a different form of temporality from the merely chronological, which it keeps in abeyance. In effect he retools non-linearity as a source of antic exuberance. So his account of his first faltering steps on the 'paths of knowledge' (*LSGP* III: 20) is unsettled, suspended, and encroached upon by the lyrical testimony of his 'gypsy pal' Jasper, the preacher Peter Williams, 'the Hungarian' (*RR* XXXIX: 223), 'the jockey' (*RR* XV: 96), and numerous

63. [Anon], '*Romany Rye*', *The Leader* 8:375 (30 May 1857): 520–1.

others. Each figure met cannot help but 'overshare', launching into their thought-adventures. The nested narratives undermine continuity and create what *The Athenaeum* saw at best as an unstructured reverie, at worst a mere farrago of thumbnail sketches.[64] Some characters, like Isopel Berners in *The Romany Rye*, or the old woman of the castle, with whom the narrator converses fleetingly in *Lavengro*'s eleventh chapter, simply vanish with no further elucidation.

While the rambling narrator often states his resolve to follow the gist of his own family's chronicle, he is profoundly suspicious of the closed-ending format, refusing to conclude his enquiries into the riddles of personal and ethno-cultural inheritance – unlike the questing protagonists in narratives by George Eliot, J. S. Mill, Charles Dickens, or Elizabeth Gaskell. As Bonamy Dobrée remarked in his positive review of the 1949 Cresset Press edition of *The Romany Rye*: 'You would be quite happy for him to go on forever with the tales about, or by, his realistico-fantastic figures, and indeed there is no reason why he should ever stop.'[65] Borrow's narrator advocates mobility that is improvised, random, and multidirectional; he limns, through both form and content, sense-impressions that rarely conform to dominant ideology or hidebound literary codes. It is no accident then that both *Lavengro* and *The Romany Rye* stop as if in mid-sentence, or what the 1899 *Speaker* termed a 'disappointingly broken off' fashion.[66] This is most apparent in the sequel, where the narrator declares casually: '"I shouldn't wonder," said I, as I proceeded rapidly along a broad causeway, in the direction of the east, "if Mr. Petulengro and Tawno Chikno came originally from India. I think I'll go there."' (*RR* 386). His aesthetic and geographical pilgrimage has further chapters yet to run, as he ponders the birthplace of the Romani language. This is followed by yet another retelling of the narrator's chronicle in a fractious 'Appendix', divided into eleven chapters. It is an elaborate metacommentary that comprises both a hymn to fierce individualism and a voicing of disenchanted bitterness at what his critics ('calumniators') dismissed as a messy two-part pseudo-autobiography.

Lavengro also ends abruptly, with what might be labelled, in Chaucerian terms, 'the postillion's tale' (Chapter C). The postillion informs the narrator and Belle that he has spotted the Man in Black, in England. His disclosure might have assumed, in a more formally conventional text, the emotional intensity of a 'cliffhanger', one to be resolved in

64. [Anon.], 'Reviews: *Lavengro*', *The Athenaeum* 1215 (8 February 1851): 159–60.
65. Bonamy Dobrée, 'The Adventurous Victorian', *The Spectator* (25 February 1949): 262.
66. [Anon.], 'Reviews: George Borrow', *The Speaker* 20:503 (19 August 1899): 184–5.

the 'sequel', *The Romany Rye*. However, Borrow's narrator has already received visits from the priest in the Dingle. So it is not immediately apparent what function the postillion's 'revelation' serves, although early twentieth-century Borrovian Edmund Kemper Broadus supplies a clue in his 1919 poem, 'Lavengro':

> Find in a mug of ale seraphic glories
> But be content with water from a spring;
> And while inspired postillions tell their stories
> Forget that time – and plots – are on the wing;[67]

By allowing the postillion's elaborate story to unfold across several chapters – delighting in this character's 'inspired' voice for its own sake – Borrow affirms a 'loitering, devious pathway' that defies time's winged chariot and the linear, schematic 'plots' that enshrine it. Closer scrutiny of how the postillion 'tells' his story is revealing in this regard:

> 'Pray,' said I, 'did you ever take lessons in elocution?'
> 'Not directly,' said the postillion; 'but my old master, who was in Parliament, did, and so did his son, who was intended to be an orator. A great professor used to come and give them lessons, and I used to stand and listen, by which means I picked up a considerable quantity of what is called rhetoric. In what I last said, I was aiming at what I have heard him frequently endeavouring to teach my governors as a thing indispensably necessary in all oratory, a graceful pere—pere—peregrination.'
> 'Peroration, perhaps?'
> (*LSGP* XCVII: 525)

On a cursory view, Borrow's literary rendering of the postillion's utterance upholds cultural stereotypes – stuttering, dysfluency, or mispronunciations as clinical speech pathologies or even moral failings among the 'low' servant class, etc. The 'poor postillion' opens his story with 'what the man who taught rhetoric would call a hex – hex –' (*LSGP* XCVIII: 529). What he tries to articulate – 'exordium' – reminds us that in *Lavengro* the layered effects and enfolding nuances of diction in travellers' tales cast a potent spell ('hex'), to bewitch an audience. By such means, the text does not draw attention to bewilderingly ragged or broken speech acts for comic effect. Instead, we revel in the salutary *derail-*

67. Edmund Kemper Broadus, 'Lavengro', *The Review* 1 (1919): 14. For closer scrutiny of Broadus's academic career, see David Chandler, '"Celtic Fielding, Realist of Dreams!": Edmund Kemper Broadus on Borrow', *George Borrow Bulletin*, 2:6 (2000): 18–24.

ing and *disruption* – through non-standard, subaltern, or non-dominant parlance – of the parroting and automatism that the narrator links with dry Westminster 'oratory'. As Broadus's poem suggests, the postillion speaks as if 'inspired' – Borrow's 1850s texts stage the *processes* of telling stories ('In what I last said') rather than storytelling per se. That the postillion articulates 'peroration' (the closing part of an oration) as 'peregrination' wittily distils the essence of *Lavengro*'s narrative arc. Borrow describes and transcribes a creative stuttering. He stretches lexis, encounters, and moods, exulting in the wayside loitering, lulls, distractions, and postponements, the accidental collisions of bodies (or stories) in motion. Vivid anecdotes are started and not concluded, extended interminably, or never quite elucidated; theological meditations on a possibly godless cosmos, the trade secrets of the pea-and-thimble man and practical tips on shoeing horses blur into each other. *The Romany Rye* buttresses this conception of a physical and intellectual trek 'more induced by chance than any particular motive; all quarters of the world having about equal attractions for me' (*RR* XXI: 124). The trajectory evinces scant interest in a rigorous sequencing of events that moves inexorably towards what Borrow construes as the formal violence of the mimetic-realist novel. Such violence dishonestly poses as romantic redemption – the closed-ending format of a 'wedding-bells' scenario. Significantly, the narrator's cherished *Belle* Berners deserts him and travels to America by herself in *The Romany Rye*, never to be seen again.

The postillion's tale shows how 'finales' in *Lavengro* and *The Romany Rye* rhyme with and *reflect* the organisation of other 'endings' in this sprawling text. Several chapters 'break off' just before, or at the same moment as, the dramatic disclosure of a stranger's identity. The eleventh chapter of *Lavengro* closes when the old woman, 'seated on a stone', declares that the derelict habitation the narrator views belongs to her own clan, 'the accursed house of Cromwell!' To this 'house of the broken-hearted' (*LSGP* XI: 70), no further mention is made, and the woman does not reappear in the sequel. A sporting gentleman in Chapter XXIV, asked by a magistrate to introduce himself, replies that '"My name is no matter [. . .] were I to mention it to you, it would awaken within you no feeling of interest"' (*LSGP* XXIV: 157–8).[68] After this dialogue, the chapter closes. We turn to a completely different and seemingly unrelated 'matter' – the narrator's brooding over the essence of 'truth'

68. This chapter ends on a question: 'What is his name?' (*LSGP* XXIV: 159). See also George M. Hyde, 'Murky Doings in Mumper's Dingle: George Borrow's *Lavengro* as a portrait of the artist (Part Two)', *Review of English Literature at Kyoto Women's University* (2002): 19–42.

and the pitfalls of reconstructing our personal life story as a coherent biography when so much memory gets buried, lost, or fragmented. The sporting gentleman's remarks – voicing a justifiable suspicion of the law's attempts to name, tame, or shame a rogue – throw into bolder relief the narrator's misgivings about unveiling his birth name. Life-writing, in Paul de Man's conception, 'seems to depend on actual and potentially verifiable events'; it belongs 'to a simpler mode of referentiality'. This genre boasts myriad 'phantasms and dreams' – and here we recall the opening sentence from *Lavengro*'s 1851 Preface, describing it as a 'dream, partly of adventure, partly of study'. For de Man, such 'deviations from reality remain rooted in a single subject whose identity is defined by the uncontested readability of his proper name'.[69] To divulge this real 'name' is for Borrow's narrator somehow *improper*, a concession at odds with the arts of trickery, concealment, and masquerade upon which he depends to sway his audience. *Blackwood's Magazine*, in its 1851 review of *Lavengro*, deplored this figure's desire to don the 'slouched hat and russet mantle' of melodrama, whispering in 'oblique hints' and 'obscure innuendoes' – an encrypted language associated with the 'world of *spirits and dreams*' (*LSGP* VI: 42; my emphasis).[70]

The crises of knowing and being that Borrow's 1850s texts present and enact stylistically – via a ceaseless probing of the stability of one's name, family, class, genre, or 'profession' – while they bemused some mid-century pundits, resonated with fin de siècle cultural producers. *The Romany Rye*'s focus on the solitary and anxious male 'tramper' (*RR* VI: 37), or what W. E. Henley termed the 'self-conscious Tinker-Quixote',[71] became for William Morris, who 'read' Borrow 'perpetually', a symbol of resistance to an established industrial capitalist system.[72] By the early years of the twentieth century, Paul Elmer More, literary editor of the *New York Evening Post*, perceived Borrow as 'one of the most enigmatical and tantalizing personalities of English literature'.[73] What proved 'tantalizing' to Elmer More and others was Borrow's unconcern for both the rote aspects of life-writing and formulaic providential plots.

69. Paul de Man, 'Autobiography as De-facement', *MLN* 94:5 (December 1979): 919–30. [920].
70. [Anon.], '*Blackwood's* Review of *Lavengro*', *The Home Journal* (New York) 15 (12 April 1851): 4.
71. William Ernest Henley, 'Borrow', *Views and Reviews*, 136.
72. [Anon.], 'Borrow's *Lavengro*', *Dublin University Magazine* 37:222 (June 1851): 712–13; J. W. Mackail, *The Life of William Morris* (London: Longman Green and Co., 1901), 220.
73. Paul Elmer More, *The Demon of the Absolute* (Princeton: Princeton University Press, 1928), 127–8. On Elmer More's reading of Borrow as a picaresque author, see also More, 'George Borrow', *The Nation* (27 June 1912): 633–6.

Downplaying these rote qualities allowed Borrow to reappraise how, for example, the postillion's speech acts, which comprise a quest for eloquent authority, also uncover absorbing quandaries of novelistic form.

My next chapter turns to *Wild Wales: Its People, Language, and Scenery* (1862), a travelogue in which the intricacies of speech acts also take centre stage. Borrow's exploration of the contours and singularities of what he terms 'Cambrian' culture is measured against Matthew Arnold's 1860s social criticism and metropolitan English newspapers like *The Telegraph* and *The Times* which situated 'the Cambrian tongue' and its sister Celtic languages as a social hindrance with little substantive role to play in a swiftly evolving market economy. 'If Wales and the Welsh are ever thoroughly to share in the material prosperity, and, [. . .] we will add the culture and the morality, of England,' the 1866 *Times* opined, then 'they must forget their isolated language, and learn to speak English, and nothing else.'[74] It is no accident that *Wild Wales* evokes '*The Times*' as a 'trumpery journal' from which one should 'expect nothing but shabby treatment' (*WW* XXXVII: 259). The *North Wales Chronicle* journalist and poet Richard Richards, though he reproached *The Times* for its 'spiteful croaking at the Welsh language', contended that 'the Scotch and the Irish have discarded their ancient languages long ago', and with no lasting damage in his opinion, so why shouldn't Wales follow suit?[75] Alongside this trend, specialised English- and Welsh-language print media outlets sought to safeguard Cambrian lore – as well as 'those cognate dialects of the Welsh', like 'the Cornish, Armoric, Highland Gaelic and Irish' (*WW* XL: 277) – from assimilation into the dominant, Anglocentric culture with which *The Times* was then linked. *Archaeologia Cambrensis*, *Bye-gones*, *The Cambrian Journal*, *Y Brython* (*The Briton*), *Y Beirniad* (The Critic), *Y Geninen* (The Leek), and *Y Traethodydd* (*The Essayist*) variously promoted Celtic studies, broadly defined. The *Cambrian Journal* sought to uncover those facets of the vernacular tongue which suggested Welsh was one of the cornerstones of modern European languages, worthy of sustained academic scrutiny alongside the law and medicine. What 'advantages', the *Cambrian* declared, 'would accrue to us as a great nation – the British – if our ancient tongue – the language of the ancient world, was cultivated, in this, our common country'.[76] Echoes of this formulation can be heard

74. [Anon.], 'Editorial', *The Times* 25598 (8 September 1866): 8. Matthew Arnold alludes to this *Times* editorial in his Preface to *On the Study of Celtic Literature* (1867).

75. Richard Richards, *Miscellaneous Poems and Pen and Ink Sketches, chiefly of Welsh Scenery and Notable Places in Carnarvonshire* (Bangor: John Kenmuir Douglas, 1868), 38, 132–3.

76. Mancenion, 'Essay on the Advantages accruing to Englishmen from a Knowledge of the Welsh Language', *Cambrian Journal* 1 (Autumn 1858): 212–13.

in the proud innkeeper's reference to Welsh as 'the ancient British language' in Chapter LXXXII of *Wild Wales*.

I trace how Borrow's travelogue both mirrored and nurtured a contemporary antiquarian fascination with Welsh philology, folk survivals, and those palpable vestiges which stirred, according to the first number of *Archaeologia Cambrensis*, 'delightful associations' synonymous with the 'very name of Wales'.[77] I compare *Wild Wales* with Arnold's more widely reviewed and seminal *On the Study of Celtic Literature* (1867). In this text, Arnold posits that it is 'by the forms of its language' that 'a nation expresses its very self': 'what a people [. . .] say in its language, its literature, is the great key'.[78] However, by stressing that 'the Welshman' and 'Irishman' should 'speak English', Arnold's *Celtic* essays seem to begrudge those peoples any claim to national self-determination. It is chiefly for this reason that critic Geraint H. Jenkins identifies Arnold's *Celtic* essays as 'the *locus classicus* of the pro-English zealot'.[79]

Borrow's travelogue is based on a walking tour he undertook through Wales and neighbouring counties in the summer months of 1854 when he was fifty-one, accompanied by his wife and stepdaughter, Henrietta.[80] Borrow began his tour in Anglesey on the north coast. He passed through '*Gwlad y Bryniau*' ('Mountain Land') to Glamorganshire in the industrialised south, thence eastward to Chepstow to inspect the castle ruins. The timing of his tour 'catches' Wales at a fateful point in the emergence of its modern national identity.[81] From the year of the inaugural nationwide census in 1801 – two years before Borrow was born – to the publication of *Wild Wales* in 1862, a predominantly agrarian society of just over half a million inhabitants, equally dispersed across a country with no large urban centres, was morphing into an advanced industrial economy.[82] By the start of the First World War, the population had swelled to nearly 2.6 million citizens, two-thirds of

77. [Harry Longueville Jones and John Williams], 'Introduction', *Archaeologia Cambrensis* 1 (January 1846): 1.
78. Arnold, *On the Study of Celtic Literature*, 334–5.
79. On Arnold's belief 'that the inexorable march of Progress rendered redundant the Celtic peripheries and their languages', see Geraint H. Jenkins, '"Wales, the Welsh and the Welsh Language": Introduction', *The Welsh Language and its Social Domains 1801–1911*, p. 9.
80. C. Dellheim, 'Imagining England: Victorian Views of the North', *Northern History* 22 (1986): 216–30; Rolant Pyrs Gruffudd, '*Landscape and nationhood': tradition and modernity in rural Wales, 1900–1950* (unpublished PhD: University of Loughborough, 1989).
81. Kenneth O. Morgan, *Rebirth of a Nation: Wales 1880–1980* (Cardiff: University Press of Wales, 1981).
82. G. E. Jones and D. Smith, eds, *The People of Wales: A Millennium History* (Llandysul, 2000).

whom resided in and around the southern industrial localities of Gwent and Glamorgan. Social historians estimate that 91 per cent of the population were Welsh speakers in 1801 (of which a significant number were also Welsh monoglots).[83] A century later, the census reports that the indigenous language had been reduced to the level of 'a minority tongue' for the first time in its history.[84]

Wild Wales ponders the linguistic, ecological, and infrastructural changes that attended what was then a boom of extraordinary demographic magnitude, 'unmatched', as Andrew Webb remarks, 'by the experience of virtually any other European nation of that period'.[85] Borrow's narrator charts how the growing awareness of North Wales as a favoured travel destination was buttressed by assorted technological 'marvels' – for example, the 'mighty' Scots engineer '[Thomas] Telford', 'flung over' the Menai Strait the first chain-link 'iron suspension bridge' (*WW* XXVIII: 191), thus linking Anglesey to the mainland. *Wild Wales* is permeated by often ambivalent allusions to how English railway magnates were 'developing' previously secluded 'landscapes' into thriving weekend getaways, sites of 'accessible otherness'[86] that attracted thousands of free-spending tourists during the summer months and in turn required a sizeable bilingual staff. This prompted Richard Richards to proclaim in 1868 that 'the extension of railways into all parts of the land' was 'the greatest of all boons to Wales' – indeed, just over 1400 miles of track were constructed between 1840 and 1870.[87]

Borrow's narrator also registers patterns of labour migration via the gravitational pull of the South Wales Coalfield. This region of blackened hills, so stark a contrast to the grand solitudes of Snowdonia, is dominated by 'terrible furnaces', streams of molten metals, slate quarries,

83. See Dot Jones, *Statistical Evidence relating to the Welsh Language 1801–1911 / Tystiolaeth Ystadegol yn ymwneud â'r Iaith Gymraeg 1801–1911* (Cardiff: University of Wales Press, 1998).

84. See Geraint H. Jenkins, ed., *The Welsh Language and its Social Domains 1801–1911*, 1–81; R. T. Jones, *Faith and Crisis of a Nation: Wales 1890–1914* (Cardiff: University Press of Wales, 2004).

85. Andrew Webb, *Edward Thomas and World Literary Studies: Writing Wales in English* (Cardiff: University of Wales Press, 2013), 8. Dudley Baines, *Migration in a Mature Economy: Emigration and Internal Migration in England and Wales 1861–1900* (Cambridge: Cambridge University Press, 1985), 277–8.

86. See Katie Gramich, '"Every Hill Has Its History, Every Region Its Romance": Travellers' Constructions of Wales, 1844–1913', *Travel Writing and Tourism in Britain and Ireland*, ed. Benjamin Colbert (Basingstoke: Macmillan 2012), 147.

87. Richard Richards, 'Nantlle and its Slate Quarries', *Miscellaneous Poems and Pen and Ink Sketches, chiefly of Welsh Scenery and Notable Places in Carnarvonshire* (Bangor: John Kenmuir Douglas, 1868), 132.

smelting houses, and unsightly 'heaps of burning' (*WW* C: 669). Many largely unskilled young labourers from towns and villages in north-west and mid-Wales, traditionally the mainstays of Welsh-speaking communities, had rejected a life of bare subsistence tending crops and cattle by relocating to towns and cities like Merthyr, Newport, Cardiff, and Swansea. Alert to the specificities of local conditions, the narrator is struck by sprawling and 'gloomy' urban centres such as Swansea, where an immigrant anglophone proletariat was generally usurping the southern nonconformist Welsh peasantry.[88] Wandering among Swansea's 'immense edifices', the narrator depicts a fractured linguistic locality rather than an ethnically homogenous enclave. Consequently, the industrial base had become, in his estimation, a cultural melting pot. This raised what Richard Richards called 'vexed questions' about the forces threatening the vitality of Welsh-language communities at mid-century. Given the unprecedented levels of inward labour migration to South Wales from Scotland, Ireland, and England; as well as metalworkers from France, Holland, and Spain, enticed by the burgeoning copper trade, what was it, Richards wondered, that 'Welsh poets and orators really meant when urging the people never to forego their Nationality, or what they understood by the term *nationality*'.[89] Borrow finds little evidence of a marked 'Cambrian' sensibility in Swansea: 'whether I was in Wales or not, I was no longer amongst Welsh. The people whom I met did not look like Welsh.' The 'women had much the appearance of Dutch fisherwomen; some of them were carrying huge loads on their heads' (*WW* C: 389).

Though *Wild Wales* remains, according to Harold Brough, 'one of the greatest of British travel books',[90] contemporary print media outlets were less enamoured of what they saw as a needlessly longwinded text. 'Mr. Borrow' was, in the *Quarterly Review*'s judgement, 'a genuine traveller', uniting 'the antiquarian, the poet, the painter, the gastronomist', and 'even the theologian, in the tourist'.[91] However, *The Saturday Review* found in *Wild Wales* a boastful *ieithgi* or self-taught language buff who foregrounds mundane frivolities, spinning out his testimony 'to a wearisome length by the dullest repetitions and by the silliest egotism. He seems to fancy that the whole world must be interested in knowing

88. D. W. Howell and C. Baber, 'Wales', F. M. L. Thompson, ed., *The Cambridge Social History of Britain 1750–1950. Vol. 1. Regions and Communities* (Cambridge: Cambridge University Press, 1990), 281–354.
89. Richard Richards, 'Hope', *Miscellaneous Poems and Pen and Ink Sketches, chiefly of Welsh Scenery and Notable Places in Carnarvonshire* (Bangor: John Kenmuir Douglas, 1868), 132.
90. Harold Brough, 'Walking Wales', *Liverpool Daily Post* (9 September 1997): 16–17.
91. [Anon.], '*Wild Wales*. By George Borrow', *London Quarterly Review* 20:40 (July 1863): 536–8.

everything he does.'[92] Critical carping was rooted in a perception that Borrow's cantankerous gypsy laureate persona was a 'bad Englishman' (*WW* XLVII: 322). This accusation is levelled at him because of his perceived disdain for 'money-making' Saxon philistines (*WW* XXIX: 206). The 1863 *London Review* seemed to echo this charge: 'We never quarrel with a few wholesome prejudices.' However, Borrow's unpatriotic narrator scarifies the genteel, reviles railroads and those that journey by them; 'such feelings are quite unworthy of a sensible writer'.[93] The subtext is clear: a 'sensible writer' surely grasps that the only publishing (and political) infrastructure that counts – the career-making literary cliques, major journalistic outlets, the concentration of influential pundits, booksellers, and advertisers, the readership with the deepest pockets and loudest voices – is based in and around the English capital. Borrow's Appendix to *The Romany Rye* attributes the muted reception of his mid-century narratives to this same metropolitan media elite and the draining promotional duties it imposed on aspiring authors. Critics rejected him because, 'having the proper pride of a gentleman and a scholar', he elected not 'to permit himself to be exhibited and made a zany of in London' (*RR* 355). While Borrow's travelogue portrays 'Saxon' metropolites in an unfavourable light, many Welsh citizens show the narrator a kindness that fills his 'eyes' with 'tears': 'How different is the reception of this despised race of the wandering stranger from that of –. However, I am a Saxon myself, and the Saxons have no doubt their virtues; a pity that they should be all uncouth and ungracious ones!' (*WW* XXXII: 220). Here he throws back at unsmiling 'Saxon' scribes the pejorative label that the 1860s *Daily Telegraph* was wont to employ in evoking the Welsh tongue – 'uncouth'. For the *London Review*, however, Borrow's unrelentingly opinionated narrator – he 'takes every opportunity of sneering' at upwardly mobile 'Saxon' utilitarians and Celtophobes – has *gone native*.[94] *Wild Wales*, in its scrutiny of the tangled relations between the national literary traditions within Britain, frequently measures the dignified 'Celt' against the boorish English, who are 'in the habit of making fun' of the locals and their language. The Welsh have for Borrow's narrator a natural edge over that gentrified 'Saxon' constituency whom the Romani matriarch Mrs Herne, in *Lavengro*, curses as 'single tongued idiots'.

92. [Anon.], 'Reviews. Borrow's *Wild Wales*', *Saturday Review* 15:375 (3 January 1863): 20–1.
93. [Anon.], '*Wild Wales*', *London Review* 6:133 (17 January 1863): 72.
94. [Anon.], 'IV: *Wild Wales*', *The Eclectic Review* 4 (January 1863): 58.

In *Wild Wales*, there is an intense identification with a 'Celtic' cultural legacy that 'has been for centuries', in the words of Borrow's biographer Edward Thomas, 'close to the main river of European literature'.[95] At the same time, the travelogue supplies an unexpectedly detailed portrait of socioeconomic ferment and intercultural dialogue in the country and its borders during the 1850s. The narrator meets, among others, a businessman born of Welsh Pennsylvanian settlers, a former slave from Antigua in Chester, Irish tinkers, and fellow 'Saxons' who have relocated across the border to settle down and raise families with Welsh wives. What emerges from these interactions is a view of domestic and foreign policy that can be parsed both as anti-imperialist and sabre-rattling, as broad-minded and spitefully reactionary, as cosmopolitan and xenophobic. The narrator's forthright reproofs of 'Saxon' smugness and 'over-reaching' (*WW* XXIX: 206) given the mishandling of Irish affairs, for example, appears to chime with the Union Repeal movement. Yet his equally barbed vignettes of post-Famine migrant Irish 'vagabonds', as well as 'Dan O'Connell with his emancipation cries' (*WW* XXV: 169), signifies a hidebound Tory in an era of awakening liberalism, for whom the only answer to the 'Irish Question' is a firming up, not a dissolving, of the Union. This is a stance closer to Thomas Carlyle's staunch support for the political status quo in *Reminiscences of my Irish Journey in 1849* or Harriet Martineau's Irish essays.[96] It becomes difficult to gauge, and reconcile, the musings of an easily riled and bearish narrator who endorses ostensibly discordant political perspectives. In one chapter, he appears to voice unequivocal support for sturdy 'Saxon' government at home and abroad, yet in another he confesses, '"I am ashamed to say that I am an Englishman"' (*WW* XXIX: 206). This is partly because, in *Wild Wales*, concepts of 'religious persuasion', ethnocultural belonging, and international relations are not crisply delimited polarities. The text not only records a geographical 'pilgrimage' to the shrines of ancient Welsh bards: it depicts the passage through, or disruption of, myriad ideologies. This is apparent from the earliest chapters, as we follow the narrator across the frontier into *anialwch* – a rural 'wilderness' far from the traffic of towns. On this tour, he queries an entrenched and continuing Anglocentric agenda that situates the Welsh (and Irish) tongue and lore as insular atavisms of annexed minorities. What the narrator specifies as '*iaith yr nefoedd*' (the 'language of heaven'), *The Times*

95. Edward Thomas, *The Reviews of Edward Thomas* (Oxford: Oxford University Press, 2010), 5, 32

96. See Thomas Carlyle, *Reminiscences of my Irish Journey in 1849* (London: Gilbert & Rivington, 1882).

notoriously branded, in its summary of the 1866 Chester Eisteddfod (at which a letter from Matthew Arnold was read out recommending the institution of a Celtic professorship at Oxford) 'the curse of Wales', for all practical purposes a 'dead language'.[97] So 'desirous' is Borrow's narrator to affirm, in riposte, 'the living people' of Wales and the varieties of what *The Times* deemed an 'unknown tongue', that he lingers in 'very remote and little-known spots' – *terra incognita* beyond the penny postman's routes.[98]

97. [Anon.], 'Editorial', *The Times* 25598 (8 September 1866): 8. 'MR. ARNOLD even recommends a deputation from the Eisteddfod to the University of Oxford, to urge the importance of establishing a chair of Celtic [. . .] we are quite willing to believe that this effusion from the Professor of Poetry at Oxford was too absurd even for the bards and other enthusiasts who assembled under the banner of the Red Dragon.'
98. [Anon.], 'Reviews: *Wild Wales*', *Archaeologia Cambrensis* 9:34 (April 1863): 174–6.

CHAPTER 4

WILD WALES: BORROW THE BAD ENGLISHMAN

Wales the Undiscovered Country

> How is it that Wales has received so little justice from tourists and literaturists? How is it that its traditions and legends have never been thrown upon the broad, white sheet of letters, from the phantasmagoria of the poet's mind? We know almost more of any country on the face of the earth than we do of Wales. [. . .] Scotland has had its poet and romancist. Every nook and corner of Westmoreland and Cumberland are laid bare and open to every vulgar eye. [. . .] But few people ever turn to Wales.[1]

The January 1863 *Eclectic Review* used the recent publication of Borrow's travelogue to bemoan the profound 'English ignorance of Wales'. While the Highlands have had a Scott, the Lake District a Wordsworth, Wales remains largely 'unbroken ground' in British land-writing and unenticing to 'sentimental idlers' who scorn it as a minoritised nation at the geographical periphery of Europe. The *Eclectic* ponders what Mary-Ann Constantine has recently labelled the 'chronic inbetweenness' of Wales both as an object of academic study and a fund of creative inspiration: 'being either too exotic (an unfamiliar language and a literature which rarely appears on any English syllabus) or not exotic enough (politically subsumed, and – language apart – not as challengingly "other" as [. . .] Ireland'.[2] The *Eclectic* goes on to invoke Londoner Joseph Downes's 1836 'romance of North Wales', *The Mountain Decameron*. In his 'Dedication' to this sequence of tales about Welsh popular customs, legends, and topographical curiosities, Downes, who had settled in the Breconshire market town of Builth Wells to pursue a medical career, presents

1. [Anon.], 'IV: *Wild Wales*', *Eclectic Review* 4 (January 1863): 55.
2. See Mary-Ann Constantine, 'Beauty Spot, Blind Spot: Romantic Wales', *Literature Compass* 5:3 (2008): 585–6.

himself 'labouring under a sort of double obscurity: not only as a man unknown, but belonging to a country (wonderful to say!) almost equally unknown, in a wide sense of that word, although the most beautiful province of the United Kingdom'.[3]

The *Eclectic Review*, in citing Downes's text, oversimplified the case. Following the publication of William Gilpin's *Observations of the River Wye* (1782) and eminent Flintshire zoologist and polymath Thomas Pennant's *A Tour in Wales* (1778–83) – Borrow's narrator pointedly mentions the latter in Chapter XVI – Wales saw an influx of 'sentimental idlers' as well as more zealous antiquarians, historians, poets, and landscape artists venturing among those hills to which weekly newspapers seldom found their way.[4] That Pennant's reappraisal of Wales was especially 'alluring to burgeoning Romantic sensibilities' is borne out by S. T. Coleridge's 1794 walking tour of Wales with his friend Joseph Hucks,[5] his later 1798 excursion, with Dorothy and William Wordsworth, to visit radical activist John Thelwall; the Shelleys' plans to settle in the Elan Valley and later at Tremadog; Thomas De Quincey's 1802 solitary tramps through Denbighshire described in *Confessions of an English Opium Eater.*[6] Romantic-era Wales was then, as Constantine notes, 'a fascinating place: part literary construct, part tourist destination', as well as 'a locus of alternative possibilities, both political and personal' that Borrow's text registers.[7] The fascination for a youthful De Quincey resided in how Wales was at once a colony overseen by England for half a millennium, whose border was easy to cross on foot, yet also a site of beguiling mystery, with an 'ancient and peculiar language' (*WW*: xxv) and mores that greatly predated Roman and Norman incursions. Borrow's narrator reinforces this sense of alterity in his Preface to *Wild Wales.* He reminds us that the country is 'still called by the Germans Welschland' (*WW*: xxv). The German adjective 'welsch' and its cognates, while etymologically linked to the name 'Wales', is also freighted, in certain contexts, with associations of 'foreign', 'odd', and 'unfathomable'. In Chapter XXVII, Borrow's narrator reflects on Wales's place in Romantic cosmology when describing a visit to the ruined castle above Beaumaris in Anglesey, a 'favourite residence of the celebrated

3. Joseph Downes, *The Mountain Decameron* (London: Richard Bentley, 1836), v–vi.
4. [Anon.], 'IV: *Wild Wales*', *Eclectic Review* 4 (January 1863): 55.
5. Joseph Hucks, *Pedestrian tour through North Wales in a series of letters* (London, Printed for J. Debrett and J. Edwards, 1795; Cardiff, UWP, 1979).
6. See Shawna Lichtenwalner, *Claiming Cambria: Invoking the Welsh in the Romantic Era* (Newark, NJ: University of Delaware Press, 2008), 97.
7. Mary-Ann Constantine, 'Beauty Spot, Blind Spot: Romantic Wales', *Literature Compass* 5:3 (2008): 577–90.

Owain Gwynedd, the father of the yet more celebrated Madoc, the original discoverer of America'. Here the narrator intones lines 'from the *Madoc* of Southey, not the least of Britain's four great latter poets, decidedly her best prose writer, and probably the purest and most noble character to which she has ever given birth' (*WW* XXVII: 190). His similarly rapt reaction to Snowdonia also carries faint traces of Wordsworth's two Welsh 'spots of time': the 1791 moonlit ascent of Mount Snowdon in the final book of *The Prelude* and the memories of a walking tour through South Wales evoked in 'Tintern Abbey'. These canonical Romantics were variously reacting to a nascent tourist industry that Pennant, as 'the first modern traveller in Wales', according to George Nicholson in 1808, had helped create with his sedulous descriptions of natural scenery, local lore, ancestral seats, commercial returns, and mineral resources.[8]

Between 1770 and 1815, around sixty-five 'Tours' through Wales were published, many of which were directly inspired by the untiring Pennant. His example, coupled with the Napoleonic Wars making 'the Continent impossible as a British playground', set 'the stream of fashion in the direction of Wales'.[9] By the time Borrow published his travelogue – a year after John Murray released its *Handbook for Travellers in North Wales* (1861) – the Home Tour had become, in Cecil Price's estimation, 'an outworn' literary trend.[10] 1860s middlebrow journalists could grumble, with some justification, that in 'these days', among 'the educated classes it is almost the exception to find a person of ordinary intelligence who has not, at some time or other, rushed into print' a 'Book of Travel'.[11] Among the popular titles dedicated to mapping the 'most beautiful province of the United Kingdom' were Edward Parry's *The Cambrian Mirror* (of which 8000 copies had been sold by 1850),[12] *Black's Picturesque Guide through North and South Wales and Monmouthshire* (1851), George Bennett's *The Tourist's Guide Through North Wales* (1853), and Thomas Roscoe's *Wanderings and Excursions in South Wales* (1854).

8. George Nicholson, *The Cambrian Traveller's Guide and Pocket Companion* (London: Crosby and Co., 1808), iii–iv.
9. [Anon.], '*Highways and Byways in North Wales*', *Athenaeum* 3722 (25 February 1899): 235.
10. Cecil Ford, 'Introduction' to George Borrow, *Wild Wales: Its People, Language and Scenery* (London and Glasgow: Collins, 1906), 11.
11. John Murray (Firm), *Handbook for Travellers in North Wales* (London: John Murray, 1861); [Anon.], 'i', *London Review* 6:133 (17 January 1863): 71.
12. The *London Literary Journal* reviewer praised *The Cambrian Mirror* for how 'it approaches more to the completeness and brevity of the Continental Handbooks than any we have seen – a real Welsh Murray'. See [Anon], 'Miscellaneous: *The Cambrian Mirror*', *London Literary Journal* 10:247 (15 July 1851): 335–6.

For the *Eclectic Review*, however, such texts had snubbed those 'glorious and magnificent by-ways' where the 'lackadaisical dilettantic tourist', steered by their Gilpin and equipped with pocket compass, maps, and sketchbook, 'would not usually like to travel'.[13]

Borrow, in the *Eclectic*'s judgement, supplied an altogether racier reaction to Cambrian geography, legends, and usages: 'These volumes are perhaps the most remarkably graphic ever penned by a tourist.' At times it was a mite too 'graphic' for the *Eclectic*'s liking, given the not-infrequent flashes of bitter bigotry directed against nonconformist religious sects and fellow travel writers. In a puckish allusion to Gilpin, Pennant, and the 'Celtic Fringe' writing industry they helped foster, the wife of Borrow's narrator consents to visit Wales since it was a 'very nice picturesque country', though 'not so fashionable as either Leamington or Harrowgate' (*WW* I: 2). Her 'sight-seeing' expectations are to some extent shaped by Gilpin's delimited aesthetic category, one that was 'born', as Timothy Heimlich remarks, 'in Wales, England's oldest and most successfully integrated' dependency – specifically the Wye Valley, whose river Borrow's narrator hails as 'the most lovely' which 'the world can boast of' (*WW* LXXXVII: 574).[14] Although the narrator himself, striking the pose of a Romantic 'man of feeling', deploys this term and the pathetic fallacy to evoke Snowdon's peaks, cataracts, and groves in Chapter XXIX, the general tendency of *Wild Wales* is to situate the 'picturesque' as a watchword of commercial tourism, exploited by 'Saxon' land-grabbers who decouple natural beauty from the utility linked with the practical business of human existence. This split is traced to what the narrator calls the 'pandemonium' of large-scale industrialisation in South Wales, evidenced by the cinder piles, leaden swamps, and 'diabolical-looking buildings' halfway between Swansea and Neath (*WW* CII: 682). The formal compositional codes and generic conventions of the 'picturesque' have become, in his estimation, an instrument of 'colonial control that evolved to maximize imperial profit'.[15] This reflects his sense elsewhere that Welsh sites of natural interest like 'Mynydd Turvey' (*WW* CVIII: 713) have been reframed by authors of Gilpinesque guidebooks as, at best, touring terrain, and at worst, a largely moribund repository of history devoid of the potent sense of continuity that cuts across periods, business initiatives, and

13. [Anon.], 'IV: *Wild Wales*', *Eclectic Review* 4 (January 1863): 55.
14. Timothy Heimlich, 'Romantic Wales and the Imperial Picturesque', *MLQ* 81:2 (June 2020): 170.
15. Timothy Heimlich, 'Romantic Wales and the Imperial Picturesque', *MLQ* 81:2 (June 2020): 170–5.

class formations to consolidate communal ties. 'Saxon' weekenders, staying in reconditioned farmhouses, perceive local products and the craftsmen who make them – often depicted as figures of uninstructed good taste in *Wild Wales* – as 'quaint' museum pieces. Artificial 'loveliness', rather than inherent organic 'splendour' (*WW* CVI: 703), is applied, at no little expense, as a pleasing varnish – a pedantic imitation of the scenic, to attract sightseers used to tourist itineraries, like the narrator's wife.

Walk (and Talk) Like a Welshman

In *Wild Wales*, picturesque tourism, under whose banner the narrator's pleasure-seeking spouse and stepdaughter rally, is measured against an aesthetic endeavour that genuinely fires Borrow's creative imagination – that is, rethinking the *picaresque* narrative form, themes, and tropes of his earlier texts, especially his runaway bestseller *The Bible in Spain* (1843), which affirms Henry Fielding as 'the most singular genius [England] ever produced' (*BIS* I: 6). This is a facet of *Wild Wales* that sets it apart from the published tours synonymous with Gilpin's and Pennant's antiquarian votaries.[16] The echoes of *The Bible in Spain* can be felt, first of all, in the narrator's full-throated reaction to Holyhead, a commercial port in Anglesey: 'the town, with its white houses placed by the seaside, on the skirt of a mountain, beneath a blue sky and a broiling sun, put me something in mind of a Moorish piratical town, in which I had once been' (*WW* XLII: 245). Approaching Tregaron in Chapter XCII he cannot help but recall 'an Andalusian village overhung by its sierra' (*WW*: 612). However, it is in Borrow's literary persona – a polyglot roving 'I/eye', a man of habitual self-concealment – that the influence of *The Bible in Spain* is most powerfully felt. *Wild Wales*'s narrator, like the resolute colporteur of the earlier text, is adept at mimicry. Indeed, his precocious aptitude for different dialects permits a protean reshaping of self. *The Bible in Spain* shows how subterfuge and linguistic sleight of hand comprises a crucial set of tactics in a sometimes-inimical Catholic expanse. In *Wild Wales*, the obsession with assumed roles is mirrored in the narrator's unplaceable accent, demeanour, and code switching. His movement between languages limns his desire to refine a multifaceted identity that draws on two cultural localities ('Cambrian' and 'Saxon'). To devise a third, hybrid dis/guise that is fluid, transitional, and somewhere in between

16. Angus Fraser, 'George Borrow's *Wild Wales*: Fact and Fabrication', *Trafodion Anrhydeddus Gymdeithas Y Cymmrodorion / Transactions of the Honourable Society of Cymmrodorion* (1980): 163–73.

a 'Welshman or foreigner' (*WW* XCIX: 663) – that is his unspoken goal. This elaborate charade – one observer calls him a 'strange fellow' whose 'Welsh sounds very different from ours' (*WW* XXXIX: 270) – suggests a desire to bring a whiff of cosmopolitan glamour to the small regional hostels at which he stays. This ploy also signals his fear of being unmasked, and shunned, as a 'Sais' (English) interloper by the local 'miners and the carters', the 'rough, unkempt fellows' whose 'discourse' (*WW* XCIX: 659) he is so keen to hear. The narrator's self-presentation as a nomadic man of mystery or citizen of nowhere – 'I was a foreign man', 'I did not say a Saxon' (*WW* LXXX: 521) – signifies deep misgivings that he is merely following in the footsteps of 'Sais' literary luminaries for whom Welsh Romanticism was 'largely a locale and a motif, rather than primarily an authorial birthright'.[17] Thus, he yearns to confound people's expectations of him, 'to be anything but what I am, one of a nation amongst whom any knowledge save what relates to money-making and over-reaching is looked upon as a disgrace' (*WW* XXIX: 206).

What he discovers on his sojourn is that even within the Welsh language itself, battle lines are drawn between 'North' Walian and 'South' Walian variants of the spoken tongue (Chapter XCVIII). A 'man' tells him: 'I see you are a Cumro', 'one of ourselves' (*WW* LXVII: 449). However, at Port Dyn Norwig his English-inflected pronunciation, syntax, and lexis are deemed so odd that the patrons, regarding their own dialect as a 'pure' Welsh, suspect he hails from South Wales. In the South, however, he is chaffed for 'pronouncing' like a North Welshman. Michael Sullivan, the impecunious book-huckster from County Mayo, 'discoursing' with the narrator during the latter's visit to Anglesey, exclaims: 'I see your hanner is a Munster man. Ah! All the learned men comes from Munster' (*WW* XXVII: 188). On the top crag of Snowdon, the narrator, after declaiming 'two curious englynion or stanzas', a Welsh gentleman approaches him and asks: 'Wyt ti Lydaueg' (Are you Breton?) (*WW* XXIX: 206). A traveller in Chapter XLIX assumes he is 'of the [United] States' (*WW*: 290–3), while a flummoxed young woman cannot decide whether he is an eccentric local or holding forth in some 'horrid English' (*WW* XLIV: 299). All these scenes accentuate how the narrator, like the travelogue in which he appears, personifies a baffling miscellany of styles, attitudes, and inflections. This discursive heterogeneity (picaresque, philological speculation, diary, ethnographic transcript, translated verse, social history) conveys the narrator's quest

17. See Laura Dabundo, 'Review of Damian Walford Davies and Lynda Pratt, eds, *Wales and the Romantic Imagination* and Shawna Lichtenwalner, *Claiming Cambria: Invoking the Welsh in the Romantic Era*', *The Wordsworth Circle* 40:4 (2009): 173.

for a 'plot' that will do justice to the myriad versions of 'Welshness' he perceives. This plot, he hopes, will not fix him as another glib 'Saxon gentleman' (*WW* XCI: 600), a retailer of 'mostly white, male, middle-class, heterosexual myths, and prejudices', treating their readers 'as eager consumers of exotic – culturally "othered" goods'.[18] It is partly because of this (doomed?) search that *Wild Wales* complicates the affective grammar and syntax of Home Tour travelogues which targeted a rapidly gentrifying audience eager to visit holiday resorts in rural North Wales given the geopolitical turbulence caused by the coeval 'Crimean expedition' (*WW* LVI: 383).

Contemporary middlebrow magazines struggled to interpret what was to them a deeply 'strange book' and what *The Spectator* later termed the mask-wearing 'poser' at its centre.[19] For the *Saturday Review*, Borrow's gallimaufry of local gossip, ethnographic lore, and personal crotchets, on top of an 'overweening love of prating', was meant to 'astonish the Welshman with the sight of an Englishman who could speak Welsh'. Here the *Saturday* slyly alludes to the fact that Pennant, as was common among the literary squirearchy of his era, published in English. Though fluent in French and Latin, Pennant understood little Welsh and relied on learned clerics from among his circle of walking companions to transcribe and translate extracts from medieval Welsh manuscripts. By contrast, *Wild Wales* parades its narrator's credentials as a self-taught and prodigious polyglot, whose translations from Welsh date from Borrow's youth, when he had hoped to build a professional career as a journalist and poet. His early correspondence implies that he would only visit Wales at such a point when he had established his public profile as an expert on an august literary tradition in a Celtic language.[20] Underlying his promotion of 'venerable bards' like Dafydd ab Gwilym ('the Welsh Ovid') and 'Iolo Goch' is a sense that Cambrian literature, as penned by Welsh authors born and bred, in their native tongue, had been utterly overshadowed by a Romanticism of Wales, a slick literary brand designed to edify those residing elsewhere, in non-Welsh, affluent, metropolitan localities. Against this trend *Wild Wales* positions ab Gwilym as 'the greatest poetical genius that has appeared in Europe since the revival of literature' (*WW* I: 6). An early review of Borrow's text in the 1865 *Y Traethodydd*, a quarterly published by the

18. Patrick Holland and Graham Huggan, *Tourists with Typewriters: Reflections on Contemporary Travel Writing* (Michigan: University of Michigan Press, 1998), viii.
19. [Anon.], 'IV: *Wild Wales*', *Eclectic Review* 4 (January 1863): 54; [Anon.], 'George Borrow and His Circle', *The Spectator* 111:4461 (27 December 1913): 1125.
20. [Anon.], 'Reviews. Borrow's *Wild Wales*', *Saturday Review* 15:375 (3 January 1863): 20–1; see also Hyde, 'Travelling Across Cultures', 331–2.

republican Denbigh printer and founder of the Welsh Land League Thomas Gee, questioned this self-advertised grasp of the ancient bards.[21] There was, however, broad consensus among contemporary Anglophone print media outlets that, 'in order really to understand' the links, interactions, and tensions between the cultures and language clusters of Wales, 'an Englishman familiar' with the indigenous tongue like Borrow 'would have great advantages over anyone else'.[22]

Speaking in Uncouth Tongues

Borrow's autodidact narrator needs little encouragement to exhibit his language talents. He initiates conversations, using English, with Welsh labourers to see how often he is greeted with the terse reply, 'Dim Saesneg'. This in turn allows him to surprise and impress his interlocutors with his mastery of 'the other tongue'. In Chapter VIII, he asks a mower, who considers himself a 'real Welshman', if he has studied Ellis Wynne's *Gweledigaetnau y Bardd Cwsg* or *Visions of the Sleeping Bard*, published in 1703. Borrow had made a translation of this text in 1860. The 'real Welshman', confessing that he is not conversant with this source text, asks the narrator,

> 'Are you a Welshman?'
>
> 'No,' said I; 'I am an Englishman.'
>
> 'And how is it,' said he, 'that you can read Welsh without being a Welshman?'
>
> 'I learned to do so,' said I, 'even as you learned to mow, without being bred up to farming work.'
>
> 'Ah!' said he, 'but it is easier to learn to mow than to read the Bardd Cwsg.'
>
> 'I don't think that,' said I; 'I have taken up a scythe a hundred times but I cannot mow.'
>
> 'Will your honour take mine now, and try again?' said he.
>
> 'No,' said I, 'for if I take your scythe in hand I must give you a shilling, you know, by mowers' law.'
>
> He gave a broad grin, and I proceeded up the hill. When he rejoined his companions he said something to them in Welsh, at which they all laughed. (*WW* VIII: 39–40)

21. [Anon.], 'Cymru trwy Lygaid y Saeson', *Y Traethodydd* (July 1865): 3. *Y Traethodydd* is the oldest magazine in the Welsh language still in publication. Online editions of this journal (1900–2007) are available via the National Library of Wales.
22. [Anon.], 'Reviews. Borrow's *Wild Wales*', *Saturday Review* 15:375 (3 January 1863): 20–1.

Borrow's narrator does not explain what the mower says to his 'companions' to trigger such mirth. For all his self-declared proficiency – 'pattering every slang, lingua and lingo, of Frank, Jew, and Gypsy', according to *Tait's Edinburgh Magazine* – he remains the butt of jokes, excluded from the farmhands' banter.[23] This sense of the linguistic and cultural outsider, whose fluency derives in large part from much-thumbed ancient tomes rather than the easy rhythms of quotidian speech, also resonates through Chapter XVII, in which he orders a 'pint of the best ale' at a 'gwestfa' (boarding house). The 'girl stared' yet 'went away apparently to fetch it' (*WW* XVII: 100). We are perhaps meant to admire, like the ostensibly dumbfounded local barmaid, the insouciant charisma of a gentleman-traveller requesting beer in Welsh. However, the scene is staged to make a different reading equally, if not more, credible. The girl, belonging to a fluid and vibrant linguistic community, cannot fully grasp what sounds like a bookish, arcane, or orotund species of 'Cambrian-English'. Like the local guide tasked with escorting the narrator to Pont Erwyd (Chapter LXXXI) who confesses that he finds the gentleman's Welsh parlance 'quite above my comprehension' (*WW* LXXXI: 531), the barmaid proceeds more by hunch than instruction. The narrator's public self-placement as one inordinately 'fond' of the native language – we recall Lavengro's boast that he was 'a perfect master in the Welsh tongue' (*LSGP* XIX: 145) – suggests his immersion in 'Owen Pugh's translation of *Paradise Lost*' (*WW* LV: 375), for example, might be better received at an Eisteddfod.[24] In the eleventh chapter he 'spoke some Welsh' to several young people 'which *appeared* to give them great satisfaction' (*WW* XI: 56; my emphasis). What the narrator perceives as 'satisfaction' could be something less gratifying to his (easily bruised) ego. Here, as elsewhere, *Wild Wales* strikes an ambiguous note. Has the autodidact narrator designed these 'interviews', vignettes, and asides to parade a sort of embarrassed self-awareness, even a flair for playful self-mockery? Or are such moments inadvertently droll for a twenty-first-century readership? That the polyglot narrator is far from 'master of the colloquial language of Wales' (*WW* LV: 375) is reinforced by his memorable encounter, while searching for Goronwy Owen's birthplace at Llanfair on Anglesey, with a humble mason who, it turns out, speaks 'very tolerable Spanish' (*WW* XXXII: 225). That the mason mistakes him for a Spaniard contains a

23. [Anon.], 'Borrow's *Bible in Spain*', *Tait's Edinburgh Magazine* 10:110 (February 1843): 75–84.

24. Jodie Matthews, 'Borrowing Welshness: *Wild Wales*, Affiliation and Identity', *North American Journal of Welsh Studies* 6:1 (2011): 53–61.

subtle joke at the narrator's expense. In the first chapter of *Wild Wales*, he exults in his ability to articulate the rolled 'R' and voiceless alveolar lateral fricative (the Welsh 'll' sound at the beginning of a word): '"Had you much difficulty in acquiring the sound of the ll?" I think I hear the reader inquire. None whatever' (*WW* I: 4–5). The Welsh 'll', the narrator explains, was easy to pronounce because he had already learned the Spanish 'll'. The mason at Llanfair however, having spent part of his professional life in Chile, assumes the lost gentleman-traveller is a 'stranger' from Iberian shores, given his bizarre intonation.

The sly comedy of manners, exposing a narrator who is vain about his linguistic expertise, is deepened in Chapter LXXII. Here he meets in Bala a 'fast young man' from Wolverhampton, precisely the kind of philistine, smug and 'coarse-hearted Saxon' tourist from whom he tries to distance himself. And yet the young man recognises in the narrator all the verbal and gestural tics of a fellow Wolverhamptonite (*WW* LXXII: 476). We note the narrator's chagrin that, no matter how much he expresses delight in all things 'Cambrian' and for cultural heterogeneity more broadly, this relish is anchored in the inherited prestige of being an affluent 'Saxon' traveller – as the 'fast young man' implies. We see this with startling pictorial vividness in Chapter XX, which concerns the narrator's visit to 'the birthplace of the great poet Huw Morris' (*WW* XX: 125).[25] With typical fondness for full-blooded dramatic gestures, he reverently removes his hat, stands in the rain, enunciates his tribute in Welsh, and then sits in the bardic chair to commence 'repeating' the esteemed poet's verses. His not-so-rapt congregation consists of a 'stout old lady, the short, buxom and bare-armed damsel' and 'John Jones the Calvinistic weaver of Llangollen':

> all of whom listened patiently and approvingly, though the rain was pouring down upon them, and the branches of the trees and the tops of the tall nettles, agitated by the gusts from the mountain hollows, were beating in their faces, for enthusiasm is never scoffed at by the noble simple-minded, genuine Welsh, whatever treatment it may receive from the coarse-hearted, sensual, selfish Saxon. (*WW* XX: 130)

The narrator's craving for acceptance and approval from those whom he fetishises (and infantilises) as 'simple-minded, *genuine Welsh*' (my emphasis) makes it inconceivable to him that such drenched

25. Helen Fulton, 'George Borrow and the Oldest Animals in *Wild Wales*', *Trafodion Anrhydeddus Gymdeithas Y Cymmrodorion / Transactions of the Honourable Society of Cymmrodorion* (2003): 23–40.

onlookers will 'scoff' in private after this heartfelt oration ends. One such contemporary scoffer was Pembrokeshire poet and Conservative MP John Henry Scourfield, whose flippant odes target Cambrophiles who glorify 'the Celt in a Coracle, fishing for Salmon', as well as the meaningless 'mummeries' of the Eisteddfod. Scourfield's *Lyrics and Philippics* (1859) lampoons a figure not unlike Borrow's narrator here – one who 'wants you to listen to Cambria's praise, / To keep up old Customs, and walk in old ways, / So snug in Humbugging, and Tomfoolery'.[26] The Borrovian narrator's resolve to show that he shares little with the 'coarse-hearted' Wolverhamptonite distances him from supposedly 'patient' Welsh onlookers as well. It is telling that his stoically reserved and soggy companions do not add their voices to his lusty recital – though it is plausible the narrator has effectively drowned out his audience, such is his performative ardour.

When the narrator encounters locals who fall far short of his ideal of the '*genuine Welsh*' – like the dissolute, ale-worshipping Wrexham couple in Chapter LXV – he suggests that they are, in fact, of English extraction, no better than the boorish Wolverhamptonite: 'genuine descendants' of 'old heathen Saxons who followed Rag into Wales'. If 'these two are a fair specimen of the Wrexham population, my friend the Scotch policeman was not much out when he said that the people of Wrexham were the worst people in Wales' (*WW* LXV: 441). The narrator does not consider Wrexham to be 'properly Welsh' anyway, as most of its inhabitants seem to speak only English. These episodes – which variously ironise the narrator's brittle fictions and fantasies of *authentic* Welshness – buttress the conceptual pattern of *Lavengro* and *The Romany Rye*, which also stage cross-border dialogues to probe intricacies and lacunae in national (hi)stories: that long, tangled chronicle of multilingualism, adaptation, migration to and around Britain, which was obscured in favour of an increasingly xenophobic, nativist, and monoglot ethos embodied by the narrator's recruiting sergeant father. A plebeian experience of mobility, mutation, frontier-crossing, and re/settlement, with its ongoing struggles for social equality and recognition, is woven into *Lavengro*'s 'interviews' featuring a vast army of casual and seasonal labourers, 'Irish' travellers, 'Armenians', and Romani ('I like you all the better for talking Rommany').

That scholars are more attuned nowadays to the comic, rather than the political resonances of the narrator's celebration of Welsh-language texts like the *Bardd Cwsg* and the 'verses of Huw Morris' ignores how

26. John Henry Scourfield, 'A Welsh Ode: Composed for the Eisteddfod', *Lyrics and Philippics* (Covent Garden: G. Norman, 1864), 27.

Wild Wales's fervid investment in Cambrian lore challenged external neo-colonial social commentaries. Key among them was the December 1847 'Blue Books' (blue being the colour of their original binding) – the *Report of the Commission of Inquiry into the State of Education in Wales*.[27] Authored by three Oxbridge-educated, Anglican, and monoglot English inspectors, this diatribe against indigenous national culture was popularly dubbed as *Brad y Llyfrau Gleision* ('The Treason of the Blue Books') – named after the *Brad y Cyllyll Hirion* ('The Treason of the Long Knives'), a pseudohistorical tale describing the massacre of British Celtic chieftains by Anglo-Saxon warriors in the fifth century. Borrow's narrator alludes to this 'infernal carnage' in Chapter LII, observing grimly: 'the Saxons derived their name from the saxes, or long knives, which they wore at their sides, and at the use of which they were terribly proficient' (*WW* LII: 355). The Welsh tongue, the 'Blue Books' inspectors concluded, together with wanton 'dissipation' fostered by nonconformist chapel culture, would fatally hamstring any effort on the part of the population to attain a competitive position in an expanding global economy.[28] The inspectors parsed putative linguistic 'backwardness' and moral turpitude as inextricably entangled: 'the Welsh are peculiarly exempt from the guilt of great crimes', but there are very 'few countries where the standard of minor morals is lower'.[29] Rhoda Broughton's 1860s fiction was no less severe in presenting 'slovenly locals' with their 'chattering harsh Welsh – the ugliest of all ugly tongues', which 'we trust, will soon be among the abuses of the past'.[30] In an 1852 report on Welsh elementary education, while serving as Her Majesty's Inspector of Schools, Matthew Arnold, though he had conceded that Welsh children were 'quick in apprehension, to a greater degree than English children', had followed the 1847 'Blue Book' commissioners. He argued that it was Westminster's direct political business to 'render its dominions, as far as possible, homogenous'. 'Sooner or later,' he averred, 'the difference of language between Wales and England will probably be effaced.'[31] John Jenkins's *Report on the State*

27. Ieuan Gwynedd Jones, '1848 and 1868: "Brad y Llyfrau Gleision" and Welsh Politics', *Mid-Victorian Wales: The Observers and the Observed* (Cardiff: University of Wales Press, 1992), 102–65; Gwyneth Tyson Roberts, *The Language of the Blue Books: The Perfect Instrument of Empire* (Cardiff: University of Wales Press, 1998).
28. *Report of the Commission of Inquiry into the State of Education in Wales. In Three Parts. Part I, Carmarthen, Glamorgan and Pembroke. Part II, Brecknock, Cardigan, Radnor and Monmouth. Part III, North Wales* (London, 1847), II, 66.
29. *Report of the Commission of Inquiry*, II, 56.
30. Rhoda Broughton, *Not Wisely, But Too Well* (London: Tinsley Brothers, 1867), 82–3; Broughton, *Red as a Rose is She* (London: Tinsley Brothers, 1870), 38–9.
31. Matthew Arnold, *Reports on Elementary Schools 1852–1882* (London: Wyman and Sons, 1908), 11.

of Popular Education in the Welsh Specimen Districts (1860), published two years before *Wild Wales*, endorsed Arnold's professional judgement by contending that Welsh was 'simply not sufficient to meet the requirements of knowledge in modern times'.[32] Any initiatives to foster some type of bilingual coexistence between Welsh and English, such as those synonymous with the Society for the Utilisation of the Welsh Language (1885) later in the century, should be resisted.

Wild Wales offers a sustained riposte to the transient experiences of the 1847 commissioners and those who declared, like the influential Flintshire barrister and bibliophile Enoch Salisbury in 1849, that 'the extermination of the Welsh language (as a *living* one) would be the greatest possible blessing to Wales'.[33] By contrast, Borrow's narrator expresses unalloyed delight in a mellifluous 'language older than Greek' (*WW* LXXXVI: 569). His discussion of its tonal richness and lyrical sophistication pushes against contemporary journalists and novelists who smeared Welsh as a 'language of the woodcutters and the fisherman, of labour and fatigue', of destitution and need.[34] This is why Borrow's translated texts, like the prolonged 'interviews' with Welsh-born barmaids, Calvinist preachers, smallholders, millers, dockhands, and shop assistants (which the *Cornhill* reviewer deemed provocatively trite) are, in fact, essential to his narrative structure. Interactions with these Welsh speakers allow us to inspect ascendant concepts of ethnicity espoused by Borrow's more garlanded contemporary Arnold, how such ideas evolved through a continual process of cultural upheaval, and where they were (con)tested by residual, dissident, or denigrated perceptions of regional 'belonging' (*WW* LXXIV: 485). More importantly, these myriad conversation 'set pieces' lend the threatened vernacular language a cultural visibility, even a public platform, one that could be savoured by Borrow's readership both within and beyond Wales.

Matthew Arnold and the Celtic-Saxon Nexus

> The attempt of Borrow, an Englishman [. . .] to give a connected account of Welsh poetry deserves high praise. [. . .] He wrote with knowledge, the result of some thirty years' reading. [. . .]

32. Quoted in Hywel Teifi Edwards, 'The Welsh Language in the Eisteddfod', *The Welsh Language and its Social Domains 1801–1911*, ed. Geraint H. Jenkins (Cardiff: University of Wales Press, 2000), 295.
33. E. R. G. Salisbury, 'A Letter on National Education, suggested by "A Letter on State Education in Wales"' (Cardiff: Smithson, 1849), 3.
34. 'Gwelai mai Cymraeg oedd iaith y cymynwyr coed a'r gwenhynwyr dwfr, iaith llafur a lludded, iaith caledi ac angen'. See B. G. Evans, 'Cymro, Cymru a Chymraeg', *Transactions of the Liverpool Welsh National Society* (1889): 22–3.

> At any rate, he went to the originals and obtained his information at first hand. A careful investigation of the sources he used shows how much more at home Borrow was with his theme than his contemporary Matthew Arnold.[35]

In 1928, Herbert G. Wright measured *Celtic Bards, Chiefs and Kings*[36] – Borrow's voluminous celebration of Cambrian culture drafted alongside *Wild Wales* but unpublished during his lifetime – against Arnold's reductive conception of the Welshman's 'land' as 'a province', his speech a feeble 'echo', 'growing every day fainter', 'gone in Cornwall, going in Brittany and the Scotch Highlands, going, too, in Ireland'.[37] As Wright indicates here, Borrow's scholarly engagement with Wales, unlike Arnold's, started early and with unusual keenness. Borrow's interest may have been piqued by his Norwich intellectual lodestar William Taylor, who, between 1804 and 1806, was corresponding with his friend Robert Southey regarding William Owen Pughe's unpublished translation of sections of *The Mabinogian*, by which Southey was particularly struck. As critic Clive Wilkins-Jones states, 'surviving British Museum readers' slips recording Borrow's use of Welsh texts appear from the handwriting to date from the years 1826–9. His manuscript translation of Ellis Wynne's *Gweledigaetheu y Bardd Cwsc* was written on paper watermarked 1829.'[38]

Wright was conscious that Arnold, from his very earliest journalistic enquiries, had framed Wales, without displaying anything like Borrow's historical or translational acumen, as a 'petty' Celtic nationality. In 'England and the Italian Question' (1859), Arnold's first published pamphlet, he claims that Wales was not like those 'great' established powers and agents of history – England, France, and Italy – whose resilience, 'freedom and dignity' were mirrored in their dogged refusal to let their legal, financial, and educational frameworks be 'absorbed' by rival European nation-states. Like Cornwall, Wales – though a cultural force in the distant past – must now be steered from London, the seat of English government. By divesting themselves of their language and embracing social uniformity, these Celtic sites will access a shared

35. Herbert G. Wright, 'Preface' to George Borrow, *Celtic Bards, Chiefs and Kings* (London: John Murray, 1928), 6.
36. *Celtic Bards* would not be published until 1928 by John Murray, although it had been 'advertised in Borrow's lifetime, at the end of the first edition of *The Romany Rye*'. See Collie and Fraser, *George Borrow: A Bibliographical Study*, 162.
37. Arnold, *On the Study of Celtic Literature*, 5.
38. Clive Wilkins-Jones, 'The Making of George Borrow's "The Welsh And Their Literature"', *George Borrow: The Unveiling of the Veiled Period and other Papers* (Oxford: Lavengro Press, 2016), 51; see also Hyde, 'Travelling Across Cultures', 331–43.

cultural domain that transcends 'historically specific group interests', thus affirming the very '"best" selves as opposed to the "ordinary" selves of people'. Arnold's strategic response, coupled with the migration of more monoglot English speakers into the rapidly industrialising south-eastern counties of Glamorgan and Monmouthshire, implied that his model of political assimilation – a 'native tongue', local institutions, breakaway religious societies, even the Welsh as a discrete ethnicity rendered extinct beneath the tread of 'enlightened' anglophone culture – would happen 'sooner' rather than 'later'. This preoccupation with ethno-cultural difference, against a backdrop of aggressive English expansionism, is the conceptual thread that runs through Arnold's social criticism, from *On the Study of Celtic Literature* (1867) and *Irish Essays* (1882) to the 1888 text 'Disestablishment in Wales'.[39] What may have been intended by the humane Arnold as a rapprochement with historically scorned neighbours was in fact a prescriptive intervention, converting 'into an object of academic study' the 'last vestiges' of 'vanquished' Celtic kingdoms.[40]

If Borrow hoped that the publication of *Wild Wales* would cement his public profile as a strongminded, erudite, and empathetic defender of 'Celtic literature' (*WW* XVIII: 112) against such colonial decrees – his friend and champion Theodore Watts-Dunton claimed that 'to be recognized as a scholar was the great ambitious dream' of Borrow's life – then it must have been especially galling to see Arnold lauded by *The Athenaeum* as 'the most cosmopolitan of islanders', one who had risen above the childish squabbles of party politics to show a peerless 'authority' on Celtic-Saxon relations. For *The Athenaeum*, that authority rested on Arnold's 'message of peace to Ireland' – he closes his *Study* by campaigning for the creation of 'a chair of Celtic at Oxford'. This led to the appointment of John Rhys in 1877, thus affording a fillip to Celtic revivalism in Wales, synonymous with the Eisteddfod Festival which Arnold had witnessed while on holiday with his family at Llandudno in the summer of 1864. Borrow may have wondered how Arnold could speak so categorically on these matters, given that the *Study* and *Irish Essays* buttress a mid-century cultural imaginary nourished by the mannered whimsies of James Macpherson and Scott's *Waverley* novels, in which the 'gay', feminised 'Celt' lacks the intellectual equipment to

39. See Matthew Arnold, *England and the Italian Question*, ed. Merle M. Bevington (North Carolina: Duke University Press, 1953), 13. Also, Daniel G. Williams, *Ethnicity and Cultural Authority: From Arnold to Du Bois* (Edinburgh: Edinburgh University Press, 2017), 34.
40. See Robert Young, *Colonial Desire: Hybridity in Theory, Culture and Race* (Abingdon: Routledge, 1995), 71.

participate fully in the policy-making of a confident nation-state. The Welshman's obdurate and prolonged 'rebellion against fact', Arnold avers, has 'lamed' him in 'the world of business and politics'.[41] Arnold's Celtic imaginary also exploits contemporary stereotypes of the nomadic, post-Famine Irish population in Wales ('undisciplined, anarchical, and turbulent').[42] *Wild Wales* challenges this picture by showing how 'Irish itinerants' (*WW* V: 25), having fled the ruinous economic fallout of the Famine, found themselves persistent targets of native chauvinism due to their perceived 'Popery' and apparent collusion in keeping wages low, especially in the burgeoning industrial heartland of south-east Wales.[43]

Like *Wild Wales*, Arnold's *Celtic* writings brood over questions of the temperamental and moral facets of Englishness, fraught Irish–British political relations, and the ennobling operations of literary criticism and translation. The need to cherish and deepen one's 'personal knowledge' of other cultures was at least as vital to the largely self-taught Borrow as it was to the upper-middle-class Professor of Poetry Arnold, who commented in a letter to his mother in January 1865: 'I hate all over-preponderance of single elements, and all my efforts are directed to enlarge and complete us by bringing in as much as possible of Greek, Latin, Celtic cultures.'[44] However, Borrow's abiding desire to translate 'The Welsh and their Literature' (the title of an article he penned for the January 1861 *Quarterly Review*)[45] is more alert to the spontaneities of everyday speech – an approach that safeguards Welsh people's human rights, cultural values, and pride in their own popular literate language. J. E. Southall, in *Wales and her Language* (1892), published shortly after Borrow's death, underscored this aspect of *Wild Wales*: 'George Borrow did not go to gaze on half effaced effigies in parish meeting houses, to describe the gables of manor houses.' Instead, 'he went to see the people, knowing not merely their language but the character of their literature'.[46]

Against Arnold's *Celtic* essays, whose ostensibly 'disinterested' scholarship validates the 'natural course of things' – namely an inexorable

41. See Malcolm Chapman, *The Celts: The Construction of a Myth* (London: Palgrave Macmillan, 1992).
42. Arnold, *Celtic Literature*, 345–6.
43. See L. Miskell, 'Reassessing the Anti-Irish Riot: Popular Protest and the Irish in South Wales, c. 1826–1882', *Irish Migrants in Modern Wales*, ed. Paul O'Leary (Liverpool: Liverpool University Press, 2004); Paul O'Leary, *Immigration and Integration: The Irish in Wales 1789–1922* (Cardiff: University Press of Wales, 2000).
44. Matthew Arnold, *Selected Letters of Matthew Arnold*, Clinton Machann and Forrest D. Burt, eds (London: Macmillan, 1993), 168; Hyde, 'Travelling Across Cultures', 341.
45. [Anon.], 'The Welsh and their Literature', *Quarterly Review* 109 (1861): 38–63.
46. J. E. Southall, *Wales and her Language*, 163.

'fusion of all the inhabitants' into one 'English-speaking whole', the 'swallowing up of separate provincial nationalities' – *Wild Wales* proffers a more expansive, even multicultural and pluralistic perspective.[47] This signifies an awareness of the unprecedented levels of immigration into Wales from other parts of the island nation and Western Europe – a trend that continued apace into the first decade of the twentieth century, when over 130,000 people arrived in South Wales alone. For an autodidact philologist like Borrow's narrator, such far-reaching historical shifts compounded the complexity of the language question in Wales – a question that Arnold's hegemonic worldview could not hope to capture. On the one hand, Borrow's narrator shuns the petty provincialism and sloganeering of a 'Wales for the Welsh'. On the other, he rebuts Arnold's tendency to construe Celtic tongues as 'the badge of a beaten race',[48] to be repressed within a lofty notion of a common cultural sphere.[49] Instead, *Wild Wales* supplies a multifaceted paradigm of Union determined by enquiry into, and often droll comparison of, ethno-cultural singularities. While Borrow's notebooks imply that encounters are sometimes embellished, restructured, or fabricated to address his publisher's concerns that the text lacked rousing 'incident,' they do reveal how he conceives *Wild Wales* through a comparative ethnic lens. He attains this by surveying habitations, superstitions (corpse-candles, fairies), and speech acts given short shrift – or ignored altogether – by Arnold and privileged ramblers seeking the Cambrian picturesque. The Borrovian narrator's Celtic fieldwork uncovers the coexistence in Wales of ethno-linguistic groups and migrant subcultures markedly different from one another. Such enclaves are enshrined in a host of 'dissonant English[es]' and Cambrian 'jargon' (*WW* XXIV: 160), as well as other national languages, such as Irish Gaelic, which the narrator's guide John Jones contemptuously dubs 'Paddy Gwyddel' (*WW* XIV: 83). As early as the second chapter, Borrow's narrator is nonplussed by a barmaid, from whose mouth proceeds Welsh sounds he was 'quite unable to understand' (*WW* II: 12). Entering the 'small village' of Rhigos between the Vale of Neath and the Cynon Valley, he overhears a deeply 'strange corrupt' form of Welsh spoken by 'grimy fellows' (*WW* CIII: 686). On Anglesey, he meets the mason with a very 'tolerable' grasp of Spanish. In Chapter XXIV, conversing in Italian with a vendor of weatherglasses, the

47. Arnold, *Celtic Literature*, 296–7.
48. Arnold, *On the Study of Celtic Literature*, 293.
49. J. E. Southall, *Wales and her Language*, 241.

narrator ponders an obscure dialect 'composed of many languages', that the Milanese 'speak amongst themselves' (*WW* XXIV: 160).

Arnold's *Celtic* essays, in stark contrast, promote a 'standard' English as monolithic as his direct knowledge of ancient Welsh poetry in translation is partial and narrow – an issue that Herbert Wright targets in his 'Preface' to Borrow's *Celtic Bards*. While Arnold's appreciation of the medieval manuscripts of Wales won him plaudits from some Welsh cultural nationalists later in the century, like Tom Ellis, it did not show anything like the same first-hand knowledge and breadth of cultural reference as Borrow's *Celtic Bards* or *Wild Wales*. Indeed, Arnold's 'Introduction' to the *Celtic* essays is explicit about the 'provisional character' of his grasp of Cambrian lore. His recourse to a restricted array of scholarly sources on Celtic antiquity – translations of the Welsh *Mabinogion*, text editions by esteemed Irish-language specialists such as O'Curry and O'Donovan – ultimately exposes the degree of his enthusiasm for the subject.

Arnold understands 'Welsh' as, at best, a cluster of fading antiquarian curiosities, and at worst, a nostalgist's affectation. It is a far cry from Borrow's conception of a constantly morphing language whose vitality is mirrored in how it is voiced by ordinary townspeople advocating a gamut of political and economic theories. This responsiveness to the phonetic tics, routines, and aspirations of the bilingual labouring class can be measured against Arnold's persistent flirtation with the more rarefied elements of nineteenth-century Arthurian mythscapes – what the 1909 *Edinburgh Review* called 'the sentimentalist's emotional illusions, the poet's rapturous contemplations'.[50] Although Borrow's narrator hails Wales as 'the land of old renown and wonder, the land of Arthur and Merlin', he does not, during his stay in Cardigan, evoke the famed Pembrokeshire village of Cilgerran and its ruined castle nearby, the Welsh Tintagel, drawn by J. M. W. Turner in 1798. This site features memorably in Thomas Warton's 1777 poem 'The Grave of King Arthur': 'Stately the feast, and high the cheer: / Girt with many an armed peer, / Cilgarran, in thy castle hall, / And canopied with golden pall'. As in *Celtic Bards*, Borrow makes scant allusions to Arthuriana – a riposte to travelogues like Thomas Roscoe's *Wanderings and Excursions in South Wales*, which caters to a readership expecting thick descriptions of crumbling castle walls and 'the chivalry or superstition that once ruled the land'.[51]

50. [Anon.], 'The Wanderer: George Borrow', *Edinburgh Review* 210:430 (October 1909): 320.
51. Art IV, '*Black's Picturesque Guide through North and South Wales and Monmouthshire*', *London Review* 11:21 (October 1858): 111–42.

Borrow's travelogue is dominated instead by witty 'interviews' or 'discourses' with humble Welsh and Irish Gaelic speakers. These linguistic set pieces imply on occasions a 'field recording' and can lead to awkward interpersonal engagements, even a sharp rebuff. In Chester, for example, the narrator, eager to present himself as a fluent roving reporter, irks a Welsh bookseller who 'did not approve of an Englishman's understanding Welsh' by 'translating a couplet into English' (*WW* V: 24). The narrator explicates the etymology of '*carn-lleidyr*' ('a thief without a house or home') to another Welsh-speaker and in a more didactic, even patronising guise, 'educates' other townspeople about their own unexamined aesthetic heritage. This rich heritage has been crafted and promoted, in the narrator's opinion, by doughty resisters, poetic malcontents, and mavericks – men after his own heart like Iolo Goch, Gronwy Owen, Twm o'r Nant, and Dafydd ap Gwilym. By such 'discoursing', the narrator sidesteps Arnold's reliance on catch-all ethnocultural categories, whose lack of systematic theoretical rigour and nuance the 1867 *London Review* saw as leading to 'vague', 'prejudiced' judgements concerning the Celtic language family.[52] The reviewer targets here Arnold's habit of deploying ethnic appellations figuratively rather than literally to evoke literary styles, patterns of thought, and behavioural oddities. As critic Joep Leerssen contends, a 'given cultural profile' may be called 'Saxon' or 'Celtic' not because 'Arnold seriously wants to argue that racial descent determines cultural proclivities, but because these ethnic terms function as handy ad-hoc labels.'[53] According to Arnold's *Irish Essays*, the Welsh side of the 'Celtic' language family were at least making modest strides on a path to civilised progress: the 'Welsh have adopted with ardour our middle-class religion, and this at once puts them in sympathy with our middle-class civilisation'.[54] Here Arnold presumably means the ever-more anglicised and commercially savvy Welsh petite bourgeoisie which had placed its faith in a conception of the modern British state as a guarantor of law, plenitude, and prosperity. Borrow's narrator notes this trend in his 'interview' with a 'respectable dame' at Valle Crucis Abbey: 'I spoke some Welsh to her, which pleased her. She said that Welsh people at the present day were so full of fine airs that they were above speaking the old

52. [Anon.], 'The Celts Vindicated', *London Review* 15:369 (27 July 1867): 104–5.

53. Joep Leerssen, 'Englishness, Ethnicity and Matthew Arnold', *European Journal of English Studies* 10:1 (2006): 63–79; Huw Pryce, 'Culture, Identity, and the Medieval Revival in Victorian Wales', *Proceedings of the Harvard Celtic Colloquium* 31 (2011): 1–40.

54. Matthew Arnold, 'The Incompatibles', *Irish Essays and Others* (London: Smith, Elder, 1882), 65–6.

language – but that such was not the case formerly' (*WW* XIII: 74). The 'Calvinistic Methodist' whom the narrator meets in Chapter XII slyly describes these upwardly mobile gentrified types, with their 'fine airs', as instrumentalist 'Saxons': 'the clebberest people in Llangollen' when it comes to 'carnal things' like making money (*WW* XII: 69). The novelist Joseph Downes was more strident in his 'Preface' to *The Mountain Decameron* (1836). He castigates Celtophobic, hard-headed philistines who favour *ariangarwch* or 'money-worship' over the ethno-linguistic wealth on their own doorstep.[55] Downes's 'Preface' is marked, as Jane Aaron's *Gothic Wales* explains, by Welsh unease about 'cultural death' in the face of dwindling numbers of native Welsh speakers and repression of Welsh cultural practices that had long predated the 1536 Act of Union.[56] However much Arnold liked to profess his own 'semi-Celtic' provenance to his immediate family, there was, as *Wild Wales* demonstrates, open disdain for that anglophile 'middle-class' viewpoint which asserted that Wales's inter/national credibility relied on effacing ethno-cultural differences with their 'Saxon superiors'.[57]

The 'interviews' in *Wild Wales* mirror a more intricately textured topography of dissension. Unlike Arnold or J. S. Mill's *England and Ireland* (1868), the narrator's trek lays bare notable civic and technological shifts at mid-century – especially how the rough terrain fostered cultural divergences in a primarily agrarian, Welsh-speaking middle and north, and a gradually anglicised south. The narrator's discoursing corroborates the May 1848 *Blackwood's Edinburgh Magazine* in its summary of Welsh public feeling in the aftermath of the release of the incendiary 'Blue Books': 'The Welsh still call themselves "the Cymry" [. . .] They still look on the English as foreigners; [they] never will unite with the Saxon race so far as to keep pace with them in what is called "improvement" and "knowledge".'[58] This is a far cry from Arnold's 'Incompatibles', the opening sally of *Irish Essays*, in which a conciliatory and protective British state certifies Union and the loyalty of Welsh subject-citizens by instilling bourgeois virtues of thrift and stoical self-discipline. Borrow's narrator meanwhile projects himself as better attuned to what critic Seamus Deane terms the 'unlovely and

55. Downes, *The Mountain Decameron*, 3–4.
56. Jane Aaron, *Welsh Gothic* (Cardiff: University of Wales Press, 2013), 61.
57. See Clinton Machann, *Matthew Arnold: A Literary Life* (Basingstoke: Macmillan, 1998), 65–7; Joep Leerssen, *Remembrance and Imagination: Patterns in the Historical and Literary Representation of Ireland in the Nineteenth Century* (Notre Dame, IN: University of Notre Dame Press, 1997). See also George Borrow, *George Borrow's Tour of Galloway and the Borders 1866*, ed. Angus Fraser (Norwich: Lavengro Press, 2015).
58. [Anon.], 'Education in Wales', *Blackwood's Edinburgh Magazine* 63:391 (May 1848): 545.

brutalised relationship' between England and its Celtic 'dominions'.[59] In *Wild Wales*, the narrator journeys beyond the alder swamps and mountain gorges to survey the 'rude pews' of conventicles where Welsh 'Calvinistic Methodists' gather unnoticed by the agents of Arnold's 'enlightened middle-class'.[60] In Chapter XV, the narrator, conscious that other English sightseers might dismiss Ruthyn as an extremely 'dull town', reminds us that he is treading 'the ground which the wild bands of Glendower had trod, and where *the great struggle* commenced', which 'convulsed Wales, and for some time shook England to its centre' (*WW* XV: 90; my emphasis). The allusion to Owain Glyndŵr's fifteen-year campaign of guerrilla warfare against the rule of Henry IV serves an important political function in *Wild Wales*. Such imagery evokes a 'great' and ongoing 'struggle' to crystallise the vision of an internationally accepted independent Welsh nation. That the narrator relishes this 'struggle' implies a desire to complicate standard narratives of a modern Wales formed after a process of conquest under Edward I in the 1280s, and after more than two centuries of subjugation, following Henry VIII's break from Rome, the emergence of an 'English Empire' in which Wales was trammelled by its neighbour's administrative machinery. Here Borrow's narrator grasps how the popular media genres of mid-century journalism, stage melodrama, and cartoons, by promoting the anodyne Arnoldian 'poetry' of a Wales in which 'every crag and dell' are 'musical with legends', ultimately ensured those legends were decoupled from any awkward reference to centuries of Anglo-Norman or English rule.[61] Such journalistic clichés of Cambrian 'crag and dell' – a more palatable figuration than seeing Wales as one of the first English colonies – tallied with Arnold's notion of the dreamy, feminised 'melancholy' and 'unprogressiveness' of the 'Welsh mind' rather than the 'hot-bed of discontent' that the 1848 *Blackwood's* noted in the urban, maritime, and agricultural milieux of Caernarvon, Merthyr Tydfil, Swansea, and 'some parts of Anglesey, where the most republican and levelling doctrines prevail extensively among the farmers'.[62] Even at the time when Arnold was preparing his *Study* for publication, a text in which the 'Celt' is a fated 'creature which

59. Seamus Deane, '"Masked with Matthew Arnold's Face": Joyce and Liberalism', *Canadian Journal of Irish Studies* 12:1 (June 1986): 11–22 (16).
60. Cyril Pearce, 'A Landscape of Dissent: Topography and Identity in three Pennine Valleys', *Landscapes* 3 (Autumn, 2002): 84–102.
61. [Anon.], 'Wild Wales. By George Borrow', *London Quarterly Review* 20:40 (July 1863): 536–8.
62. [Anon.], 'Education in Wales', *Blackwood's Edinburgh Magazine* 63:391 (May 1848): 545.

had lived its cycle',[63] an increasingly confident, economically literate, and bilingual Welsh cognoscenti – that would evolve into the Cymru Fydd/The Wales to Come movement at the fin de siècle – were refining political strategies synonymous with the chiefly Protestant 'Young Ireland' activists to nurture the growth of an official institutional framework, such as the University of Wales (founded in 1893).[64] Core to Cymru Fydd policy – and imbuing travel texts such as Owen Morgan Edwards's *Cartrefi Cymru/Homes of Wales* (1896) – was Disestablishment in Wales (the title of one of Arnold's final essays), and the consecration of an ancient yet *living language* that underpins Borrow's travelogue.[65]

On the Road

That Borrow's Welsh is rendered as evolving and rich in regional variation – as opposed to Arnold's static conception of the native tongue as a dreary heritage exhibit – is due chiefly to the narrator's curiosity about how speech modes limn complex multicultural subjectivities. He gauges the effects and functions of regional vernaculars, idiolects, and how code switching ('the use of more than one language in the course of a single communicative episode') reinforces the mimetic operation in literary dialogue.[66] For all his paeans to the grave sonorities of medieval bardic verse, the narrator savours the theatrical possibilities of chance encounters on his route, whereby 'Englishes' and informal (even earthy) varieties of spoken Welsh are compared or blended. This notion of a speech act troubles orthodox assumptions that languages are separable entities; it also reveals how roadside dialogues in *Wild Wales* often become an intricate play of power relations. We see this in the narrator's reflections on inter-community friction due to exponential industrial growth in Monmouthshire and Glamorgan. In such localities the narrator treats 'Englishes' as a malleable linguistic archive shared and reforged among different geographical, religious, and class constituencies. In Llan Rhyaddr, for instance, the narrator meets a young carter who fails to answer his amiable English salutation except with a brusque '*Dim Saesneg*' ('I don't speak English').

63. [Art. II], '1. *Reports of the Commissioners of Inquiry into the State of Education in Wales.* 1847', *Quarterly Review* 87:174 (September 1850): 341.
64. Kenneth O. Morgan, *Rebirth of a Nation. Wales 1889–1980* (Oxford: Oxford University Press, 1981).
65. See Katie Gramich, 'Narrating the Nation: Telling Stories of Wales', *North American Journal of Welsh Studies* 6:1 (2011): 2–19.
66. See Monica Heller, ed., *Codeswitching: Anthropological and Sociolinguistic Perspectives* (Berlin: de Gruyter, 2000), 1; Hyde, 'Travelling Across Cultures', 338–43.

However, the boy goads and whips his team of horses up a slope with colourful English 'cursing':

> I allowed him and his team to get to the top of the ascent, and then overtaking him, I said in Welsh: 'What do you mean by saying you have no English? You were talking English just now to your horses.'
>
> 'Yes,' said the lad, 'I have English enough for my horses, and that is all.'
>
> 'You seem to have plenty of Welsh,' said I; 'why don't you speak Welsh to your horses?'
>
> 'It's of no use speaking Welsh to them,' said the boy; 'Welsh isn't strong enough.'
>
> 'Isn't *Myn Diawl* ['By the devil!'] tolerably strong?' said I.
>
> 'Not strong enough for horses,' said the boy 'if I were to say *Myn Diawl* to my horses, [. . .] they would laugh at me.'
>
> 'Do the other carters,' said I, 'use the same English to their horses which you do to yours?'
>
> 'Yes' said the boy, 'they'll all use the same English words; if they didn't the horses wouldn't mind them.'
>
> 'What a triumph,' thought I, 'for the English language that the Welsh carters are obliged to have recourse to its oaths and execrations to make their horses get on!'
>
> (*WW* LXVIII: 458)

As is his conversational custom, the narrator situates the boy as a sociolinguistic insider, informant, or 'mole', one who unwittingly divulges crucial data about the rhetorical expressiveness of localised, and sometimes closely guarded, speech behaviours and laws governing their use. The 'same English words' implies a transferred habit – a bilingual speaker applies features from one language to another, like the honorific '*Gwr Boneddig*' ('noble sir') a few Welsh-speaking characters utilise when addressing Borrow's narrator. That the Welsh lad exploits the 'oaths and execrations' of the 'Saxon' class is suggestive. His reply – 'Welsh isn't strong enough' – reverberates on two levels. First, it seems a tacit admission that, in larger struggles for cultural ascendancy, the Welsh language is not robust enough to withstand or repel the ceaseless infiltrations of a hegemonic anglophone polity whose loud 'voice' *is* the international lexicon of commerce and technology. Second, the boy enjoys (or momentarily performs?) what he judges to be the coloniser's brute authority and kudos – distilled in the fierce tone of Saxon 'oaths' – while also distancing himself from an unpopular centralised government that has devised such forceful, unlovely terms to quell Welsh man and beast alike. This scene also functions as a sidelight on a cultural phenomenon that sociolinguists Ferguson and Fishman designate as 'diglossia', whereby certain languages, tones, or registers perform lofty or respectable functions – the polite spoken Welsh that the boy might utter among close family members, employers, or clients – and the 'low' English 'execrations' he reserves for swearing at his disobedient horses.[67]

The narrator's sarcastic account of this Saxon language 'triumph' is the more notable given his appreciation elsewhere for how widely Welsh literary culture is known among the plebeian classes. However, he is not above baiting those locals whose appetite for 'speaking proper' takes precedence over rediscovering indigenous literary archives, attitudes, and customs. In Chapter LXI, the narrator finds himself on the linguistic and geographical 'borders'. He seeks guidance from those who reside in 'some small grimy-looking huts':

> At the door of the first I saw a girl. I spoke to her in Welsh, and found she had little or none. I passed on, and seeing the door of a cabin open, I looked in—and saw no adult person, but several grimy but chubby children. I spoke to them in English, and found they could only speak Welsh. [. . .] 'Truly,' said I to myself, 'I am on the borders. What a mixture of races and languages!' The next person I met was a man in a collier's dress; he was a stout-built fellow of the middle age, with a coal-dusty, surly countenance. I asked him in Welsh if I was in the right direction for Wrexham, he answered in a surly manner in English that I was. [Again] I spoke to him in Welsh, whereupon, looking at me with a grin of savage contempt, and showing a set of teeth like those of a mastiff, he said, 'How's this? why, you haven't a word of English! A pretty fellow, you, with a long coat on your back, and no English on your tongue [. . .] Why, here am I in a short coat, yet I'd have you to know that I can speak English as well as Welsh, aye, and a good deal better'. 'All people are not equally clebber,' said I, still speaking Welsh. 'Clebber,' said he, 'clebber! what is clebber? why can't you say clever? Why, I never saw such a low, illiterate fellow in my life;' and with these words he turned away, with every mark of disdain, and entered a cottage near at hand. (*WW* LXI: 417–18)

As in his exchange with the young carter, the narrator's eagerness to place himself at the centre of every linguistic event – impelled by that

67. See Mark Sebba et al., eds, *Language Mixing and Code-Switching in Writing. Approaches to Mixed-Language Written Discourse* (London: Routledge, 2012).

'mighty desire to know' indigenous lore through 'discourses' – leaves him vulnerable to charges of ego-tripping, even verbal 'slumming'. While he professes that listening is a core article of his personal creed, he is not averse to employing 'discourses' as an excuse for rhetorical skirmish, baiting, and provocation. Although the 'stout-built fellow' does not pretend to be among any cultural elite, he is openly derisive of the narrator's *apparent* ignorance of – or rather bizarre refusal to converse in – 'standard English', despite his demeanour signifying sartorial and class refinement. That the polyglot narrator wilfully mispronounces (still speaking Welsh) 'clever' as 'clebber' might be parsed as a ruse to sound like a labouring son of the soil. His misadvised ploy reflects his interest elsewhere in the long history of regional word usage and the literary conventions of representing nonstandard dialects (e.g. phonetically motivated respellings) in published form. 'Clebber/est' is woven into the narrative fabric of *Wild Wales*; it appears approximately twenty times across the volume – a peculiar lexical 'specimen' (*WW* LXV: 441), pinned and mounted on the printed page.

This heated exchange, like many others in *Wild Wales*, crystallises how linguistic negotiations in a bicultural atmosphere are fraught with forms of social aspiration and unease. Members of all classes – though colliers, as well as financially straitened tradespeople, have the most at stake in *Wild Wales* – realise that their cultural literacy is calibrated by the way they 'pronounce' (*WW* I: 5).[68] The 'surly' fellow, though sporting a 'short coat' and with 'teeth like those of a mastiff', emulates his perceived social betters by voicing faith in the uplifting prestige of standard 'English' – it is the Arnoldian benchmark, the desired norm, in this scenario. By the time *Wild Wales* was published, the phonology, morphology, lexicon, and grammar of the national 'standard' was already synonymous with educational polish, hard-working respectability, and a progressive social democratic orientation. These qualities were trumpeted by affordable conduct manuals, tracts, and puristic pronunciation guides, many influenced by Knowles's *A Pronouncing and Explanatory Dictionary of the English Language* (1835) or A. J. Cooley's *A Dictionary of the English Language* (1861), aimed at rural and industrial labourers.

The narrator's stress on the semantic and cultural connotations of 'clebber' in this episode also highlights how contemporary patriotic philologists argued that Arnold's proposed classroom diktats and regulations while working as a school inspector carried the polluting imprint

68. Lynda Mugglestone develops this argument by focusing on how accent became the 'dominant social construct of the age' in *Talking Proper: The Rise of Accent as Social Symbol* (Oxford: Oxford University Press, 2003), 21.

of Norman French. Borrow's fascination with the use of direct dialogue in regional idiom implies that it is the Arnoldian pedant-enforcers, asserting the professional virtues of 'speaking proper', who are ironing out the sheer fullness, vibrancy, and antiquity of Welsh. That the narrator's 'clebber' performance impugns, for example, the collier's attitude to informal spoken Welsh chimes with Borrow's impatience elsewhere in his published oeuvre with those self-designated wardens of 'gentility' who hold forth on the perceived faults of provincial idioms. The amusingly thunderous diatribe against metropolitan journalists in the Appendix to *The Romany Rye* is arguably the most striking instance. This railing against speech acts governed by trifling rules of politesse lends a peculiar force to those passages in *Celtic Bards, Chiefs and Kings* in which Borrow, as a hater of humbug and pretension, laments 'the miserable rage for gentility so prevalent amongst all classes of the English' – and, as in the collier's case, some Welsh speakers.[69] The orthographic representations – the collier views nonstandard dialects as *substandard* – goad an already contemptuous 'fellow' into a further parade of verbal aggression. His outburst – ('why can't you say clever?') – reveals how the collier makes sense of and constructs his public persona in a swiftly changing linguistic, pedagogical, and civic terrain.

This encounter prompts us to view the tetchy 'fellow' in this example as a partial product of the 'Welsh Not' educational drive. Though not official government policy, the measure empowered schoolmasters, especially those influenced by Arnold's 1850s educational reports, to stigmatise, and in some cases beat young children found speaking Welsh in class. The bilingual 'coal-dusty' man has, to some extent, internalised the 'Welsh Not' conception of the native tongue – along with aberrations of regional accents and dialects – as slovenly, shameful, and, as he calls it here, 'low'. Borrow's narrator affirms those 'clebber', non-standard locutions and 'low' vulgarisms that Blue Book authors sought to eradicate through root-and-branch spelling reforms. How can there be, as Theodore Watts-Dunton proposed in his introduction to *Wild Wales,* a single Arnoldian 'standard English' given the 'energy, military or commercial' of the anglophone people who carried their language/s 'all round the globe', 'building up new English-speaking communities' each with its own unique vernacular vigour?[70] If the meaning of 'ramble' extends to the dynamic phenomenon and performance of bilingualism in *Wild Wales*, then it proves that even Arnold's lofty 'standard English' contains complex foreign influences, loanwords, and other *borrowings*. This notion

69. George Borrow, *Celtic Bards, Chiefs and Kings* (London: John Murray, 1928), 4.
70. Theodore Watts-Dunton, 'Introduction', *Wild Wales*, x.

also shapes how the narrator recounts his formative school experiences in Edinburgh in *Lavengro*, or exchanging 'a pack of cards' for Irish lessons from his friend and 'language-master' Murtagh. Both scenes highlight the vernacular piquancy of 'borderland' expressive techniques, and how the daily use of several languages in different contexts was fast becoming a norm in certain parts of the island nation. In this way, Borrow brings an Arnoldian idea of the mother tongue into proximity with frowned-upon, threatened, or 'uncouth' linguistic models, such as 'Scotch' (Lowlands Scots) and Romani 'canting'. For Arnold, however, cultural diversity is accessed and savoured only through the libraries of a well-appointed elite university.

In *Wild Wales*, the regional play of linguistic differences, and the 'incompatible', subaltern, or dissenting philosophies they embody, furnishes the narrator with a richer feeling for what 'Englishes' can (and can't) do as he treks from North to South. Arnold's published criticism, anchoring 'Wales' as a locus of Celtic mystique, tries to steady a ship that might be interestingly drifting into new waters. Borrow's account ratifies this drift by presenting Wales as a site for socioeconomic cross-currents, ebbs, and flows of internal and external migration. In short, Borrow's Home Tour becomes a vital 'occasion' on which to 'discourse' about geopolitics, cosmopolitanism, and how divergent language habits resist, undercut, or transmute power relations and identity construction (what is a '*real* Welshman'). This was a bold gambit given that the concept of Wales as a multicultural society was barely broached in 1860s public life. *Wild Wales* replaces Arnoldian stereotypes about the fey or doomed 'Celt' with a more finely grained appraisal of the infections, interactions, and discords between native Welsh sensibilities and a hegemonic 'English civilisation'.[71] *Wild Wales* achieves this through a distinctive form of Celtic fieldwork. To adapt the terms of Ann C. Colley, whose astute analysis of S. T. Coleridge's notebooks reveals a rambler with a spatial imagination as much haptic as visual, Borrow's Cambrian odyssey is 'not only bound to the autocracy of the eye but also to the pace and tread of his feet'.[72] We are frequently reminded that Borrow's ambulant narrator's efforts to capture the 'soul' of Wales involves navigating 'all kinds of paths' – a tactile, companionable yet taxing pursuit. This release of the corporeal self into 'wild' spaces is keenly felt through the 'soles' of his increasingly tattered footwear –

71. Matthew Arnold, 'The Incompatibles', *Irish Essays and Others* (London: Smith, Elder, 1882), 66; see also George Hyde, 'Travelling Across Cultures', 331–43.

72. Ann C. Colley, 'Coleridge Walks: Boots and the Measure of the Landscape', *Romanticism* 27:1 (2021): 28.

which partially explains the narrator's many 'interviews' with boot-boys and shoemakers (*WW* XI: 61) in and around the taverns along his route. Walking puts him in a kinetic dialogue with the 'frightfully miry' terrain around Swansea, for example, which is reflected in the halting rhythm of the prose cadence – amplifying the structural parallels between his 'treading' (*WW* XV: 90) and his text. Here is a productive co-existence of *making* (moves), thinking, and 'scribbling' (*WW* LIX: 396). He makes marks in his hiker's journal to record his arrival at Glandwr, noting frictions between individual direction and the unexpected, even hazardous 'turns' of the industrialised milieu. The landscape *marks* him with mud from 'top to toe' – an inescapable outcome of his immersion in the palpable and social fabric of what Tim Ingold dubs the Cambrian 'weather-world'.[73] The scene also recalls the encounter between a 'plentifully bespattered' narrator and the suspicious national guard in Chapter X of *The Bible in Spain*.

> Arrived at a place called Glandwr, about two miles from Swansea, I found that I was splashed from top to toe, for the roads were frightfully miry, and was sorry to perceive that my boots had given way at the soles, large pieces of which were sticking out. I must, however, do the poor things the justice to say, that it was no wonder that they were in this dilapidated condition, for in those boots I had walked at least two hundred miles, over all kinds of paths, since I had got them soled at Llangollen. (*WW* C: 677)

While Arnold pronounces on a Celtic sensibility *ex cathedra* in a book-lined study – knowledge production that functions on a profoundly disembodied plane – Borrow's 'splashed' narrator explores the depth and range of everyday experience both along treacherous 'paths' and in the myriad guesthouses where he stays. In these venues, he expresses his inordinate liking for 'public-house conversation', from which he derives as much 'amusement' as 'edification' (*WW* XXIV: 205).

TOO MUCH PUBLIC-HOUSE CHAT?

In a letter dated 20 December 1862, the poet Edward FitzGerald enthused to his friend George Crabbe:

> My dear GEORGE,
>
> . . .I have been, and am, reading Borrow's 'Wild Wales,' which *I* like well, because I can hear him talking it. But I don't

73. See Tim Ingold, 'Footprints through the weather-world: walking, breathing, knowing', *Journal of the Royal Anthropological Institute* (2010): 121–39.

> know if others will like it [. . .] Then, no one writing better English than Borrow in general[74]

FitzGerald's friendship with Borrow dates from mid-1853, and the former's correspondence contains admiring allusions to the travelogue's dialogic prose. A facet of this conversational vim, FitzGerald proposes, is the ability to distil the ephemeral, shifting, and continuous facets of spoken language in an artfully packaged literary production, which is of course discrete, fixed, and enduring. Borrow's talent – his handling of a highly contrived written medium to signal how 'talking' unfolds on a moment-by-moment basis – is such that FitzGerald feels he is being directly addressed as by word of mouth. He 'can hear' an incorrigible buttonholer of everyone he meets along the toll roads and muddy paths. J. E. Southall, however, some decades later in *Wales and her Language* (1892), found it more difficult to 'like' Borrow's facility for implying the flows, stutters, and hesitations of transcribed spontaneous speech in a literary medium that should be reserved for more solemn cultural pursuits. Southall, as a member of the Society of Friends who penned *Quakerism as a Factor in the World's History*, took an unsurprisingly dim view of the 'public-house chat' with which *Wild Wales* is suffused. Southall prioritised other facets of Borrow's '*ingenium*':

> Perhaps my readers will pardon my making a short digression, to give some account of Borrow, although his book on *Wild Wales* is doubtless familiar to some of them. [. . .] As he was of Cornish descent on one side, he possessed a certain *ingenium* which I have no doubt much facilitated the acquisition of Celtic languages. However that may be, he was not content with a mere smattering of Welsh, but acquired a sufficiently extensive knowledge of it, to read almost anything in the bards. [. . .] His work is marred by the introduction of a good deal of public-house chat, but it betrays an acquaintance with Welsh literature far more extensive than is to be found in the works of half-informed English tourists of an earlier date, whose works are looked up to as standards, and in vain we search [Thomas] Pennant [. . .] for the kind of information we get here.[75]

74. Edward FitzGerald, *The Letters and Literary Remains of Edward FitzGerald*, ed. William Aldis Wright, 3 vols (London: Macmillan, 1889), I: 289; also Clive Wilkins-Jones, 'A Friendship made in Oulton: Borrow and Edward FitzGerald', *George Borrow Bulletin* 36 (2008): 46–62.

75. John Edward Southall, *Wales and her Language Considered from a Historical, Educational and Social Standpoint, with remarks on modern Welsh literature and a linguistic map of the country* (London: E. Hicks, 1892), 162–3.

To Southall, Borrow epitomises both a tireless Cambrian traveller and an enlightened visionary to those 'Saxon' outsiders prepared to embrace a bilingual ethos. Borrow's lifelong appreciation of the native language made him, in Southall's estimation, a shining 'example worthy to be followed' by those 'great men' who had not yet openly declared the aesthetic and academic virtues of Wales's national culture. The anecdote of the young 'Oxonian' who stays at Pengwen Hall in Chapter XVIII of *Wild Wales* to revise for his yearly collegiate exams and emerges two months later with a 'marvellous' fluency in Welsh to match that of many locals reinforces Southall's conviction that familiarity with Borrow's favourite 'bards' not only sharpens one's cognitive abilities – as argued by the Cambrian Society of South Wales, for example – but also deserves to be taught more widely at university level. A few pages later, Southall posits that Borrow's '*ingenium*' regarding 'Celtic languages' stands in sharp contrast to 'Matthew Arnold', who was 'naturally unable to take a comprehensive view' of them. Consequently, Southall implies that Arnold's 'flat' use of identity as an analytical tool fails to account for the sheer diversity of Welsh-language constituencies, how they view themselves, their friendship and professional networks, individual stories, and histories.[76]

Southall's text is helpful for how it situates Borrow in relation to earlier Cambrian antiquarians like Pennant, as well as mid-century professional journalists influenced by Arnold's cultural criticism. More importantly, Southall furnishes a closely reasoned response to why Borrow's travelogue should be parsed, as 'the only book in the whole circle of English literature which illustrates fairly-well the literary side of the Welsh character'.[77] This did not blind Southall to the text's 'blemishes' – for example, Borrow's narrator lauds some aspects of Welsh (and Irish) culture while retaining a scholarly outsider's readiness to snub, devalue, or veto others. Moreover, the 'public-house chat' at which Southall baulked emerges as a key facet of the narrator's Celtic fieldwork. Growing bored of conversation with lawyers at Machynlleth – as he does elsewhere with the squirarchy, land-grabbers, and parsons – the narrator enters the inn-yard and enjoys 'a great deal of learned discourse with an old ostler about the glanders in horses' (*WW* LXXVIII: 508). This is one example of what critic Jodie Matthews terms 'plebephilism' in *Wild Wales*. In Chapter XIX, impressed that a miller's children should know poet Huw Morris's work, the narrator argues this is a major 'difference' between a

76. R. Brubaker and F. Cooper, 'Beyond "Identity"', *Theory and Society* 29 (2000): 34.
77. Southall, *Welsh and her Language*, 150–1, 164.

cultured 'Welshman' and the figures exposed to tainted industrial Englishness like the young carter in the previous section: 'What would a Suffolk miller's swain have said if I had repeated to him verses out of Beowulf or even Chaucer, and had asked him about the residence of Skelton'. Similarly, he comments on 'a scene in a public-house, yes! but in a Welsh public-house. Only think of a Suffolk toper repeating the death-bed verses of a poet; surely there is a considerable difference between the Celt and the Saxon' (*WW* XXI: 142).[78]

Borrow's merger in *Wild Wales* of citation and dialogue in these linguistic events – what the *London Quarterly Review* decried as entering into 'conversation with every man, woman, and child' in the drabbest localities – underscores that dramatic feeling for how everyday 'discourses' both reveal and conceal important cultural resonances.[79] The narrator's fascination with the rhythms of 'public-house chat' mirrors his conviction that what Arnold saw as a 'standard' English was actually a hybrid, intricately layered entity comprised of numberless regional and historic nuances.[80] It is through (sometimes highly charged) speech acts in hostels and inns that *Wild Wales* maps the divergences between what an indigenous community terms 'good Welshmen' (*WW* XIX: 122) as opposed to a polyglot 'Sais' (Englishman). Like the Gorgio snoop Lavengro who faces the wrath of Mrs Herne for making known the Romani language of the roads, Borrow's narrator meets with opprobrium from several characters in *Wild Wales*. Such figures bridle at his grasp of the native tongue: 'I will tell you plainly that we don't like to have strangers among us who understand our discourse, more especially if they be gentlefolks' (*WW* XCIX: 663). In terms of the narrator's self-stylisation, the success of infiltrating a closely guarded drinking den like the inn at Gutter Vawr in Chapter XCIX relies on his being a 'stranger' to it – he must demonstrate skill at getting in even when watchful locals remark his suspiciously 'long nose' ('Mind that he ain't nosing us'). He wishes to break bread with this community but does so from a position that tends to reassert his 'Sais' background and training.

A striking example of this elaborately staged bar-room back-and-forth is found in Chapter XV. Here the narrator recounts his impressions of the venerable '*Tafarn Tywarch*' ('Turf Tavern'), near the Vale

78. See Jodie Matthews, 'Borrowing Welshness: *Wild Wales*, Affiliation and Identity', *North American Journal of Welsh Studies* 6:1 (2011): 53–61.

79. [Anon.], '*Wild Wales*. By George Borrow', *London Quarterly Review* 20:40 (July 1863): 536–8; Hyde, 'Travelling Across Cultures', 331–43.

80. Joep Leerssen, *Remembrance and Imagination: Patterns in the Historical and Literary Representation of Ireland in the Nineteenth Century* (Cork: Cork University Press, 1996), 96–100.

of Clwyd. This episode riffs upon his earlier encounter with a 'strapping' Welsh 'chambermaid' in Chapter II. With this girl the awkwardly aloof narrator 'scraped acquaintance, not [. . .] for the sake of the pretty Welsh eyes which she carried in her head, but for the sake of the pretty Welsh tongue which she carried in her mouth' (*WW* II: 12). The Turf barmaid by contrast is a more abrasive custodian of what George M. Hyde designates a 'hard-shelled culture': she cannot – or more likely, will not – 'understand' him. As a migrant Englishwoman explains to the narrator on his way to Machynlleth, Saxon settlers become 'poor lone creatures in a strange land, without a soul to speak to but one another'. The Welsh 'take good care that we shouldn't pick up a word of their language' (*WW* LXXVII: 503). In the Turf Tavern the narrator tries in vain to order ale in what must have sounded an ornate Welsh out of keeping with a homely venue. The narrator's Welsh-speaking, as one old man reminds him in Chapter XLIII, 'is different from ours, and of course better, being the Welsh of the grammar. Ah, it is a fine thing to be a grammarian' (*WW* XLIII: 295). That the narrator reproduces this comment indicates that he sees himself pursuing a high philological calling – keeping maligned national languages active as vital repositories of culture – an implicit rebuke to Arnold's imagery of fossilised Celtic lore. This is not the same thing as a 'native' speaker, however. The Turf barmaid's pique reveals her deeply held belief that only one born and raised in Wales can 'pronounce' the language – a witty inversion of what an upwardly mobile anglophile might call 'speaking proper'. As the increasingly tetchy exchange unfolds, the narrator protests at being treated as a caricature of the 'Saxon' interloper – a determinedly monolingual species that the 1864 *Pembrokeshire Herald* dubbed 'one-tongued emigrants locating themselves in our parishes'.[81]

> 'You are a Welshman?' said she.
>
> 'No, I am not,' said I, 'I am English.'
>
> 'So I thought,' said she, 'and on that account I could not understand you.'
>
> 'You mean that you would not,' said I. 'Now do you choose to bring what you are bidden?'
>
> 'Come, aunt,' said John, 'don't be silly and cenfigenus, but bring the breakfast.' (*WW* XV: 85)

The narrator's guide, John, finds the barmaid's demeanour '*cenfigenus*' – spiky and ungenerous towards a learned and courteous

81. [Anon.], 'Letters', *The Pembrokeshire Herald and General Advertiser* (8 January 1864): 3.

visitor. She objects to the appropriation of her language by one she perceives as an agent of the dominant Saxon culture: 'what right' have self-identified English migrants and tourists 'to come here speaking Welsh, which belongs to the Welsh alone'. She evinces little of that 'inclusive patriotism' for which the bilingual activist Southall campaigns in Chapter Six of *Wales and her Language* – namely the readiness to appraise 'strangers' as 'a part of the Welsh unity' by virtue of their sincere attempts to acquire the rudiments of the native tongue. Such study, Southall claims, would facilitate the crossing over from one linguistic enclave to another – a cooperative, not adversarial relationship affirming shared social experience and the refinement of new literary forms. Instead, the barmaid, in no mood to foster amicable associations across the linguistic gulf, exhibits what the narrator implies is a kind of siege mentality – one that is glimpsed in later pub scenes when angry Welsh drinkers (r)eject him when he tries to get served.[82]

The gruff female gatekeeper of the Turf Tavern claims that no Englishman 'could speak Welsh', because 'his tongue was too short'. This droll barb impugns not only the narrator's imperfect phonology, but his projection of extrovert vitality too. So surprised is he at the quick-witted and acerbic hostess that he starts to wonder whether he is ensnared in an escalating verbal spat or a bizarre courtship ritual. He reacts by reheating a commonly voiced 'Sais' taunt that the woman's 'long tongue' manifests her dishonesty. The only way the narrator can reassert his linguistic sway, and by extension his manly vigour, is by berating the barmaid, who is 'inclined to talk nonsense about no Englishman's understanding Welsh' or 'knowing anything of Welsh matters' (*WW* XV: 87). When he enquires if she knows the Welsh term for 'salmon', the barmaid assumes that it is no different from the English. This 'ignorance' gives the narrator immense satisfaction, since he informs her that it is, in fact, '*eawg*' (or '*eog*'). That the barmaid is unaware of the 'proper' Welsh word functions to salve the narrator's bruised vanity, as George M. Hyde notes.

This exchange also casts a sobering sidelight on the diminished richness of the barmaid's 'native tongue', given how languages are shaped – or in this scene vitiated – by embodied discursive habits and cultural traditions which are unceasingly sedimenting across time. Over generations of colonisation of a geographically peripheral area (and attendant standardisation of the written national majority language), some Welsh phraseology has been almost buried beneath

82. Southall, *Wales and her Language*, 241; Hyde, 'Travelling Across Cultures', 341–43.

English *borrowings* – especially lexis which signals how a plundering Saxon populace has profited (both in stomach and pocket) from Welsh natural resources (*gleisiaid* or salmon; trout; coal; water; wood for heating; housing; and medicine). An old man caustically notes this history of violence when, after the narrator enquires: '"Any thieves about?"', he answers: '"No, no thieves here, but what come from England," and he looked at me with a strange, grim smile' (*WW* LXXIV: 491). Chapters LXXVIII (focusing on poaching) and XCI variously reinforce how highly prized are the local salmon to English entrepreneurs (or 'thieves'). That the narrator claims privileged knowledge of '*eog*' in this episode is due to his championing of Daffydd ap Gwilym's verse, especially that included in Robert Gurney's *Bardic Heritage: A Selection of Welsh Poetry in Free English Translation*, which contains the poem 'To the Salmon' ('I'r Eog'). As if to crown his philological and 'manly' victory here over the bewildered barmaid, he specifies the gendering of the word for 'salmon': '*cemyw*' for the male, '*hwyfell*' for the female.

An equally complex representation of Welsh rural pub culture – as compassionate and convivial as the Turf Tavern exchange is fraught and uncomfortable – occurs later in Chapter LXIV. These two scenes mesh to remind us how 'Wales' in this text signals a highly variegated space of cross-cultural f(r)ictions and negotiations: between mono- and bilingual; 'unschooled' and 'lettered'; industrialised South and agrarian North-east; highland and lowland; so-called 'proper speech' and 'corrupt jargon'. As the 1877 *Hull Packet* averred, although *Wild Wales* 'is of no particular use as a guidebook', it delineates with unusual subtlety the social and technological forces transforming quotidian 'Welsh life' and speech, especially in the farming communities of Denbighshire and Flintshire.[83] Arnold's *Irish Essays*, like his earlier report on Welsh elementary education, posited that there was little to be gained from the Welsh 'hinterland' defending its native tongue, since its chances of survival in the linguistic battleground were slim indeed, while English was fast becoming a global *lingua franca*. In contrast, Borrow's staging of 'public-house chat' asserts the crucial importance of exploring, and cherishing, the cultural and linguistic deviation/s that are an inevitable byproduct of cross-border trade, marriage, and proselytising ('Methodists, going about to raise recruits' [*WW* IV: 17]). This is evidenced by the narrator's fortuitous encounter with an illiterate waggoner in a small village ten miles from Llangollen. For the *London Review*, such episodes typified Borrow's exasperating tendency to swell out 'three

83. See [Anon], 'Literature: Extracts and Selections', *The Hull Packet and East Riding Times* (21 September 1877): 3.

thick volumes' with 'disjointed' trivialities.[84] However, the dialogue – and the patterns of thought it exposes – rewards a more measured appraisal:

> I went to a small inn, or public-house, sat down, and called for ale. A waggoner was seated at a large table with a newspaper before him on which he was intently staring.
>
> 'What news?' said I in English.
>
> 'I wish I could tell you,' said he in very broken English; 'but I cannot read.'
>
> 'Then why are you looking at the paper?' said I.
>
> 'Because,' said he, 'by looking at the letters I hope in time to make them out.'
>
> (*WW* LXIV: 431)

This ostensibly humdrum scene throws into tragicomic relief some of the most consequential geopolitical events of the 1850s. The narrator notes the fierce concentration that the waggoner believes will enable him, after prolonged 'staring', to decode a Welsh-language newspaper – one filled with doleful 'accounts from the seat' of the Crimean War (*WW* LXIV: 432). Here a chiefly Welsh-speaking audience, long used to debating the latest views/news in the community hub of a 'small inn', now finds popular culture and current affairs enshrined in the permanency of cheap print. The oral as the principal medium of modern information exchange is giving way to a phenomenon at which the editor Alexander Andrews marvelled in his 1859 *History of British Journalism*. After the repeal of the remaining newspaper stamp duty in 1855 – the so-called 'taxes on knowledge' – the average 'workman', Andrews remarked, could savour a host of regional and national print media, in both Welsh and English, at a price which 'he can spare without missing from his week's wages'.[85]

Borrow's text furnishes then an unusually vivid portrait of Welsh pub culture in which a platter of radical nonconformist and more mainstream secular weekly newspapers are served up alongside the narrator's ale, bread, and cheese. Becoming fully literate, not just speaking in 'broken English', will be crucial for the news-hungry and politically savvy rural community to which the waggoner belongs. Given the way such regional print media is reshaping contemporary public discourse –

84. [Anon.], 'Wild Wales', *The London Review* 6:133 (17 January 1863): 71–2.

85. Alexander Andrews, *The History of British Journalism, from the foundation of the Newspaper Press in England to the Repeal of the Stamp Act in 1855*, 2 vols (London: Richard Bentley, 1859), II, 340.

and Wales's socio-cultural self-image – the narrator urges the waggoner to attend 'an evening school' forthwith. The narrator elects not to specify the newspaper whose 'dismal' report on 'Crimea' he reads out to the attentive waggoner ('the Russians are beating us and the French too'). Given the Denbighshire location of this modest inn, it is likely the narrator is perusing the seminal Welsh-language bi-weekly *Yr Amserau* ('The Times', 1843–59). This was one of the 'euphonious titles' included among a list of politically significant 'Welsh papers' in Alexander Andrews's *History of British Journalism.*[86] Unlike the *Cumro*, an 'excellent Welsh journal written in the interest of the [Anglican] Church' that the narrator peruses at the Mallwyd inn (*WW* LXXV: 490), *Yr Amserau* prioritised more radical, agrarian, and dissenting opinion. Published and distributed around Merseyside (which boasted a notable Welsh immigrant population), *Yr Amserau* was, by the 1850s, popular enough to reach even those secluded rustic taverns where Borrow's narrator sups. Indeed, the voluble and conceited 'man in grey', a poet manqué whom the narrator meets in Chapter XXXVII, deems 'the Liverpool Times, the Amserau' a sufficiently reputable beneficiary of his 'pennillion [verses]' (*WW* XXXVII: 259). Based on Matthew 16:3, the eye-catching masthead of *Yr Amserau* – '*oni fedrwch arwyddion yr amserau?*' ('can ye not discern the sign of the times?') – implies the paper's close regard for geopolitical controversies and convulsions. It also furnishes a poignant commentary on the waggoner's linguistic plight.[87] Though desperate to 'make out' the printed 'signs' which chronicle turbulent 'times', the embarrassed waggoner cannot face the prospect of learning his letters at 'evening school' because 'the children would laugh at me' (*WW* LXIV: 432).

What appears then as inconsequential bar-room 'chat' in *Wild Wales* frequently offers a small-scale drama of language attitudes, cultural il/literacy, and regional affiliation, staged by a cosmopolitan narrator fond of proclaiming that he has 'been everywhere' (*WW* XCIX: 663). Such scenes expose the dynamics of speech acts as well as the suitability of languages for specific local occasions and in reaction to historical turmoil or demographic pressures (increased migration, 'innovations' in elementary school pedagogy, improving literacy rates, evolving communication networks and transport technologies) acting

86. Andrews, *History*, II, 337
87. For a subtle and wide-ranging account of *Yr Amserau*'s place in the history of Victorian Welsh-language journalism, see Aled Jones, 'The Welsh Language and Journalism', *The Welsh Language and its Social Domains 1801–1911*, ed. Geraint H. Jenkins (Cardiff: University of Wales Press, 2000), 379–403.

on speakers like the waggoner and their chosen vernacular/s. These cultural pressures – helping create an empire of words – are, to the narrator's mind, frequently entangled with the follies and fictions of an expansionist Westminster government mired in 'disasters and disgraces' both at home and overseas, like 'the Crimean expedition' (*WW* LVI: 383). This is apparent not only in the way he engages with Welsh speakers and their varied reactions to the 'Sais'; it also moulds his fascination with other clusters from the beleaguered 'Celtic' language family, especially Irish economic migrants like Michael Sullivan, a County Mayo man whose hardscrabble existence is revealed when the narrator reaches Bangor in Chapter XXVII. Borrow's Irish adventures, memorably sketched in *Lavengro*, resonate forcefully through *Wild Wales* to the extent that the 'recurrent Irish motif' becomes 'a unifying theme'.[88] Indeed, the narrator's first extended 'interview' with a family of 'Irish itinerants' occurs as early as Chapter IV.

For Arnold in *Celtic Literature* and *Irish Essays*, the 'Irish Question' had become one of the thorniest political conundrums. *On the Study of Celtic Literature*, released over the course of several months by *The Cornhill* in 1866 – five years after *Wild Wales* was published by John Murray – was contemporary with Reform League demonstrations (culminating in the 1866 Hyde Park riots) and escalating Irish nationalist activism in North America and Ireland in the middle years of that decade. The republican-nationalist ferment, and the subsequent reaction by a counter-insurgent British state which refused to entertain any repeal of the Union as a viable option for easing civic unrest, persuaded Arnold, and many other like-minded liberal opinion-formers, that there was 'no vital' connection 'between [the Englishman] and the races he has annexed'. His 'Welsh and Irish fellow citizens are hardly more amalgamated with him now than they were when Wales and Ireland were first conquered'.[89] As his 1852 Report on Welsh schools implied, English efforts to build community consensus and shape responsible citizen-subjects in its 'dominions' (Ireland and Wales) must be secured through racial 'incorporation' – linguistic consistency would, he hoped, buttress a shared sense of Britishness in the aftermath of the 1800 Act of Union. By the time Arnold's *Irish Essays* was published, a year after Borrow's death in 1882, the election of Charles Stewart Parnell to Westminster as leader of the Irish Parliamentary Party on a Home Rule

88. Collie and Fraser, *George Borrow: A Bibliography*.
89. Matthew Arnold, *On the Study of Celtic Literature*, *The Complete Prose Works of Matthew Arnold*, 11 vols, ed. R. H. Super (Ann Arbor: University of Michigan Press, 1962), III, 386.

ticket (May 1880), coupled with the *Cogadh na Talún*, or Irish Land War (1879–82), had shown that Arnold's proposed 'work of fusion' had been an absurdly naïve fantasy. His top-down and paternalistic cultural programme, stressing a coherent British ethnocultural integrity, could not mitigate what *Wild Wales* shows to be grievous religious as well as socio-economic problems, resulting in a deep-seated 'suspicion of the Saxon' (*WW* XLIX: 346). Arnold's 'The Incompatibles', a lengthy piece which opens *Irish Essays*, posits (with little to no documentary evidence) that 'Scotland, Wales, and Cornwall' are 'blended in national feeling with us' (the English). Ireland, however, shows signs of 'fatally and irresistibly drifting to a separation, and a miserable separation, from England' and the 'enlightened' technological modernity it epitomises. Arnold, for all his carefully pondered prose and honest campaigning for Anglo-Irish landlords to espouse a 'larger and sweeter temper', cannot match the Borrovian narrator's unblinking scrutiny of how a basic 'incompatibility' flows from unappeasable historic wrongs. 'The English have forgot that they ever conquered the Welsh [and the Irish],' he proclaims, 'but some ages will elapse before' these ethnic groups 'forget that the English have conquered them' (*WW* XLIX: 346).[90]

Asking the Irish Question in *Wild Wales*

In the backroom of a 'little hostelry' in Chapter XXI, an 'intoxicated' private in the Denbighshire Militia admits feeling 'the greatest dread of being sent to Iwerddon [Ireland]'. To this 'stout young fellow', Borrow's narrator offers some reassurance:

> 'You ought to rejoice in your chance of going there,' said I, 'Iwerddon is a beautiful country, and abounds with whisky.'
>
> 'And the Irish?' said he.
>
> 'Hearty, jolly fellows,' said I, 'if you know how to manage them [. . .]'.
>
> Here he became very violent, saying that I did not speak truth, for that he had seen plenty of Irish camping amidst the hills, that the men were half naked and the women were three parts so, and that they carried their children on their backs. (*WW* XXI: 140)

This 'interview' with the militiaman reveals the narrator's enigmatically ambivalent attitude to 'Iwerddon' throughout *Wild Wales*. The private's conception of 'half naked' Irish nomads is little better than

90. Matthew Arnold, 'Preface', *Irish Essays and Others* (London: Smith, Elder, 1882), vi.

the xenophobic and grotesque mid-century *Punch* cartoons depicting a simian or savage tribe on empire's very doorstep. By contrast, the narrator's affectionate tribute to a 'beautiful country' populated by 'jolly fellows' seems, at first blush, to debunk these offensive *Punch* stereotypes, as well as Arnold's thesis of a recalcitrant, lamentably premodern 'Ireland', perpetually at variance with the British political establishment. However, the narrator's use of the conditional – 'hearty fellows [. . .] *if* you know how to manage them' – is slippery and not without condescension, hinting at the firm paternalistic hand required to ensure that Irish conviviality does not descend into self-destructive antics.[91] This tendency – infantilising the boisterous Irish – is more marked in the narrator's later dispute with Pat Flanagan: 'How fortunate it is that the Irish have the English among them, to prevent their cutting each other's throats' (*WW* C: 672).

The proudly (and loudly) Anglican narrator, for all his attempts to persuade the militiaman of the merits of the Irish temper and largely unspoilt landscape, can, when nettled, reheat the reductive *Punch* stereotypes of an Irish 'Papist' population lacking any common sense, or worse an atavistic enclave comprised of 'fierce looking' 'vagabonds', subsisting by 'plunder' (*WW* XIV: 83–6). These tropes stand in contrast to Borrow's *The Bible in Spain*, in which his 'wandering heretic missionary' persona hails priests at the Irish College at Salamanca in 1837: 'Honour to Ireland and her "hundred thousand welcomes!" Her fields have long been the greenest in the world; her daughters the fairest; her sons the bravest and most eloquent' (*BIS*: 277). In *Wild Wales*, after the Methodist Edward Jones informs him about a few Catholic families scattered around Flintshire, the narrator concludes that their belief system betrays merely a modified Hinduism: 'Indians and sepoys worship stocks and stones, and the River Ganges, and our Papists worship stocks and stones, holy wells, and fountains' (*WW* IX: 49). It is not always clear whether the narrator voices such nuance-free opinions (in which Irish religion and politics are inextricably merged) out of conviction or a liking for histrionics, rhetorical jousting, and provocation for its own sake. On the road to Swansea, for example, he meets 'a small, well-made fellow, with reddish hair' named Pat Flanagan (*WW* C: 671), who wishes that 'the ould Shanavests and Caravauts were fighting still, and I among them. Faith! there was some life in Ireland in their days' (*WW* C: 672). Flanagan's attitude to rural resistance and class upheaval in Ireland between 1760 and 1840 – distinguished by an intensifying

91. M. Wynn Jones, *In the Shadow of the Pulpit: Literature and Nonconformist Wales* (Cardiff: University of Wales Press, 2009).

series of nationalist protests, uprisings, and movements against corrupt Anglo-Irish governance – the narrator dismisses as bloodthirsty bravado.[92] His gambit, if it is meant to trigger prolonged verbal skirmish with Flanagan, succeeds:

> 'How fortunate it is that the Irish have the English among them, to prevent their cutting each other's throats.'
>
> 'The English prevent the Irish from cutting each other's throats! Well, if they do, it is only that they may have the pleasure of cutting them themselves. The bloody tyrants! too long has their foot been upon the neck of poor old Ireland.'
>
> 'How do the English tyrannise over Ireland?'
>
> 'How do they tyrannise over her? Don't they prevent her from having the free exercise of her Catholic religion, and make her help to support their own Protestant one?'
>
> 'Well, and don't the Roman Catholics prevent the Protestants from having the free exercise of their religion, whenever they happen to be the most numerous, and don't they make them help to support the Roman Catholic religion?'
>
> 'Of course they do, and quite right! Had I my will, there shouldn't be a place of Protestant worship left standing, or a Protestant churl allowed to go about with a head unbroken.'
>
> 'Then why do you blame the Protestants for keeping the Romans a little under?'
>
> 'Why do I blame them? A purty question! Why, an't they wrong, and an't we right?'
>
> 'But they say that they are right and you wrong.' (*WWC*: 672–3).

That the dialogue ends with a handshake and a cordial agreement to differ suggests that the narrator's goal is not to browbeat Flanagan regarding the supposed glories of the English state apparatus, whose civilising mission shows imperialist coercion insidiously veiled as humanitarian care. Flanagan, it is implied, has seen first-hand the immiseration created by the cultural imposition of an Anglican church, and especially the custom of *Regium Donum* that compelled his fellow Irish Catholics to pay taxes for the upkeep of a Protestant religious infrastructure that had no relevance to their daily existence ('Don't they [. . .] make' Ireland 'support their own Protestant one?'). Rather

92. The Welsh conservative politician and poet John Henry Scourfield targets, and mocks, such bravado in *Lyrics and Philippics* (1859): 'We'll give a hiding to the Saxons for riding / On poor old Ireland's back this many a day'. See 'The Repealer', *Lyrics and Philippics* (1859; Covent Garden: G. Norman, 1864), 17.

this language event is designed to underscore how quickly competing ethno-cultural practices can cause tragic and pointless cycles of sectarian strife, nurtured by the binary logic to which the narrator himself is prone. Like Thackeray before him in the *Irish Sketch Book* (1843), the narrator grapples with what he sees as a country of bitter, bewildering disputes and paradoxes. However, unlike Thackeray's text, *Wild Wales* poses more urgent philosophical questions regarding the nature, causes, and consequences of 'religious persuasions', and how a 'faith position' can calcify into tribalist slogans and internecine conflict.

Flanagan's zeal for 'the Catholic religion' furnishes a telling contrast to the mercenary Donnybrook-born fiddler who, it emerges, 'plays' for both sides of the religious divide in Chapter XXV. This self-declared 'Catholic to the backbone', having performed at a loyalist lodge since abjuring 'the repalers [repealers] and emancipators' led by 'Dan O'Connell' (*WW* XXV: 169) – whose vigorous political campaign prompted Wellington's government to pass the Roman Catholic Relief Act of 1829 – now finds 'Orangeism' far less lucrative.[93] This has prompted his reversion to the 'Popery' of his younger days. The narrator bribes this 'professor of music' with the princely sum of a shilling, instructing him to play the 'blackguard Orange' song 'Croppies Lie Down' which Borrow had learnt while his recruiting sergeant father was stationed at Clonmel and which Lavengro performs with malicious gusto in front of a Fenian insurgent in the eponymous 1851 novel.[94] The narrator in *Wild Wales* portrays this 'fiddler' using terminology not far removed from the visual and verbal clichés that distinguish mid-Victorian anti-Irish satirical cartoons: 'red shock hair and very red features', 'ragged coat and breeches, and a hat which had lost part of its crown, and all its rim' (*WW* XXV: 165). This typecasting obscures an awkward truth, however: is not the Irish fiddler also practising – to survive financially – a version of the code switching and mimicry that the 'Saxon' narrator adopts,

93. In Chapter 42 of *Lavengro*, when the narrator's friend, the blithe man-about-town Francis Ardry, explains O'Connell's strategies for securing higher offices and leadership roles for Irish Roman Catholics, including membership of Parliament, the narrator remarks: 'I wish him success in the cause he has taken up – I love religious liberty' (*LSGP* 252). Borrow, it seems, was in far less charitable mood when O'Connell, now an MP and buoyed by the passing of the Emancipation Act, sought the repeal of the 1800 Act of Union and restoration of an autonomous Irish parliament. On 4 April 1843, Borrow remarked to his publisher John Murray III: 'I hope the old Duke will at last give salt eel to that cowardly bawler vagabond O'Connell [. . .] I think the end of the Dublin bully will be a disgraceful one.' Quoted in Knapp, *Life*, II, 323.

94. See Colm Kerrigan, *George Borrow in Tipperary, 1815–1816* (Norwich: Lavengro Press, 2017); A. Byrne, '"He will bid me cross the border": George Borrow's *Wild Wales*, O. M. Edwards's *Cartrefi Cymru* and the Imagined Nation', *Studies in Travel Writing*, 18: 2 (2014), 148–59.

and savours, as part of his Celtic fieldwork? For the narrator and his local guide John Jones, however, the fiddler is little better than the Irish 'vagabonds' whose increasing visibility in rural Wales has alarmed community leaders. Jones's disdainful reaction gives the lie to the (still widely held) conviction that the historical experience of cultural domination by 'Saxons' had made the Welsh unusually compassionate towards other racialised minorities. For Jones, these 'savage, brutish *Gwyddeliad*' (Irish scoundrels) are as intemperate and superstitious in behaviour as they are unkempt in appearance, a fact reinforced when the narrator meets Johanna Colgan, a 'bedivilled woman from the county of Limerick', garbed 'in rags and tatters' (*WW* CV: 692). Jones's notion of a *gwyddelod* evokes the Irishman both as a coarse atavistic throwback and a scourge: 'in general without shoes and stockings', this ethnic group continues, in the aftermath of the potato blight, to 'infest these parts'. Jones's argument is that the bellicose Irish contaminants have, given their superior numbers, ousted those wandering families Matthew Arnold judged as a pronounced case study in Celticism, namely the 'dark, handsome Gipsiaid' with their brightly coloured 'vans and carts', the 'men buying and selling horses', while 'the women told fortunes' (*WW* XIV: 81). Jones's objections suggest that, by the time the narrator begins his trek in the 1850s, Romani families were finding it near impossible to carry out their already marginal traditional crafts in Wales, resorting instead to covert acts of criminality on the shabbier fringes of industrial towns and cities like Newport, Merthyr, and Cardiff. Unsurprisingly, the narrator is keen to learn details from Jones of the language habits of these Irish trespassers. The *Gwyddeliad* are at least as financially savvy as the Romani whose camps they have gradually overrun:

> 'Are these Gwyddelod poor?'
>
> 'By no means, sir; they make large sums by plundering and other means, with which, 'tis said, they retire at last to their own country or America, where they buy land and settle down.'
>
> 'What language do they speak?'
>
> 'English, sir; they pride themselves on speaking good English, that is to the Welsh. Amongst themselves they discourse in their own Paddy Gwyddel.'
>
> 'Have they no Welsh?'
>
> 'Only a few words, sir; I never heard one of them speaking Welsh, save a young girl – she fell sick by the roadside as she was wandering by herself – some people at a farmhouse took her in, and tended her till she was well. During her sickness she took a fancy to their quiet way of life, and when she was recovered, she begged to stay with them and serve them. They consented; she

became a very good servant, and hearing nothing but Welsh spoken, soon picked up the tongue.' (WW XIV: 82)

Jones's animus is such that he does not perceive the indigenous Irish tongue as a national language to which its speakers attach culturally shared attitudes, responsibilities, and inalienable rights; instead, it is criminal patois, canting, or 'jergo' (*WW* XXIV: 161). Jones's narrow-minded conception prompts comparison with the prejudices of Lavengro's sergeant father, who claims the 'Irish' have 'a bad language' derived from aboriginal 'fiends, half naked, with their hair hanging down over their bosoms'. His visceral distaste for the simian London Irish anticipates the pseudo-Darwinian science of racial pre-eminence that informs sketches of the 'Irish Yahoo' in the 1860s *Punch*: 'A creature manifestly between the Gorilla and the Negro [. . .] it belongs in fact to a tribe of Irish savages' which 'talks a sort of gibberish'.[95] Jones's anecdote of the young Irish girl who is redeemed and assimilated through the ministrations of a kindly Methodist rural clan – instructing her in the Welsh language and a 'purer' form of worship than her Roman Catholic 'heathen crefydd [religion]' – does nothing to suggest that Jones believes the 'Paddy' capable of any substantive moral and spiritual improvement.

In Chapter XCVIII, the narrator meets a disgruntled Romani traveller on the road to Birmingham whose experiences appear to corroborate Jones's account of a fast disappearing 'Gipsiaid' whose campsites and precarious livelihoods have been seized by 'dirty' Irish 'fellows' ('Hindity mescrey') and their 'women'.[96] Here the 'woild Irish', so often the victims of verbal abuse and systematic discrimination in Wales, measure the 'Romani foky' according to their own caste system, and judge them, quite literally, as beyond the pale: Wales is now teeming with 'Hindity mescrey, woild Irish, with whom the Romani foky stand no chance. The fellows underwork me at tinkering, and the women outscream my wife at telling fortunes—moreover, they say the country is theirs and not intended for niggers like we' (*WW* XCVIII: 654).

Wild Wales rarely addresses Ireland's post-Famine reconstruction era explicitly. Moreover, Borrow's surviving unpublished correspondence sheds little light on how he felt about the potato blights of 1845–9, which caused a decline of just over two million in the population of Ireland from emigration and deaths. As Angus Fraser observes: 'It would

95. Quoted in Roy Foster, *Paddy and Mr Punch: Connections in Irish and English History* (London: Allen Press, 1993), 183–4.

96. In his *Romano Lavo-Lil*, Borrow defines 'Hindity-mengré / Hindity-mescré, s. pl.' as 'Irish. Dirty, sordid fellows'.

have been illuminating to know what Borrow made of Clarendon's tenure' of the office of Lord Lieutenant of Ireland from 1847 to 1851. Clarendon 'had to cope at the sharp end with the doctrinaire conviction of Lord John Russell and the Treasury that the famine was best left to the operation of natural causes'.[97] However, *Wild Wales* shows how a Westminster government has compelled many thousands of migrants ('Hindity mescrey') to seek employment, gainful or otherwise, across the Irish Sea, especially in the South Wales ports and coalfields, Cornish tin-mines, and the textile manufactories of Liverpool and Manchester. Army deserters, tinkers, professional musicians, and (as the narrator implies) commercial sex workers were prominent among these 'vast numbers'. Wearing his 'priestly' social guise in Chapter CVIII, the narrator advises an Irish girl who barely earns pennies selling 'needles' not to sell herself, to which the girl replies: 'All Irish women have a dread of striopachas. It's the only thing that frights them' (*WW* CVIII: 717–18). In this exchange, both the narrator and the girl resort to a euphemism derived from the Middle Irish *striapach* ('prostitute', 'whore', based on Latin *stuprum*), as if a 'decent' language like Arnold's 'standard' English cannot be used to signify such corrupting transactions.

The narrator's steady focus on the customs of the nomadic Irish in the Welsh hinterlands complicates Arnold's critique – and John Jones's derogatory 'witness statements' – by inspecting 'Celticism' through a comparative ethnic lens.[98] This is reflected in the narrator's notion that a serious translator must immerse themselves in the 'Irish Question', which is of a piece with his explication of linguistic singularities among other ethnic groups such as the Romani in *Lavengro*. This methodical survey of denigrated and overlooked national languages of Britain is fundamental to what critic Jodie Matthews terms Borrow's projection of deep respect for Celtic 'cultures to shape his own sense of self on the page'.[99] Matthews reminds us that pedestrianism, for Borrow's narrator, allows one to limn a more socially diverse enterprise, one that prioritises the vivid life-experiences of harried, non-dominant, or subaltern subjects, unlike the hegemonic authorities which infantilise them. While Arnold's *Celtic* and *Irish Essays* tend to trade in national and cultural stereotypes – many of which are reproduced in John Jones's complaints

97. Angus Fraser, 'Borrow's Political Views (Part 3): Ireland', *George Borrow Bulletin* 18 (1999): 18; Byrne, '"He will bid me cross the border"', 148–59.
98. Gerry Smyth, '"The Natural Course of Things": Matthew Arnold, Celticism and the English Poetic Tradition', *Journal of Victorian Culture* 1:1 (1996): 49.
99. Jodie Matthews, 'Borrowing Welshness: *Wild Wales*, Affiliation and Identity', *North American Journal of Welsh Studies* 6:1 (2011): 53–61.

in *Wild Wales* – Borrow's narrator collects captivating individual testimony behind the catch-all categories. While noting the sorry appearance of the Bangor Irish – 'loud and dissonant', 'ragged and red-haired', wild 'looked the men yet wilder the women' – the narrator nevertheless admires their 'free, independent, and almost graceful carriage': 'they were fine specimens of humanity' (*WW* XXVII: 189). What is apparent from his many 'interviews' with the peripatetic Irish in Wales is his often-amused ethnographic curiosity – a stark contrast to Jones's undiluted fear and loathing of other racialised minorities:

> I sat down on the stool. 'You are not from these parts?' said I, addressing myself to the man.
> 'We are not, your haner,' said the man; 'we are from Ireland.'
> [. . .]
> 'And what trade or profession do you follow?' said I.
> 'We do a bit in the tinkering line, your haner.'
> 'Do you find tinkering a very profitable profession?' said I.
> 'Not very, your haner; but we contrive to get a crust and a drink by it.'
> 'That's more than I ever could,' said I.
> 'Has your haner then ever followed tinkering?' said the man.
> 'Yes,' said I, 'but I soon left off.'
> 'And became a minister,' said the elder female, 'Well, your honour is not the first indifferent tinker that's turned out a shining minister.'
> 'Why do you think me a minister?'
> 'Because your honour has the very look and voice of one. Oh, it was kind in your honour to come to us here in the Sabbath evening, in order that you might bring us God.' (*WW* IV: 21–2)

This passage, in which the narrator accepts an invitation to sit and converse with a family of Irish tinkers, is remarkable for several reasons. First, his willingness to enter a space of sympathetic camaraderie is measured against John Jones's wary resentment. The narrator's normally blithe and assertive guide nervously skirts around 'a place which is called Allt Paddy, because the Gwyddelod are in the habit of taking up their quarters there' (*WW* XIV: 83). Second, the narrator's rueful reflections on his own struggles in the 'tinkering line' evoke the period of penury and poor mental health chronicled in *Lavengro*. Indeed, his 'discourse' with the Irish 'tinker' is as controlled and respectful – the travellers address him throughout as 'your haner/honour' – as John Jones's lexis is vituperative and paranoid. That the Irish clan deems the narrator to have 'the very look and voice' of a 'shining minister' – they eventually address him as 'your Reverence' – seems no mere blandishment. These travellers plead with the narrator to 'pull out the Holy Book' and give them 'God' (*WW* IV: 23). There is, of course, a mordant irony in this whole episode. The narrator, whom the Irish mistake for 'a good minister', dines and sups at nearly every alehouse on his route, sometimes offering lavish rhetorical tributes to the transformative power of beer and the eye-catching landladies who serve it. This chapter is no throwaway comedy of manners, though, in which the Irish are luckless dupes, their native tongue reduced to 'local colour', a mere embellishment extraneous to textual meaning. Instead, the scene reinforces how *Wild Wales* provides a more nuanced cultural appraisal that has its roots in the narrator's peripatetic course and chequered educational career documented in *Lavengro* and *The Romany Rye*. The dialogue signifies the narrator's ardent desire to become proficient in spoken Irish, despite or perhaps because the military men serving under Lavengro's father claim that even 'the respectable people' of Ireland 'do not speak it, only the wilder sort' (*LSGP* IX: 59):

> 'O sir, do give us God; we need Him, sir, for we are sinful people [. . .]'
>
> 'Bi-do-hosd,' said the man: Irish words tantamount to 'Be silent!'
>
> 'I will not be hushed,' said the woman, speaking English. 'The man is a good man, and he will do us no harm.' (*WW* IV: 23)

Here, as elsewhere, 'Englishes' operate in embodied, mundane interactions and reverberate alongside other 'minority' languages, which have their own operative laws, layered histories, and affective energies. This is reinforced by the staging of the printed page. Where we expect the flagging of single-word 'foreign' loan terms and conversational code switching through juxtaposition of 'normal print' (Saxon English as the primary medium of expression in this exchange) and italics (the visual othering of the Irish tongue), Borrow's text resists such typographic conventions or signposting. This visual feature operates to query the ethno-cultural and linguistic pre-eminence encoded in 'standard' English. Gatekeepers of this standard, influenced by Arnold's 1850s commentaries on the discursive fabrication of a great European polity, might deplore the deliberate code switching of bilingual speech communities as defective competence or even a menacing, conspiratorial ploy to thwart Saxon monoglots. The narrator, by contrast, as a participant observer, valorises and renders the two lexical repertoires upon which these Irish travellers draw and drift between. The Irish phrase used also gives rise to vivid cues that can attain an array of interactional goals, such as citation, exclamation, injunction, verbal repackaging, or an implied finessing of intonation which is a facet of spontaneous speech. Even the polyglot narrator, with his privileged access to the cultural background of numerous languages, is not necessarily privy to all the semantic and cultural connotations of the man's decree 'Bi-do-hosd'. That the narrator glosses the command as 'Irish words tantamount to. . .' makes us ponder the editorial manipulations and limits of his translational strategies. When and to what degree does the narrator use syntactical irregularity to evoke the rhythms of a 'foreign' tongue, or phonetically adapt certain Irish tags to the host language, for example? We imagine what exists beyond the narrator's confident gloss: the Irishman's timbre, gaze, posture, and gestural mannerisms as he speaks sternly to his partner, who imprudently wishes to confess to a relative stranger how 'sinful' her (normally vigilant, even secretive) 'people' are. Crucially then, 'Ireland' – as a complex lexicon (as opposed to John Jones's vilification of 'Paddy Gwyddel' patois), as an independent nation, as an imperilled yet storied culture – will not 'be hushed' (*bí i do thost!*).

Some of the narrator's most memorable displays of code switching in *Wild Wales* are performances of 'Irishness'. Like *Lavengro* before it, the travelogue lays bare the 'Saxonist' bigotries that convert 'Ireland' into 'a laboratory in which to experiment with various methods of exercising colonial power'.[100] *Wild Wales* furnishes a salutary corrective to imperialist conceptions of a lower Irish lifeform, physically and affectively stunted. This corrective is, however, marked by a riddling contradiction. While Borrow's empathetic narrator tries to better grasp, even inhabit, a subaltern position, these interactions also reveal a countervailing impulse to expose, even guy, agents of a 'Popish' religion that, in his opinion, exploit the illiterate and nomadic poor. One social mask that he dons is that of the Irish priest 'Father Toban' (*WW* IV: 23), who is referenced in the interaction just cited; the other is *Brian Bóramha* 'Brian Boru', the celebrated monarch 'slain at the battle of Clontarf' (*WW* XCV: 631). In Chapter XLI, the narrator encounters a hard-pressed group of Irish tinkers, many 'armed with shillealahs' (a type of cudgel) and led by a man whose face is an admixture of 'savagery and roguishness'. This leader, convinced the narrator is in fact Father Toban, whom he has often heard recite mass, menaces him with 'a good big bating' if he refuses to bless the

100. Gerry Smyth, '"The Natural Course of Things": Matthew Arnold, Celticism and the English Poetic Tradition', *Journal of Victorian Culture* 1:1 (1996): 37.

'dirty steamer' on which he and his confrères are scheduled to sail for 'ould Ireland'. Instead of losing his temper – these 'blackguards' warrant being 'bridled, ridden violently down to Holyhead or the Giant's Causeway' and drowned 'like the herd of swine of old' (*WW* XLI: 282) – the narrator devises a 'holy' ritual, more experimental than sacramental. When he asks this belligerent fellow, 'how shall I give the blessing?' the leader replies:

> 'Och, sure your reverence knows very well how to give it.'
>
> 'Shall I give it in Irish?'
>
> 'Och, no, your reverence – a blessing in Irish is no blessing at all.'
>
> 'In English?'
>
> 'Och, murder, no, your reverence, God preserve us all from an English blessing.'
>
> 'In Latin?'
>
> 'Yes, sure, your reverence; in what else should you bless us but in holy Latin?' (*WW* XLI: 282)

In *Wild Wales* the peripatetic Irish have an array of linguistic modes at their disposal, whether it is to foil Saxon busybodies like the narrator when it senses its indigenous lore is threatened, or to mark familiarity and closeness and to consolidate social ties among its own membership. The tinkers, while they treat their own 'native tongue' as apt for everyday interactions and affirming fraternal bonds, imply it is ill-suited to capture the ceremonial gravitas – and by extension perceived ontological potency – of a 'holy' benediction. Rendering that 'blessing' in English – the language of Arnold's cultural criticism and the colonial overlords who treat Ireland as lacking any sovereign claims, political mandate, or historical validity – would be far worse than a curse to these fellows ('Och, murder'). What this passage demonstrates is how such verbal flourishes, tics, and behaviours ('God preserve us all from an English blessing') are especially pronounced in the case of a subjugated community, or – as the narrator concedes in later chapters – when a bardic Welsh register has lapsed into desuetude, smothered by another, supposedly more 'refined' language from without, like Arnold's 'standard' English.

The narrator's elaborate pose as 'Father Toban' also resonates through his dialogue with 'Mary Bane', a hawker of soft goods from County Cork in Chapter XCV. Mary asks the narrator his name, so that she can identify him to her 'spiritual director', the very same 'Father Toban'. Mediated and framed by an erudite and historically savvy narrator, this 'interview' blends puckish humour and sad irony:

> 'Shorsha Borroo,' said I.
>
> 'Oh, then I was right in taking your honour for an Irishman. None but a raal Paddy bears that name. A credit to your honour is your name, for it is a famous name, and a credit to your name is your honour, for it is a neat man without a bend you are. God bless your honour and good night!' (*WW* XCV: 631)

'Shorsha' (Irish 'Seoirse' for George) 'Borroo' (Borrow) puns on one of the most fearless and unifying rulers of medieval Ireland. That the pedlar considers the narrator 'a raal Paddy' wittily echoes the narrator's earlier debates with innkeepers, farmhands, and fellow drinkers as to what defines 'a real Welshman' (*WW* V: 27). The glaring inconsistency here relates to how the narrator's desire for companionship and bonhomie that transcends 'Saxon', regional ('Norfolk'), and bourgeois family affiliations is achieved through an underhand, even dishonourable *passing* as a 'Paddy' or a 'Cumro'. We watch a social chameleon, adapting himself to fit a range of roadside scenarios, appealing to various marginalised ethnic and professional groups. His hope is that they will confide in him because they assume he belongs to their tribe ('I was right in taking your honour for an Irishman'). It is telling that, alongside the lengthy encomia to medieval bards, *Wild Wales* also documents the 'celebrated hero of Tregaron', Tom Shone Catti (Chapter XCIII). Catti's 'disposition to roguery and mischief' – 'his disguises were innumerable and all impenetrable' (*WW* 615) – suggests the narrator's own veiling of his Saxon origins, as 'one of the seed of the Coiling Serpent' (*WW* XX: 130). That the narrator repeats Taliesin's 'Coiling Serpent' figuration at least six times on his sojourn reflects his troubled sense that he is a product of a hegemonic and metropolitan Saxon culture that masquerades as a composite identity to ensure that the peoples of four different nations are subservient to a larger political project. So a 'neat man without a bend' or critic Gavin Young's conception of an 'innocent stroller'[101] is precisely what the narrator, with his peculiar blend of the furtive and the flaunting, *is not*. What complicates this episode is the narrator's staging of ethnic selfhood: 'Borroo' was esteemed in the *Annals of Ulster* as 'High King of the Gaels of Ireland and the Norse outsiders and the Britons', an Augustus of north-western Europe. We are invited to compare the venerable culture over which this noble 'Borroo' once presided with a nineteenth-century Ireland whose people are presented in *Wild Wales* as destitute, dispersed, and governed from afar by a craven, punitive, and 'ignominious' Saxon administration (*WW* LVI: 383).

101. Gavin Young, 'Greening of the Valleys', *The Observer* (8 January 1989): 31.

'Welsh and Saxons Together will Conquer the World!'

What the 'interviews' with members of the Irish diaspora share is an obsession with military adventurism, colonial mismanagement, and how such behaviours give rise to 'ethnocentrically superior attitudes to "other" cultures, peoples, and places'.[102] That the narrator, for all his cosmopolitan credentials, is himself prone to casual bigotry is revealed as early as Chapter III. His mask of amused forbearance occasionally slips when roused by familiar bugbears such as 'teetotal nonsense' and other 'perfect' specimens of 'humbug' (*WW* XLII: 285). For example, when visiting Chester, he encounters a 'brutishly ugly' black ex-slave, 'his features scarcely resembling those of a human being'. The man, a 'native of Antigua', is a 'blacksmith by trade': 'He said that any black might live in England without working; that all he had to do was to attend religious meetings' and 'speak against slavery and the Americans' (*WW* III: 16). This exchange indicates how the extraordinary growth in the coal industry and especially merchant shipping by mid-century had attracted many black seafarers to Wales from North America, West Africa, and the Caribbean. Nettled by this fellow's apparent reluctance to practice smithing, or indeed any other professional craft in his new home, the narrator tars him as one of those 'rascals' whose idleness makes a compelling case for why 'negro slavery' was instituted in the American South (*WW* III: 16–17). Though the narrator reveals elsewhere his antipathy to slavery, there is in this episode a refusal to condemn the secessionist Confederate states – a political stance shared by 'Lord Palmerston' and some other Tory 'gentlefolks in London' (*WW* C: 669). Palmerston, though some of his most notable parliamentary oratory impugned slavery, looked unfavourably on the North's Republican administration during the American Civil War, and even expressed hope that the Union might founder, thus opening potentially lucrative new trade routes for British manufacture in the South.

The narrator's later sojourn in Holyhead brings him 'in contact with a fellow dressed in a turban and dirty blue linen robes and trowsers. He bore a bundle of papers in his hand', one of which was 'stuffed with religious and anti-slavery cant'. This paper describes the man's 'captivity which he had undergone amidst savage Mahometans'. Rather than dwell on the myriad racisms, brutalities, and exclusions this man may have endured, the narrator depicts a deeply unreliable witness, with a 'dark, cunning, roguish countenance'; he has, supposedly, 'all the appearance of a Jew' (*WW* XLII: 284). Such moments signify that

102. Holland and Huggan (1998), viii.

even with an empathetic narrator well versed in the customs of many nations, who boasts of having 'been everywhere', his social conditioning means that he fixes 'the fellow dressed in a turban' not as a victim but as a potential miscreant. Such colour prejudice is more troubling here given the narrator's obvious enjoyment of the '*roguery* and mischief' (my emphasis) embodied by the famous Welsh thief Tom Shone Catti (*WW* XCII: 604). The narrator repeatedly manipulates 'appearance' along his route, staging language events in which he assumes the life stories and identities of others, such as the Irish Catholic priest Father Toban.

The posing of the 'Irish Question' in *Wild Wales* is linked, via a complex web of imagery, to other (sometimes pernicious) attitudes to identity formation, ethnicity, and language linked with a British empire at the apex of its power. Such discriminations and taxonomies expose his own dogmatic reactions as an inescapably white, moneyed, politically Protestant gentleman-traveller. His outspoken representations of ethnic minority clusters also raise wider questions about who is and isn't regarded as a 'real Welshman', who can claim membership of the national family, and the exercise of citizenship rights and equality which that access permits. The unsparing vignette of the turbaned 'fellow' is, first, a sharp reminder that a focus on ethno-cultural strife between 'Celt' and 'Saxon' should not supplant engagement with other racialised divisions and geopolitical rifts in Borrow's text. Second, his narrator's remarks expose a tension between his lofty ambition to portray Wales as a distinct culture and 'ancient language' (*WW* XIX: 122) as well as a space that is not only humane, but internationalist, progressive, and hospitable to all ethnicities.[103]

The narrator is especially exercised by the Anglo-French expedition to 'Sebastopol' during the Crimean War (1853–6). The affective resonance of what he terms a 'disagreeable subject' – a war of expediency, conducted to buttress Turkish sway over much of Eastern Europe and undermine Russian imperialism – is keenly felt in the travelogue's later chapters. Regarding this 'war', the narrator counsels the nervous Denbighshire militiaman in Chapter XXI that it is the 'duty of every gentleman' to be ready 'at all times to lay down his life in the service of the Queen'. It is this fierce sense of duty which will ensure 'Cronstadt could be taken' (*WW* XXI: 139–40).[104] As *Wild Wales* unfolds, however, the narrator's tone alters, and there will be no ritualised affirmations of British martial triumphalism. The striking absence of macho

103. See Charlotte Williams, Neil Evans, and Paul O'Leary, eds, *A Tolerant Nation? Revisiting Ethnic Diversity in a Devolved Wales* (Cardiff: University of Wales Press, 2015).

104. Cronstadt [Kronstadt] had resisted the Anglo-French fleets during the Crimean War.

rodomontade or sabre-rattling in his brooding on the long Siege of Sebastopol (1854–5) is chiefly because Anglo-French belligerence was directed against 'a mighty country' (*WW* XVIII: 107) and a people for whom Borrow felt affection during his time as a Bible Society colporteur in St Petersburg (1833–5), a city 'so fine' that 'neither Bristol nor Hereford is worthy to be named in the same day with it' (*WW* XCIX: 664). Borrow found ordinary Russians to be congenial, welcoming, and 'more tolerant to people of a different faith to themselves than the Roman Catholics'.[105] His narrator's dialogue with Mr Jones, a Llangollen tradesman in Chapter XVIII, is telling:

> I said [. . .] that we ran no risk from Russia; that the only power at all dangerous to Britain was France, which though at present leagued with her against Russia, would eventually go to war with and strive to subdue her, and then of course Britain could expect no help from Russia, her old friend and ally, who, if Britain had not outraged her, would have assisted her, in any quarrel or danger, with four or five hundred thousand men. (*WW* XVIII: 107)

Here the true imperial aggressor, for the narrator at least, is not Russia, whose autocratic government offended the so-called liberal principles of 'Lord Palmerston' (*WW* C: 570). Instead, it is France. As Borrow's choleric Appendix to *The Romany Rye* makes explicit, the Normans have been, historically, the 'scourgers' and 'torturers' of Saxon and Celt alike, 'the plunderers of their homes, the dishonourers of their wives, and the deflowerers of their daughters' (*RR*: 320). *Wild Wales* underlines how all such histories of violence end in the ruin of both occupying force and colonised subject. In the Vale of the Dyfi (Chapter LXXVII), the narrator meets the 'poor creature' Dafydd Tibbot. His surname, for the antiquarian narrator, carries an echo of bygone battles; indeed, this lowly 'creature' could be a 'descendant of some desperate Norman Tibault who helped to conquer Powisland under Roger de Montgomery'. The cheerless fate of this roadside labourer is proof perhaps that 'descendants of proud, cruel, and violent men – and who so proud, cruel, and violent, as the old Normans – are doomed by God to come to the dogs' (*WW* LXXVII: 505). In *Wild Wales*, then, the British campaign in Russia – which in the narrator's oft-stated opinion, is also going 'to the dogs' – represents a distraction from far more sinister geopolitical threats much closer to home. More importantly, it

105. Borrow (*c.*1835) quoted in Angus Fraser, 'Borrow's Political Views (Part 4): Foreign and Imperial Affairs', *George Borrow Bulletin* 19 (2000): 8.

is an 'outrage' perpetrated against a former 'friend and ally'. In Chapter CVII, the narrator illustrates how this military fiasco can barely be broached by a Welsh populace made increasingly fretful by press reports concerning the dire living conditions and poor physical and mental health of British soldiers, sailors, and cavalry. The son of a local mine-owner is 'in the Crim – fighting with the Roosiaid' (*WW* CVII: 709). It is one of the irascible narrator's most peculiar 'blind spots' that he can reject the contemporary anti-slavery movement as 'humbug' yet dwell on the grotesque follies of an Anglo-French alliance against far better drilled, fed, and motivated 'Roosiaid'. The litany of British strategic blunders in the Crimea are inextricably meshed in his mind with Lieutenant Parry, on whose fate he reads an 'excellent article' while resting at the Owen Glendower Inn (*WW* XXIII: 150). Referred to only as 'poor Lieutenant P', the unassuming son of a businessman without genteel pretensions, his 'crime was trying to defend himself with fist and candlestick from the manual attacks of his brutal messmates' (*WW* XLV: 310). *Wild Wales* alludes to the courts-martial at Windsor in July–August 1854 of James Edward *Perry* of the 46th (The South Devonshire) Regiment of Foot. What Borrow's narrator deplores as a travesty of justice garnered much adverse publicity, with the London *Standard* noting how the dismal proceedings had only 'strengthened the opinion of the public that the entire system of courts-martial needs a sweeping reform'.[106] What *Wild Wales* portrays as an 'infamous' episode of snobbery and yobbery in the '"service"' – exposing the hierarchical, elitist, and corrupt nature of the mid-Victorian officer corps – was already woven into the polemical fabric of *The Romany Rye*. Its Appendix devotes two embittered paragraphs to the sufferings and trial of an unnamed 'Lieutenant' (*RR*: 330):

> It was quite right and consistent with the justice of God that the British arms should be subjected to disaster and ignominy about that period. A deed of infamous injustice and cruelty had been perpetrated, and the perpetrators, instead of being punished, had received applause and promotion; so, if the British expedition to Sebastopol was a disastrous and ignominious one, who can wonder? Was it likely that the groans of poor Parry would be unheard from the corner to which he had retired to hide his head by 'the Ancient of days,' who sits above the cloud, and from thence sends judgments? (*WW* LVI: 383)

106. [Anon.], 'Second Court-Martial on Lieutenant Perry', *The Standard* 9353 (29 July 1854): 3.

The narrator's strength of feeling is mirrored in the self-conscious artifice of his rhetoric. As with his later meditations on the bloodthirsty, conquering Normans ('who so proud, cruel, and violent, as the old Normans are *doomed by God* to come to the dogs') the narrator argues that British military failures in Crimea show divine retribution at work. His disillusioned summary chimes with the remarks of the Welsh groom in the opening chapter from whom the narrator claims to have memorised his first phrases of 'the Cambrian language'. The groom laments the numberless miseries of 'poor British soldiers, and the tyranny of haughty British officers', one of whom may even have perished at the hands of his own enraged men, rather than 'under enemy fire', as was 'announced publicly' (*WW* I: 5). That the narrator voices sympathy for Parry's predicament is consistent with *Lavengro*'s depiction of the eponymous protagonist's humble sergeant father whose career has stalled while better connected, more moneyed but far less courageous officers were fast-tracked into vital leadership roles for which they were profoundly unsuited by temperament – and which may explain why the 'expedition to Sebastopol' was becoming a debacle.

Pointed allusions to warring empires in Crimea thicken the depictions of overbearing 'Saxon' attitudes to a 'lowly' Welsh language and mores. In *Celtic Bards, Chiefs and Kings*, drafted alongside the travelogue, Borrow loses no time in speculating on the etymology of 'Crimea' and 'Cymru':

> The Welsh style themselves Cymry or Cumry, a word which, in their language, means a number of people associated together. They were the second mass of population which moved from Asia into Europe. They followed and pushed forward the Gael or Gauls; were themselves impelled onward by the Teutons, who were followed by the Slowaks [. . .] who were themselves hunted, goaded, and pestered by a wild, waspish race of people, whom, for want of a better name, we will call Tatars or Tartars. The Cymry have left their name behind them in various regions far eastward of the one where they now sojourn. The most easterly countries which still bear their name, or modifications thereof, are Cambria, [. . .] and the Cryme or Crimea.[107]

Borrow's extravagant thesis that the 'Crimea' and 'the Cymru' enjoyed cultural links stretching back to the Bronze Age – which bears the intellectual imprint of his Norwich mentor, the polyglot and political radical

107. Borrow, *Celtic Bards, Chiefs and Kings*, 27; Hyde, 'Travelling Across Cultures', 339–43.

William Taylor – enlivens the opening pages of *Celtic Bards* and reverberates through Chapter XCIV of *Wild Wales*.[108] Although it shares little with methodically evidenced ethnolinguistic scholarship, this argument about common provenance and solidarity ('people associated together') chafes against the jingoistic sentiments the narrator hears on the streets of Llangollen – 'Welsh and Saxon shall conquer the world!' – at the misleading early news of 'Welsh Fusiliers' breaching Russian barricades only then to suffer 'horribly' (*WW* LVI: 380). Here the disenchanted narrator's stress on the enormous human cost of this conflict stands in stark contrast to the 'wild excitement' Borrow recorded in his 1854 diaries when the allies' expedition to Sebastopol was still in its initial phase: '(28 Sept. 1854) [. . .] Certain old pensioners [. . .] swear that the English will always conquer – God grant that they may conquer in the present instance'; and '(2 Oct.) Sudden clang of bells in the distance. Peth yw y matter says John Jones to a postman hurrying on in a cart – Sebastopol taken!'[109]

The narrator's perception of the waste, recklessness, and futility of the Crimean campaign is underscored in the closing chapters of *Wild Wales*. As his tour reaches its final week, he calls at the Brynaman Inn (Gutter Vawr), and hymns the glories of Russia, its cities, cultural treasures, and its emperor. Then, in Newport, reading a newspaper report of the grisly but inconclusive 'Battle of Inkerman' (5 November 1854), he muses gloomily, 'In my childhood [. . .] the Russians used to help us against the French; now the French help us against the Russians. Who knows but before I die I may see the Russians helping the French against us?' (*WW* CVII: 711).

The narrator's reflections on the 'Cymry' and 'Crimea' in *Wild Wales* operate as another reminder of the grave repercussions of what the high-minded Arnold euphemistically dubbed attempts at 'reconciliation' between rival states, political models, and national languages. In Arnold's *Celtic Literature* and *Irish Essays*, as critic Seamus Deane concludes, nonconformist Welsh speakers and Irish Catholics are 'really an absence for Arnold', catchalls in a thesis which 'has as its goal the ratification of the great project for a perfectly formed and perfectly irresistible English civilisation'. Against Arnold's paternalistic 'talking down' – a European nation-building enterprise in which 'standard' English is historically embedded – *Wild Wales* stages intercultural dialogues and weighs bi- or multilingual solutions to sociopolitical challenges.

108. See David Chandler, 'William Taylor of Norwich', *George Borrow Bulletin* (Spring 1994): 8–16.

109. *The Diaries of George Borrow*, Hispanic Society Museum and Library, New York.

This is seen in how the travelogue evokes rituals of 'talking with' members of minority language clusters as the narrator treks from Anglesey to Glamorgan. Such rituals show the far-reaching cultural effects of centuries of monolingualising nationalist ideology. Consequently, Borrow's text attains a more complex feeling for the interplay of discordant perceptions, cadences, and beliefs, gauging 'various religious persuasions' among, for example, Welsh 'Baptists', 'Independents', and 'Calvinistic-Methodists' (*WW* V: 25), as well as resisters of all political stripes.[110]

The narrator's yearning to be 'of a people', sharing with them his sincere 'love of the Welsh tongue' cannot hide an unresolved contradiction, however. In learning myriad languages and pretending to be a 'Cumro' or – as in the case of 'Father Toban' – a Catholic 'Irish' priest, does he not weaken his own thesis regarding the so-called 'purity' and legitimacy of a threatened culture whose historic vigour flows from that culture's speech economy? Anyone with the narrator's grasp of the native tongue could masquerade as 'a genuine Welshman', surely? In Chapter XI, the narrator's reaction to a man who recounts the mythic history of Madoc, son of Owain Gwynedd and said to have discovered America, is telling. The man proclaims that 'his people are still to be found in a part of America speaking the pure iaith Cymraeg better Welsh than we of Wales do'. 'That,' the narrator replies, 'I doubt [. . .] However, the idea is a pretty one; therefore cherish it' (*WW* XI: 60). Ultimately, his status as what Nigel Musk terms a 'floater' – one who professes to feel equally 'at home' in speaking Welsh and English – supplies a flexible, *impure*, and extempore notion of 'Welshness' that relies on frequent (and self-preening) displays of code switching and mimicry.[111] It was this very same facility – Borrow as a conversational chameleon – to which a young Wyndham Lewis alluded in his 1917 fictional manifesto 'Code of a Herdsman': '*Borrow from all sides* mannerisms of callings and classes to enrich your personal bastion of language' (my emphasis).[112]

While the narrator's conception of 'Welshness' draws intellectual sustenance from the bardic past, the travelogue's investment in this august 'literary' Welsh is often overshadowed by lively intercultural dialogues that consecrate hybrid, non-standard, or vernacular voices.

110. See Jodie Matthews, 'Borrowing Welshness: *Wild Wales*, Affiliation and Identity', *North American Journal of Welsh Studies* 6:1 (2011): 53–61.

111. Nigel Musk, 'Performing Bilingualism in Wales with the Spotlight on Welsh' (unpublished PhD: Linköping University, Sweden, 2006).

112. Wyndham Lewis, 'The Code of a Herdsman', *The Essential Wyndham Lewis*, Julian Symons, ed., 123.

These earthier accents mirror what the 1863 *Archaeologia Cambrensis* labelled Borrow's 'evident spirit of vulgar, democratic feeling'.[113] The authors of the 1847 'Blue Books', and to a lesser extent Arnold, set forth, using a tone of unruffled impartiality, an educational agenda geared towards replacing a 'vulgar' Cambrian tongue with fidelity to a culturally conservative, unionist political vision. *Wild Wales*, however, evinces a more partisan, even pugnacious verve that stresses popular struggles against obvious social injustices, like 'Rebecca of the toll-gates' that captured national press and parliamentary attention (*WW* XVI: 93). As in *Lavengro*, the narrator is easily irked by establishment civil and religious bureaucracies, and instead claims kin with those nomadic and subaltern (white) speakers who contest 'the principle of centralisation' – the 'most fatal for national spirit and natural freedom that can be devised', according to the 1848 *Blackwood's Edinburgh Magazine*.[114]

By the end of *Wild Wales*, we are left with the impression that Borrow's narrator is preaching this idiosyncratic, pick-and-mix Cambrian gospel to near-empty pews. Although the travelogue presents a narrator judged a prodigy, a cultural curiosity, who has laboured strenuously to win over a watchful indigenous population, such efforts ultimately reinforce the persona he projects when first venturing into Wales with his wife. He remains the burly English gentleman-traveller who fails to rewrite the ethno-cultural assumptions, crotchets, and behaviours separating 'Saxon' from 'Welsh' tribes: 'the English cannot make friends amongst the Welsh. The Welsh won't neighbour with them', as one disaffected English settler explains. They are 'as jealous of strangers hearing their discourse as if they were plotting gunpowder treason' (*WW* LXXVII: 504) – a tendency shared by gypsy matriarch Mrs Herne, who tries to kill the busybody narrator with a poisoned cake in *Lavengro*. Mrs Herne, like some Welsh townspeople, deplores the arrogance of learned trespassers who claim that they appreciate the historic value and sonority of minority tongues a great deal more than those to whom it properly belongs. Another Welsh local tells the narrator frankly that he will '[d]o anything for him but answer questions or let him hear my discourse'. He deems it,

> wise to be mum, quite mum. Know what he comes about. Wants to hear discourse of poor man, that he may learn from it poor man's little ways and infirmities, and mark them down in one small, little book to serve for fun to Lord Palmerston and

113. [Anon.], 'Reviews: *Wild Wales*', *Archaeologia Cambrensis* 9:34 (April 1863): 174–6.
114. [Anon.], 'Education in Wales', *Blackwood's Edinburgh Magazine* 63:391 (May 1848): 563.

> the other great gentlefolks in London. Nice man, civil man, I don't deny; and clebber man too, for he knows Welsh, and has been everywhere—but fox—old fox—lives at Plas y Cadno. (*WW* C: 668–9).

To this gracious yet guarded interviewee, the narrator is no harmless rambler. Rather, the 'small, little book' signifies the avatar of an illiberal state apparatus which executes surveillance for reasons of manipulation and 'ridicule' (*WW* LVI: 382). The allusion to 'Plas y Cadno' (loosely translated as 'Fox's Court') implies that warren of trickery and deceit, 'London', where the 'great gentlefolks' reside (*WW* C: 669). These remarks indicate that, no matter how much the narrator revels in bar-room bonhomie, code switching, and costume changes – seen early in his fascination with local protest movements like the 'Rebecca riots',[115] in which 'men dressed in women's clothes' (*WW* XVI: 93) – some canny locals tag him as a shady metropolite. The fellow's unbending resolve to 'keep mum' denotes that the 'treachery' of the 1847 *Blue Books* had been neither forgiven nor forgotten.

In my next chapter, I scrutinise how Borrovian tropes 'wandered' into a broad range of early twentieth-century cultural production.[116] Such was the potency of the 'Borrow brand' by the interwar period that allusions to his literary career could be found in the unlikeliest of places. The London Transport Authority utilised *Lavengro* in 'The Art of Travel' (1921), a vivid advertising poster by Ethel Gabain. This poster quotes from Kenneth Grahame's *Pagan Papers* to extol the quiet pleasures of joining 'Lavengro' in 'driving his tinker's cart' – though of course, it may be sensible for the less resilient to 'get a good start by Motor Bus'.[117] The first-person narrator of Walter Starkie's travelogue *Raggle-Taggle* (1933) was all too conscious of the relative comforts of motor travel when compared to the practical snags of following on foot 'the example of George Borrow in a Europe teeming with police and customs officials, where the vagabond is looked on with

115. See Rhian E. Jones, *Petticoat Heroes: Gender, Culture and Popular Protest in the Rebecca Riots* (Cardiff: University of Wales Press, 2015); Byrne, '"He will bid me"', 148–59.

116. See Lou Charnon-Deutsch, *The Spanish Gypsy: The History of a European Obsession*, 15. Roger Ebbatson, 'Henchard and George Borrow', *The Thomas Hardy Journal* 19:3 (2003): 82.

117. Kenneth Grahame, 'The Romance of the Road', *National Observer* (14 February 1891). See Grahame, *Pagan Papers*, sixth ed. (London: John Lane, 1898), 16. Ethel Gabain's advertising poster (ref. no. 1983/4/1141) is featured on the London Transport Museum website at: https://www.ltmuseum.co.uk/collections/collections-online/posters/item/1983-4-1141 (accessed 11/6/2022).

Figure 1 Ethel Gabain, 'The Art of Travel' (1921) ©TfL from the London Transport Museum collection

suspicion'.[118] Mindful of a redrawn European map, shrewd advertisers of the Triumph Ten Saloon and Austin Seven invoked Borrow to boost their 'Call of the Road' initiative to a more prosperous suburban demographic. *Lavengro*, we are told in rapt terms, 'awakes within us the nomadic instinct of our long dead forefathers' – who sadly couldn't savour the 'virgin splendour of spring' from the comfy seat of a charabanc.[119] Dylan Thomas gently debunked this trend in his *Portrait of the Artist as a Young Dog* (1940), whose character Mr Emlyn Evans, resident of a 'small villa' called 'Lavengro', might have found his head turned by such glossy ad campaigns.[120]

Half a century earlier, few could have forecast this Borrovian renaissance. When the gentleman-gypsy's death 'was announced in 1881', according to the *Morning Post*, 'many, even among those who

118. Walter Starkie, *Raggle-Taggle* (London: John Murray, 1933), xviii. On Starkie's self-identification as 'a writer of Gypsy books and a Borrovian', see Jacqueline Hurtley, *Walter Starkie: An Odyssey* (Dublin: Four Courts Press, 2013), 295.
119. [Anon.], 'The Call of the Road', *Bognor Regis Observer* (29 March 1933): 3.
120. Dylan Thomas, 'Where Tawe Flows', *Portrait of the Artist as a Young Dog* (London: Everyman, 1982), 98.

were seriously interested in English literature, were surprised to hear that he had not died years before'.[121] Ardent Borrovian and eminent literary critic George Saintsbury was determined to keep that memory alive. In a searching 1886 essay for *Macmillan's Magazine*, he argued that the often jaunty, oblique, and haphazard structure of *Lavengro* and *Wild Wales*, scorned as perverse idiosyncrasy at mid-century, appeared fresh at the fin de siècle. He applauded his subject, without any trace of irony, as 'a romancer in the true [. . .] sense of the word', who 'has not been approached in merit by any romancer who has published books in our days'.[122] Borrow's status as romancer would prove enticing to decadent poets disillusioned by the commercial and religious bromides of an antiseptic mid-Victorian respectability. Leonard Woolf also noted how, due in part to Edward Carpenter's zealous advocacy of 'open-air habits', Borrow's name was tied to a 'new romanticism'. This vogue had 'swept up greedily into its embrace fresh air and the road' and 'all stray vagabonds and scoundrels'.[123] Threaded through such cultural phenomena – specialist literary journals, rambling clubs – was what Roger Savage calls 'Gypsophilia', the 'late-Victorian and Edwardian idealization and rather selective emulation' of Borrow's 'Gypsy traveller'.[124] By 1913, the *Sheffield Daily Telegraph* could claim:

> We may not all be Borrovians yet, but the Heavens be praised that the army is ever increasing. Thirty years have passed since the [. . .] disappointed spirit went to his rest, but only now is he coming into his own. [. . .] *Lavengro* has lived to be regarded as one of the books of the nineteenth century.[125]

Perhaps surprisingly, given their suspicion of literary luminaries associated with a 'wondrous Victorian Age' – to cite D. H. Lawrence's sardonic phrasing from his 1923 novel *Kangaroo* – Anglo-American modernists extended Borrow's 'afterlife' well into the 1930s. James Joyce weaves terms from Borrow's *Romano Lavo-Lil* into the verbal

121. [Anon.], 'George Borrow', *Morning Post* (13 March 1899): 8.
122. George Saintsbury, 'George Borrow', *Macmillan's Magazine* 53:315 (January 1886): 170–83.
123. See Edward Carpenter, *My Days and Dreams: Being Autobiographical Notes* (London: Allen and Unwin, 1916), 208; Leonard Woolf, 'The World of Books: George Borrow', *The Nation and the Athenaeum* 35:8 (24 May 1924): 262.
124. Roger Savage, 'Vaughan Williams, The Romany Ryes, and the Cambridge Ritualists', *Music & Letters* 83:3 (August 2002): 383–417.
125. [Anon.], 'George Borrow', *Sheffield Daily Telegraph* (6 November 1913): 13.

fabric of *Finnegans Wake*.[126] Djuna Barnes, the self-described 'most famous unknown' novelist of the twentieth century, explained in a 1935 letter why *Nightwood* would make a more effective title than the original 'Bow Down': '[*Nightwood*] makes it sound like nightshade, poison and night and forest, and tough, in the meaty sense, and simple yet singular, like *Lavengro*'.[127] These years saw an array of technically ambitious verbal, visual, and performative texts in which representations of Romani, outcast, and nomadic communities played a crucial part: comparative mythography, psychoanalysis, bohemian fashion, vanguard dramaturgy, and especially the travelogue. In an interwar period marked by the rise of fascist and totalitarian regimes in Europe and a global economic depression, the Borrovian travelogue offered Lawrence, Wyndham Lewis, Walter Starkie, and other restless cosmopolites an opportunity to depict geopolitical convulsions in ways that were not always feasible in more familiar literary genres.

126. Angus Fraser, 'Borrow as a Source for James Joyce', *George Borrow Bulletin* 14 (Autumn 1997): 50–2.

127. Djuna Barnes, unpublished letter, Djuna Barnes to Emily Holmes Coleman, 23 June 1935.

CHAPTER 5

A NEW ROMANTICISM, OR BORROWED SCENES?

In Praise of Tramping

> I find it difficult, even now, to describe the extraordinary impression produced on me by this book. [. . .] *Lavengro* – the reading of which was to change my entire life – strangely disturbed me, at the age of nine, and made me realize, beyond any doubt, that my existence would, in future, be somehow bound up with that of the Gypsy people.
>
> [. . .] There was no question of 'liking' *Lavengro* as I liked other books, or, as I liked, say, the Russian Ballet. This was something more primitive. I did not guess, then, that I, myself, had gypsy blood.[1]

In 'Finding Borrow', the fifth chapter of her 1939 memoir *Life's a Circus*, the novelist Lady Eleanor Smith (1902–1945) explains that she owed her popular success partly to a 'tremendous discovery' in her well-stocked family library when she was still a child. The eldest of conservative politician Frederick Edwin Smith's three children and a debutante friend of Evelyn Waugh's, Smith published fiction whose picturesque sentimentalities and Romani backdrops furnished a blueprint for the 'Gainsborough' movie melodramas of the mid-1940s, such as *Caravan* (1946), starring Stewart Granger and based on Smith's 1942 novel of the same name. Like Irving Brown's *Nights and Days on the Gypsy Trail* (1922), in which the 'discovery' of Borrow's volumes stirs Brown's 'Romani fever',[2] Smith's account suggests a moment of multiplied perception among the bookshelves: '*Lavengro* fascinated and frightened

1. Eleanor Smith, *Life's a Circus* (1939; New York: Doubleday, Doran & Company, 1940), 31–5.
2. Irving Brown, *Nights and Days on the Gypsy Trail* (New York: Harper, 1922), 8.

me at the same time'.[3] Reading this text triggers an epiphany, one couched in terms of a naïve yet fervid primitivism. What Smith finds most 'primitive' about Borrow is his authorial self-construction as a learned, socially untrammelled wanderer – or, in W. E. Henley's terms, 'the one exemplary artist-tramp the race has yet achieved', the 'tinker who can write, the horse-coper with a twang of Hamlet'.[4] This imagery is, we will find, restated, refined, and complicated in Anglo-American cultural production across the first half of the twentieth century.

Smith's memoir reflects an extraordinary second flowering of mainstream and academic fascination with Borrow. Harry Roberts's *The Tramp's Handbook* (1903) invokes the gypsy gentleman Borrow to speak in 'Defence of Vagabondage' – instructing overwhelmingly white middle- and upper-middle-class sub/urban males 'how they may most simply nourish and protect their bodies without sacrificing their spiritual lives at the altar of the devil of the commercial age'.[5] Mindful of this cultural trend, the folklorist Cyril J. Inglis posited in 1912 that 'gypsy' and nomadic lore was no longer a 'closed' field or niche pursuit for budding antiquarians. Instead, it was 'a national topic of interest', amenable to 'the humblest reader', as mirrored in enthusiastic coverage by metropolitan newspapers and 'current magazines' like *The Tramp*.[6] Inglis's article on 'The Folk-Lore Revival' appeared in the *Romanitshels' Didakais' and Folk-Lore Gazette*, one of three periodicals – along with the Dublin-based *The Gypsy* (1915–16) and the more prominent *Journal of the Gypsy Lore Society* – which specifically appealed to 'Amateur Lavengros'.[7] Anglo-American publishing houses also targeted this growing constituency. In 1889, the Minerva Library reissued *The Bible in Spain*.[8] Theodore Watts-Dunton, hailed by Virginia Woolf as 'steeped in every sort of literary knowledge and memory',[9] edited *Lavengro* for the same series in 1893. Watts-Dunton's edition sparked a run of mass-market reprints of the novel which produced one or more almost every year for over half a century thereafter. *Lavengro* was included in Macmillan's 'Illustrated Standard Novels' series in 1896, Methuen's 'Little Library'

3. Smith, *Life's a Circus*, 35.
4. William Ernest Henley, 'Borrow', *Views and Reviews*, 136.
5. Harry Roberts, *The Tramp's Handbook* (London: John Lane, 1903), 1–3.
6. Cyril J. Inglis, 'The Folk-Lore Revival', *The Romantisshels' Didakais' and Folk-Lore Gazette* 1 (1912): 47–51.
7. [Anon.], 'Amateur Lavengros Beware', *The Romantisshels' Didakais' and Folk-Lore Gazette* 1 (1912): 46.
8. See [Anon.], 'Our Bookshelf', *The Illustrated Missionary News* 23:8 (1 August 1889): 127.
9. Virginia Woolf, *The Essays of Virginia Woolf, Volume II 1912–1918*, ed. Andrew McNeillie (London: Hogarth Press, 1987), 110.

in 1901, and 'Everyman's Library' in 1906. Moreover, Watts-Dunton's novel *Aylwin* (1898), ticketed by Joseph Conrad as a 'curiosity success' in an 1898 letter to Aniela Zagorska,[10] bolstered efforts to promote Borrow as 'the Great High Priest of the Ungenteel'.[11] Watts-Dunton was family lawyer to Ford Madox Ford, whose own tribute to *Lavengro* and *The Romany Rye* is woven into the discursive fabric of *The Cinque Ports* (1900), as well as a lengthy review of Clement Shorter's 1913 volume *George Borrow and His Circle*.[12]

Watts-Dunton's designation of a proudly ungenteel Borrow simultaneously resisted and reflected a swiftly expanding leisure industry, especially the 'open-airism' associated with Robert Blatchford's romantic socialism. Blatchford's *Clarion* newspaper, launched in 1891, coupled with his *Ramblers' Handbooks*, measured the healing potency of Borrovian 'flower-starred meadows' and 'still green woods' against the 'gloomy lanes, the fever beds and the vice traps of horrible Liverpool, [. . .] horrible London' and 'horrible Glasgow'.[13] If Borrow's imagery furnished Blatchford and his back-to-nature allies with a model for ethical and educational reform, it also proved inspirational (and lucrative) for popular novelists. Jeffrey Farnol's historical romance *The Broad Highway* (1910) sold just over 500,000 copies in Britain and North America. Maurice Hewlett's *Open Country* (1909) utilised Borrow's thematic motifs to rebrand the English countryside, especially Hardy's Wessex ('Dorsetshire Downs'), as a site and source of elemental splendour, embodied by 'Pan and the Nymphs'. Chapter XXI, 'The Tramp's Testament', tells of a 'man called Thursfield, who had what they call misfortunes'. Because of these adversities, he elects to begin, or live again, beyond the philosophies of productivity. Hewlett's account pushes against economist Henry George's notorious and paranoid 1883 conception of the white tramp as chronically indolent, 'a poisonous pariah, avenging on society the wrong that he keenly, but vaguely, feels has been done him'.[14]

> His children grew up and went into the world; his wife tired of him and went her way also. He was left in middle life with nothing but some thousands a year and a house or two. Odd as one

10. Joseph Conrad, Frederick R. Karl, and Laurence Davies, eds, *The Collected Letters of Joseph Conrad Volume 2 1898–1902* (Cambridge: Cambridge University Press, 1986), II, 137–8.
11. See [Anon], 'Literary and Art Gossip', *Leeds Mercury* (14 July 1884): 7.
12. Ford Madox Hueffer, *The Cinque Ports: A Historical and Descriptive Record* (Edinburgh and London, 1900), 219–20.
13. Robert Blatchford, 'The Two Nations', *The Scout* (June 1895): 6.
14. Henry George, *Social Problems* (Chicago and New York: Belford, Clarke & Co., 1883), 179.

> might think it, they didn't satisfy him. He let them all go; I believe that he endowed a charity with them—an almshouse of sorts. I found him some two years ago in a hollow of the Dorsetshire Downs, inhabiting a shepherd's wooden hut, living mostly on what he could coax out of the unthrifty soil. He quoted George Borrow to me: 'There's night and day, brother, both sweet things; there's likewise the wind on the heath!' He called these the Good Things, and said that they were good enough for him.[15]

Hewlett's portrayal of the Borrovian in *Open Country* – a 'hail-fellow' outside the familiar domestic and financial structures, joining 'all the gipsies, tinkers, horse-stealers, and *rascaille* on the road' – depends on treating the white 'tramper or vagabond' (*RR* VI: 39–40) as synonyms rather than distinct, even contrasting social entities. In *Lavengro* and *The Romany Rye*, the narrator is a self-styled idler, a blithe nomad across regions, cultures, and languages, homeless only figuratively. He enjoys the scope to switch between the social roles of Grub Street hack, trainee blacksmith, and snake charmer. The 'vagabond', meanwhile, as *The Bible in Spain* demonstrates, is excluded from those regimes of leisure and pleasure that Hewlett's *Open Country* identifies above as 'Good Things'. Rather the Iberian 'vagabonds' and 'undesirables' that Borrow's narrator observes are doomed to destitution.

Hewlett's popular chronicle of one who 'lived in a tent of his own stitching', with a deep 'knowledge of England's recesses' that 'must have equalled Cobbett's or Borrow's'[16] helped elevate *Lavengro* to the level of secular Scripture among an Edwardian tramping cadre seeking respite from the debilitating ennui that interwar rural historian H. J. Massingham linked with 'the prison of the pavement'.[17] However, *Open Country* shows scant awareness of a shrinking countryside, or what it means to be genuinely dispossessed, ejected from the social body and compelled to roam and beg 'on the roads of England' (*RR* VI: 39–40) – little better than the 'refuse of all classes' that Marx describes in *The 18th Brumaire*.[18] Edward Thomas's *George Borrow: The Man and His Books*, published in 1912, coupled with his book reviews for *The Morning Post*

15. Maurice Hewlett, *Open Country: A Comedy with a Sting* (New York: Scribner's, 1909), 248–9.
16. Hewlett, *Open Country*, 22. See also Martin Gosling, 'Jeffery Farnol and Shades of Borrow', *The George Borrow Bulletin* 2:15 (Autumn 2017): 20–3.
17. H. J. Massingham, *English Downland* (The Face of Britain Series) (London: Batsford, 1936), 14, 40.
18. Karl Marx, *The 18th Brumaire of Louis Bonaparte* (New York: International Publishers, 1997), 75–6.

and *The Daily Chronicle*, nuances Hewlett's misperception of *Lavengro* as a guidebook to an England of tangible bucolic nooks.[19] For Thomas, Borrow's exact place in the English countryside canon was uncertain, since *Lavengro* and *The Romany Rye* are not primarily concerned with tracing a long history of rural deprivation, itineracy, and placelessness. William Cobbett, riding through the English south-western counties around the same time as Borrow, witnessed scenes of 'unemployed working folk dizzy from starvation', as did Wordsworth tramping across Salisbury Plain after the French Wars.[20] However, Thomas wonders how Borrow can see only the mysteries of the Standing Stones, without recording the miseries of those unhoused and penniless families drifting through the locality. Borrow's account seems more in tune with the timeless world and characters of Fielding's *Joseph Andrews* (1792) or Goldsmith's *The Vicar of Wakefield* (1766).

> It would be difficult for one describing a journey to give a less realistic account of the country, the roads, and the conditions of travel. [. . .] Borrow's country [is] the country of his soul. It may be felt in his Spain, in his Wales, in his London, in his Salisbury Plain, but it is essentially an imaginative country, the product of his studies and of his temperament, with those early memories of Ireland as an airy groundwork.[21]

Borrow sketches an obscure inland empire of lyric feeling – soul over soil. His conception of 'Salisbury Plain' as 'the product' of fond, if hazy recall presents a sharp contrast, Thomas implies, with Richard Jefferies's more 'realistic', closely observed rural sociology in journalism like 'Drought and Water' (1870) and 'The Prospects of Farming' (1877). Borrow's 'journey' says surprisingly little about the relative balance between rural and suburban populations, which altered irretrievably in the time between the 1871 census – a year before the second edition of *Lavengro* appeared – and 1912, when Thomas's biography was published. As Thomas knew only too well, the decade or so after 1871 witnessed the first absolute decline in the rustic population since census

19. See Edward Thomas, 'Book review: *Artemision, Idylls, and Songs*, by Maurice Hewlett', *The Morning Post* (26 April 1909); Edward Thomas, 'Book review: *The Agonists*, by Maurice Hewlett', *The Daily Chronicle* (4 May 1911); Edward Thomas, 'Book review: *Helen Redeemed and Other Poems*, by Maurice Hewlett', *The Daily Chronicle* (12 March 1913).
20. David Williams, *A World of his Own: The Double Life of George Borrow* (Oxford: Oxford University Press, 1982), 37.
21. Edward Thomas, *A Literary Pilgrim in England* (New York: Dodd, Mead, and Co., 1917), 247–8.

accounts started.[22] By the time *George Borrow: The Man and His Books* went to press, more than half the population of England and Wales resided in towns of over 100,000 inhabitants. For H. J. Massingham in *Where Man Belongs* (1946), this represented a 'landslide of the dispossessed poor from a decaying countryside' into urban centres, especially after the Housing and Town Planning Act (1909).[23]

Like Thomas's *George Borrow*, E. M. Forster's *Howards End* (1910) throws these startling demographic and social convulsions into high relief. Forster does so primarily through his depiction of the pallid insurance clerk Leonard Bast, 'grandson to the shepherd or plough-boy whom civilisation had sucked into the town'. To Bast, given his 'cramped little mind', Borrow personifies the world of greatly expanded horizons that Hewlett's *Open Country* lauds. However, what Thomas labels Borrow's 'imaginative country' – a topographical record of the regions of his literary predecessor's mind – is for Forster a medley of stale pastoral whimsies, epitomised by Rickie Elliot's *Pan Pipes* volume in *The Longest Journey* (1907), Forster's earlier *bildungsroman*.

> [For Bast. . .] Borrow was imminent after Jefferies—Borrow, Thoreau, and sorrow. R.L.S. [Robert Louis Stevenson] brought up the rear, and the outburst ended in a swamp of books. [. . .] Within his cramped little mind dwelt something that was greater than Jefferies' books—the spirit that led Jefferies to write them; and his dawn, though revealing nothing but monotones, was part of the eternal sunrise that shows George Borrow Stonehenge.

Forster's placement of Borrow alongside 'Jefferies' is artful. The final sentences of Jefferies's *The Amateur Poacher* (1879) – 'Let us get out of these indoor narrow modern days' into the 'sunlight and the pure wind. A something that the ancients called divine can be found and felt there still' – implies a sentiment that Bast can only enact by stumbling among brambles and gorse in the 'Nature' of Wimbledon Woods. Bast's fantasy of redemptive release from the endless monotony of office work forms an insipid counterpart to the Borrovian narrator's apprehension of the wild treeless isolation around 'Stonehenge' in *Lavengro*. Bast is one of those for whom the 'Country' exists only 'in inverted commas', as Ford Madox Ford wryly put it.[24] Bast's dilemma is that the Borrovian

22. Patrick Wright, *On Living in an Old Country: The National Past in Contemporary Britain* (Oxford: Oxford University Press, 2009).
23. H. J. Massingham, *Where Man Belongs: Rural Influence on Literature* (London: Collins, 1946), 82.
24. Ford Madox Ford, *The Heart of the Country*, 23.

ethos of rambling across sparsely cultivated parts of the island nation, which may have energised 'Jefferies', 'R.L.S.', and Hewlett in *Open Country*, only underlines Bast's stymied social mobility and unavailing nostalgia. These features also distinguish Ford Madox Ford's sketch of the frustrated 'bank clerk' in Chapter III of *The Soul of London* (1905). For Bast, playing the Borrovian nomad, seeking ancestral imprints or sudden revelations in the smallest 'hedgerow events',[25] is an expensive and time-consuming exploit. He savours brief 'movement' away from the city, but without fruitful or enduring 'self-improvement'. Bast's faltering footsteps cannot compete with the relentless 'March of Bricks and Mortar'.

Three years after the publication of *Howards End*, Arthur Conan Doyle drafted a short story for the *Pall Mall Magazine* – '"Borrow"-ed Scenes' (1913) – that was even more trenchant in its reaction to Hewlett's promotion of the 'Earth as an artistic cult'[26] and Borrow's guru status for weekend wanderers like Leonard Bast. In his memoir *Through the Magic Door* (1906–7), Doyle declared that Borrow was one of his 'favourite authors'.[27] He appeared, in Doyle's judgement, 'a very strange man' – vinegary, fickle, and implacably hostile to those he dismissed as grey-faced functionaries. Coupled with this was the acute tension between the unhindered freedoms associated with Borrow's geographical wanderings and the rooted, even fanatical enmities of one who lost no opportunity to lambast the Roman Catholic Church and its agents. 'So far,' Doyle claimed, 'his catalogue of qualities does not seem to pick him as a winner. But he had one great and rare gift. He preserved through all his days a sense of the great wonder and mystery of life – the child sense which is so quickly dulled.'[28] In light of this, Conan Doyle's story, which opens with a brief '*extract from an unpublished paper upon George Borrow and his writings*', strikes a surprisingly sour note, especially when measured against that vein of tender mockery in Kenneth Grahame's *The Wind in the Willows* (1908). In Grahame's second chapter, Mr Toad, the proud owner of a 'gipsy caravan, shining with newness, painted a canary-yellow', reacts in rapt – if transient – fashion to the 'poetry' implicit in what Grahame terms the 'England' of 'by-lanes and village greens' – that is, 'the England

25. Harold Nicolson, *England: An Anthology* (London: Macmillan, 1944), 2–3.
26. E. M. Forster, *Howards End* (Harmondsworth: Penguin, 1996), 88, 116.
27. Arthur Conan Doyle, *Through the Magic Door* (New York: The McClure Company, 1908), 94.
28. Arthur Conan Doyle, *Through the Magic Door* (New York: The McClure Company, 1908), 96–7.

of *Lavengro*'.[29] It is this fantasy of England to which Conan Doyle's deluded narrator clings.

Recent critics have treated 'Borrowed Scenes' as, at best, a *jeu d'esprit*, at worst a laboured parody of the roving central protagonist, formal tactics, and set pieces of Borrow's 1850s mock memoirs.[30] However, the text, depicting a superfan or literary groupie who is 'soaked in George Borrow, especially in his *Lavengro*' is far from throwaway.[31] Conan Doyle explores how budding Borrovians in this period, by modelling their sartorial style, beliefs, and speech patterns 'very carefully upon those of the master',[32] felt as if they were making a lifelong companion in and through fiction. 'Borrowed Scenes' is, in short, a sly and sustained commentary on what we nowadays label parasocial phenomena, how bonding with a narrative persona conditions and interplays with the public and private behaviours, skills, and mindset of adults.[33] The pratfalls of Conan Doyle's narrator bear out Augustine Birrell's 1892 response to *Lavengro*: 'If one was in search of a single epithet most properly descriptive of Borrow's effect upon his reader, perhaps it would best be found in the epithet "contagious".'[34] Having caught the Borrovian 'bug', Doyle's narrator positions himself as a 'country cousin to the metropolitan *flaneur*'.[35] Aspiring to be a self-reliant individualist in the mould of his 'master', Conan Doyle's narrator is stirred by the factitious, not fact-based aspects of marginalised Romani lives. The slapstick is revealing not only about the road fantasies concocted by 'Amateur Lavengros' who purchased tramping texts like Leonard Bast. Doyle also ponders Borrow's role in the dissemination of contemporary discourses of bucolic English national belonging,

29. Kenneth Grahame, 'A Bohemian in Exile', *St James's Gazette*, 27 September 1890. See Grahame, *Pagan Papers*, sixth ed. (London: John Lane, 1898), 137–8. Grahame is not parodying this conception of England in a later episode of *The Wind in the Willows* when Toad sells a horse he has stolen from the washerwoman to the gypsy.
30. '"Borrow"-ed Scenes' (later 'Borrowed Scenes') first appeared in the September 1913 edition of the *Pall Mall Magazine*, with seven illustrations by Thomas Derrick. It later appeared in *Danger! And Other Stories*, a volume of ten collected short stories published by John Murray in 1918.
31. Conan Doyle, 'Borrowed Scenes', *Danger! And Other Stories* (New York: George H. Doran Company, 1919), 163.
32. Conan Doyle, 'Borrowed Scenes', 163.
33. See J. Ingram and Z. Luckett, 'My friend Harry's a wizard: Predicting parasocial interaction with characters from fiction', *Psychology of Popular Media Culture* 8:2 (2019): 148–58.
34. See Augustine Birrell, 'George Borrow', *Res Judicatae: Papers and Essays* (London: Elliot Stock, 1896), 110.
35. Melanie Tebbutt, 'Rambling and Manly Identity in Derbyshire's Dark Peak, 1880s–1920s', *Historical Journal* 49:4 (2006): 1149.

where an aestheticised male tramper, with conveniently deep pockets, is insulated from the harsh actualities of being landless and without a fixed home. For Doyle in this story, 'the essential Borrovian' exiles himself by choice, for aesthetic and pecuniary gain, and lacks deep insight into the lived experiences of forced itinerancy and economic precarity in an era in desperate need of radical social housing initiatives. Apathetic to the local customs of Sussex villages, Doyle's narrator discovers that Don George's rank as the self-admiring navigator of hazardous wilds, with supernatural powers as horse-sorcerer are a sham, not shamanic.[36] In fact, the nomadic communities and topographical nooks ('dingle') that 'the master' evoked in the mid-nineteenth century do not seem to exist anymore, if they ever did.

> 'Some other day,' said I, 'I may visit you in your camp in the dingle and read you the master's book about the Romanys.'
> 'What's Romanys?' asked the man.
> *Myself.* Romanys are gipsies.
> *The Man.* We ain't gipsies.
> *Myself.* What are you then?
> *The Man.* We are hoppers.
> *Myself (to Henrietta).* Then how did you understand all I have said to you about gipsies?
> *Henrietta.* I didn't.[37]

Conan Doyle apes Borrow's ostensibly capricious shifts to the playlet mode to show how the narrator tries to be, like his 'master' in *Wild Wales*, the linchpin of every conversational set-piece. Other characters in Doyle's tale, like Henrietta, function as bit-part players or 'shadow-shapes, a mere background' to the narrator's full-throated performance of vagrancy, one that offers little locally focused scrutiny of the genuine problems, injustices, and estrangements linked with gruelling rustic labour, such as seasonal crop-picking.[38] The narrator's phrasing begs the question: what is his exact relationship with, and social purpose in, the 'Sussex village of Swinehurst'? Doyle's narrator has little obvious link to the lanes through which he saunters in search of the next fleeting frisson. This severance from the *genius loci* that the playlet conveys stands in contrast to the lyrical feeling of umbilical attachment to bucolic hinterlands that Borrow's protagonist cultivates through long years of travel in *Lavengro* and *The Romany Rye*. Doyle's narrator drifts

36. [Anon.], 'The "Redoubtable Borrow"', *Saturday Review* 66:1710 (4 August 1888): 144–5.
37. Conan Doyle, 'Borrowed Scenes', 181–2.
38. [Anon.], 'George Borrow', *Manchester Guardian* (5 March 1912): 4.

between those reading constituencies at which metropolitan magazines like *The Idler* and *The Tramp* were aimed. The latter publication, in its first number of March 1910, hoped to catch the eye of the 'open-air man, the artist, the literary man, and the general reader'. It is an irony that, despite being 'soaked in George Borrow' and an earlier Wordsworthian peripatetic tradition, Conan Doyle's narrator seems little more than a poverty tourist who cannot accurately *read* the runes of his topographical setting. If he tries to present his own peregrinations as valid aesthetic 'labour', bringing a revived sense of community cohesion to a fractured countryside still reeling from the myriad economic and environmental crises of the 1890s, then the project is an abject failure. This is because Conan Doyle's Borrovian narrator, parading his impenetrable antiquarian knowledge of 'Chinese poet Lo-tun-an' and 'Grunelda, the daughter of Hjalmar' cannot adapt to a grave new world of improving infrastructure ('the railway-station') and ceaseless sub/urban expansion.[39]

'Borrowed Scenes', through knockabout farce, debunks the Edwardian tramper's intense investment in Borrow as 'one who possessed the key to the romance of the countryside'.[40] The narrator's jejune antics remind us that, despite arriving in Britain in the early 1500s as part of the Romani diaspora, the 'gypsy' is frequently framed as, at best, a quaint, prettified primitive and outsider. This is catnip to Conan Doyle's narrator. He hopes to uncover exotic human specimens (the girl Henrietta puts him in 'mind of the peerless Belle' from *Lavengro*) by staging 'wayside boxing adventures which were so common in the olden times'.[41] This stilted tribute act, in which the narrator recites a garbled 'Romani lil', indicates Doyle's belief that Borrow's major works had nearly 'exhausted' the 'quarry' of colourful vagrant patois.[42] However, for a surprising number of Anglo-American modernist vanguardists, variously invested in reconfiguring the 'savage', the 'subaltern', and the 'primitive', Borrow's descriptive sketches of roaming mendicants furnished a rich seam to mine. These cultural producers endeavoured to make the 'Borrowed' fresh while simultaneously distancing themselves from an 'easily circumstanced' town class of rambler that Conan Doyle chaffs.[43]

39. Conan Doyle, 'Borrowed Scenes', 173.
40. [Anon.], '*Lavengro* and Norwich', *Manchester Guardian* (7 July 1913): 8.
41. Conan Doyle, 'Borrowed Scenes', 173, 176.
42. [Anon.], 'Reviews: *Lavengro*', *Christian Examiner* (Boston) 50 (1851): 504–5.
43. Ford Madox Ford, *The Heart of the Country*, 23.

Modernist Makeovers? Lewis, Ford, Bloomsbury

> The joys of a tramp's life, the attraction of the open road and the fascination of travel have, during the last few years, been written into us and talked into us – dare I say – *ad nauseam*.[44]

In the September 1910 number of Douglas Goldring's short-lived modernist magazine *The Tramp*, Lord Congleton voiced irritation at cultural myths of 'the open road' that Conan Doyle targets in his skit. Congleton evokes the prefatory quotation from Walt Whitman's 'Song of the Open Road', which greeted readers of *The Tramp*'s first number in March 1910. That Congleton's weary assessment was included in *The Tramp*, a magazine devoted to the manifold 'joys of travel' at home and overseas, signalled the editor Douglas Goldring's determination to mirror a broad spectrum of opinion about 'open-airism'. The aesthetic significance of Goldring's 'editorial adventure', as critic Helen Southworth explains, was belied by its mayfly existence.[45] Indeed, *The Tramp* sheds a vital sidelight on Borrow's modernist afterlives because the journal's diverse contents manifest an intriguingly ambivalent position on those facets of advanced technological modernity that *The Romany Rye* deplores. Goldring's literary goal for *The Tramp* was to capture, as he reminisced in his 1943 memoir *South Lodge*, that 'distinction of personality or force of conviction' associated with the authors showcased by Ford Madox Ford's *English Review* (Goldring had served as Ford's sub-editor).[46] Before Goldring joined Ford's staff, he had been an apprentice at *Country Life* magazine, which printed numerous articles on Borrow's oeuvre, such as 'Picturesque East Anglia' (1906).[47] *The Tramp*'s unevenness of tone is to some degree the outcome of Goldring's effort to fuse two conflicting editorial agendas: Ford's insistence on reawakening his audience to an appreciation of the finest writing, and the commercial clout of *Country Life* – a vehicle for the 'glitter of a popular statement' that the *English Review* shunned, according to its high-minded mission statement.[48]

Lord Congleton's piece suggests how *The Tramp* reflected the growing craze for weekend treks across unspoilt Celtic hinterlands while

44. Lord Congleton, 'The Tramp in London', *The Tramp* (September 1910): 522–3.
45. Douglas Goldring, *South Lodge: Reminiscences of Violet Hunt, Ford Madox Ford and the English Review Circle* (London: Constable, 1943), 57–61. See also Helen Southworth, 'Douglas Goldring's *The Tramp: An Open Air Magazine* (1910–11) and Modernist Geographies', *Literature & History* 18:1 (2009): 35–53.
46. Goldring, *South Lodge*, 24.
47. W. A. Dutt, 'Picturesque East Anglia', *Country Life* 19:489 (19 May 1906): 719–20.
48. See Violet Hunt, *The Flurried Years* (London: Hurst and Blackett, 1926), 27.

simultaneously charting more glamorous, neo-primitivist motifs, pursuits, and figures – for example, the hobohemians Jack London and Augustus John – by inviting more conceptually audacious contributions. In the early numbers of *The Tramp* is it startling to find, alongside elegiac pieces by Edward Thomas, W. H. Davies, Arthur Ransome, and Fabian socialist Holbrook Jackson, F. T. Marinetti's 'Futurist Declaration' – a hymn to the revolutionary potential of the motorcar.[49] Placed several pages away from Marinetti's eye-catching work in the August 1910 number is 'Breton Innkeeper', a piece by a young man whom Goldring judged a writer of 'outstanding merit' – a 'P. Wyndham Lewis'.[50]

We might expect Lewis, whose *BLAST*-ing of snobbish Borrovians opens this book, to execrate Goldring's editorial plans as the epitome of bourgeois blandness – think Clive Holland's anodyne May 1910 *Tramp* article 'Summer Wanderings in the Hardy Country'. However, this misconstrues, as Southworth and other modernist scholars note, the complex if contradictory *Tramp* ethos. Numerous contributors evinced an Edwardian relish for hiking paraphernalia, resource conservation, rural crafts, and indigenous lore, as well as a preoccupation with the glitzy trappings of steam ships, trains, and foreign destinations like Corsica and Venice.[51] Personifying the magazine's ideological and tonal incongruities to a large degree was Lewis himself, after leaving the Slade School in London. The self-avowed 'enemy' of Borrovian dilettantes who bowed the knee to 'wild Mother Nature' in *BLAST 1* posits in his first critical essay 'Our Wild Body' – it predates his foundational futurist-vorticist screeds – that '[w]alking and talking are the two finest exercises in the world, and for the requirements of health no man needs any other'.[52] This scans like a coded tribute to Borrow's heroic feats of pedestrianism and taletelling in *Lavengro*.

Lewis placed no fewer than five pieces in Goldring's magazine between 1910 and 1911.[53] Some of these semi-fictional, semi-ethnographic

49. Filippo Tommaso Marinetti, 'Futurist Declaration', *The Tramp* 1:5 (August 1910): 487–8.
50. Goldring, *South Lodge*, 61. See also Southworth, 'Douglas Goldring's *The Tramp*', 35–53.
51. See, for example, Constance, Countess of Warr, 'Corsica and its Beauties', *The Tramp* (May 1910): 224; Emmeline Samuelson, 'Impressions of Venice', *The Tramp* (October 1910): 79.
52. Wyndham Lewis, 'Our Wild Body', *The Complete Wild Body*, 254. This critical essay first appeared in A. R. Orage's 1910 *The New Age* magazine.
53. See P. Wyndham Lewis, 'A Spanish Household', *The Tramp* (June/July 1910): 356–60; 'A Breton Innkeeper', *The Tramp* (August 1910): 411–14; 'Le Pere Francois (A Full-Length Portrait of a Tramp)', *The Tramp* (September 1910): 517–21; 'Grignolles (Brittany)', *The Tramp* (December 1910): 246; 'Unlucky for Pringle', *The Tramp* (February 1911): 404–14. See also Southworth, 'Douglas Goldring's *The Tramp*': 35–53.

texts were reimagined as *The Wild Body* (1927), a story collection in which he dismissed the earlier versions as a 'few hasty notes of very early travel'.[54] The *Tramp* sketches, based on memories of sojourns in Northern Spain between 1902 and 1907 as a hard-pressed art student, are rich in sociological detail and invite close comparison with Borrow's narrative strategies. Lewis's most memorable texts document experiences of living among the Breton-speaking locals of north-western France, a region of *pensions* and religious *pardons* (a cross between a penitential ritual and a riotous communal fiesta or regatta).[55] Lewis's formal-stylistic practice in these *Tramp* pieces – he later explained that 'My literary career began in France', 'what I started to do in Brittany, I have been developing ever since'[56] – is better parsed in relation to his fictional manifesto 'The Code of a Herdsman', drafted around 1914 and published in the 1917 *Little Review*:

> Borrow from all sides mannerisms of callings and classes to enrich your personal bastion of language. Borrow from the pulpit, from the clattering harangue of the auctioneer, the lawyer's technicality, the pomposity of politicians. = Borrow grunts from the fisherman, solecisms from the inhabitants of Merioneth.

Here 'Borrow' operates, first, as a transitive verb. Lewis's speaker exhorts aspirant authors to collect, scrutinise, and reimagine a babel of voices – from the 'grunts' of ordinary 'fisherman' to phraseology associated with more rarefied social regimes or stations. 'Borrow' is also the surname of 'a great writer' in 'The Code' who, Lewis asserts, 'knew what he was doing'.[57] Like Leonard Woolf a few years later, who bridled at Leslie Stephen's misperception of Borrow as one whose authorial tactics and precepts were 'lucky flukes',[58] Lewis signifies that Borrow's tales of wanderlust (the 'inhabitants of Merioneth' feature in *Wild Wales*) display an adroit rendering of verbal and gestural oddities.[59] Lewis's desire to bolster one's 'personal bastion of language' by recording both

54. Quoted in Wyndham Lewis, *The Wild Body: A Soldier of Humour and Other Stories* (Harmondsworth: Penguin Modern Classics, 2004), x.
55. Paul O'Keeffe, *Some Sort of Genius: A Life of Wyndham Lewis* (London: Pimlico, 2015), 80–8.
56. Lewis, *Rude Assignment*, 121.
57. Wyndham Lewis, 'The Code of a Herdsman', *The Essential Wyndham Lewis*, Julian Symons, ed., 123.
58. Leonard Woolf, 'The World of Books: George Borrow', *Nation and Athenaeum* 35:8 (24 May 1924): 262.
59. On Lewis's awareness of Borrow's work, see David G. Farley, *Modernist Travel Writing: Intellectuals Abroad* (Columbia, MO: University of Missouri Press, 2010), 108; Peter Carter, 'Lewis, Borrow, John and the Gitanos: a Note on a Misunderstanding', *Wyndham Lewis Annual* 2 (1998): 23–30.

endemic and exotic, mundane and grandiloquent speech acts affirms Borrow's facility for multilayered conversation set pieces in published texts which reconfigure the accepted boundaries between fiction and non-fiction. What Roland Barthes later terms 'an oral style', a 'spoken level of writing' is apparent in the sensuous immediacy of Lewis's early 'Breton Journal'. He captures 'a particular and invariable *mood* in the speaker' through the 'harsh celtic [*sic*] tongue' of native dockhands, the 'wearisome drawl' of Swedish sailors and the 'speech of Russians of the better classes'.[60] The deliberate mixing of homely and elevated registers in *The Bible in Spain*, for example, conveys the dialogic, in-the-moment staging of wrangles or clashing of cadences, when the peripatetic narrator confronts arrogant civic or religious officials. Lewis would have found this textual practice especially appealing when, in December 1909, he began drafting the prose sketches based on his continental trips to the Breton villages of Moëlan, Quimperlé, Le Pouldu, Plouhinec, and La Faouët in the previous years.

That Lewis, in his mid-twenties, found Borrow a congenial literary guide while devising his 'Brittany sketches' (1909–11) for *The Tramp*, the *English Review*, and the *New Age* was not something he wished to advertise later in his second autobiography, *Rude Assignment* (1950). In this revisionist account, Lewis takes pains to veil the nature of Borrow's influence on the style, thematic content, and assumptions of prewar vignettes which supplied 'the bedrock for his literary (and artistic) career'.[61] Instead, Lewis perpetuates what was then a caricature of the gypsy gentleman reminiscent of Conan Doyle's 'Borrowed Scenes':

> 'Wildness' of some kind or other—often more personally picturesque and romantic than mine—has been by no means an infrequent thing with the Anglo-saxon [*sic*]. As a reaction no doubt against the respectability of English life, many, like George Borrow, have gone to live in 'dingles', wandered about the earth with gypsies.[62]

Lewis's glib reference, echoed by Geoffrey Grigson in *The Shell Country Alphabet* (1966) – 'the raffish' Borrow 'expressed the century's rather

60. Roland Barthes, *Writing Degree Zero and Elements of Semiology*, trans. Annette Lavers and Colin Smith (London: Jonathan Cape, 1967), 71–2. Wyndham Lewis, 'A Breton Journal', *The Complete Wild Body*, ed. Bernard Lafourcade (Santa Barbara: Black Sparrow Press, 1982), 197.
61. See Louise Kane, 'Pre-War Writing' in *Wyndham Lewis: A Critical Guide*, Andrzej Gasiorek and Nathan Waddell, eds (Edinburgh: Edinburgh University Press, 2015), 5.
62. Wyndham Lewis, *Rude Assignment: A narrative of my career up-to-date* (London: Hutchinson & Co., 1951), 118.

inexact romantic yearnings for a gypsy freedom [. . .] in words often moving, often stilted and thin'[63] – belies the extent to which Lewis's literary evocations of the Pyrenees and the North-Western French coast utilise *The Bible in Spain*.

Lewis's aesthetic 'borrowings' – hybrid formal designs, a shifty English reporter-narrator, descriptive portraits of braggarts, swindlers, and Central European refugees in a rugged *mise-en-scène* – feature in early prose experiments like 'Crossing the Frontier'. Evoking the perils and possibilities of the Spanish border zone, this merger of travelogue, observational commentary, and Defoe-flavoured picaresque is powered by awareness of Spanish minutiae which reveal (and conceal) personality traits. Lewis's 'Bestre', 'A Spanish Household', 'Les Saltimbanques' (i.e. 'The Showmen')', 'A Soldier of Humour', *Filibusters in Barbary* (1932), and *The Revenge for Love* (1937) – all these works extend Borrow's preoccupation with the causes, functions, and consequences of social imposture, sleight of hand, and self-dramatisation. Some of the most telling encounters in *The Bible in Spain* reveal the narrator's obvious zest for legerdemain – hoodwinking potential foes on hazardous Peninsular trails. In Chapter XXX, for example, Borrow's narrator is accused of rascality, carrying 'many waistcoats about you, by means of which you disguise yourself, and appear tall or low according to your pleasure' (*BIS* XXX: 289). It is little surprise then to find that '*role*' is among the most frequently used French terms in Lewis's *Tramp*-era sketches which depict canny social actors and charlatans, garbed in 'fanciful clothing', in quest of a biddable audience with deep pockets. Perhaps the most effective example is Lewis's third *Tramp* text, from the September 1910 number, 'Le Père François', subtitled 'A Full-Length Portrait of a Tramp'. Discovered 'in front of a crowd of awestruck children', this tipsy old 'French vagabond' 'brandishing three ruined umbrellas' views himself 'as a giant in a fairy tale'.

> he wore a full grey beard and long hair falling over his shoulders, growing with an heroic and characterless sinuosity. His eyes were like a woman's—large, dark, and insinuating—his face handsome and theatrical. To look at him one would have said that the only emotion he had ever experienced was that provoked by the topical and sentimental songs of his country. He had become a very disreputable embodiment of them.[64]

63. Geoffrey Grigson, *The Shell Country Alphabet: From Apple Trees to Stone Circles, How to Understand the British Countryside* (London: Michael Joseph, 1966), 63.
64. Lewis, *The Complete Wild Body*, 277.

'Nothing,' Merleau-Ponty later explains, 'is more difficult than to know precisely what we see.'[65] Borrow is committed to this exacting perceptual exercise. We are reminded of *The Zincali*'s core claim that 'it is in the eye more than in any other feature' that the Spanish Romani 'differ from other human beings'.[66] Borrow's wandering eye in *The Zincali* invests the observing (and observed) nomad with a symbolic vitality. This prompts comparison with the embodied experience of watching closely in Lewis's *Tramp* texts, which dramatise failures to translate others' sartorial semiotics, behavioural quirks, and 'hobbyhorsical eccentricity'.[67] Lewis would later maintain, in *Time and Western Man* (1927), that he was a 'philosopher of the eye', and it is 'in the service of the things of vision that my ideas are mobilised'.[68] However, Lewis's 'Le Père François' signals and enacts the *impossibility* of apprehending 'what we see' when confronted by a 'loose-limbed' Breton ne'er-do-well who confounds the notion of a productive citizen. Lewis goes further than Ford Madox Ford's *The Heart of the Country* (1906), in which tramps are likened to 'summer ghosts', 'haunting the same countryside'. Their 'congenital lack of candour, the desire to please their interlocutor, sheer muzziness of brain, or sheer ferocity, make it difficult to discover what may be the ideal of this brown flotsam'.[69] In 'Le Père François', Lewis exploits ambiguous, oddly impersonal, and conditional clauses (especially the subjunctive) to challenge sociological generalities that seek to define 'this brown flotsam' living between the hedgerows. Lewis asks: how do we theorise a figure given that their most striking attribute is their inassimilable strangeness or enigmatic excess? What if too great a zeal for taxonomic exactitude distorts? While Borrovian cultural histories like Sir Arthur Bryant's *The National Character* (1934) and Petre Mais's *England's Character* (1936) discern essential features of the island nation in and through readable local personalities, Lewis's term 'characterless' implies a meeting with opacity, in which one must, in Édouard Glissant's lexis, 'give up this old obsession with discovering what lies at the bottom of natures'.[70]

65. Maurice Merleau-Ponty, *Phenomenology of Perception*, trans. Colin Smith (London: Routledge, 2008), 70–4.
66. George Borrow, *The Zincali: An Account of the Gypsies of Spain* (London: John Murray, 1841), 354.
67. Wyndham Lewis, *Time and Western Man*, ed. Paul Edwards (Santa Rosa: Black Sparrow Press, [1927] 1993), 455–6.
68. Wyndham Lewis, *Time and Western Man*, 392, 134.
69. Ford, *The Heart of the Country*, 43.
70. Édouard Glissant, *Poetics of Relation* (Ann Arbor: University of Michigan Press, 1990), 190.

Lewis puns on the tramp as a popular 'type' or 'character' (a mark impressed or engraved on a surface) to signify that this 'disreputable' vagabond's body is far from legible; indeed, it seems rather a blank canvas. Lewis's syntactic tentativeness ('one would have said') subverts the ordering force of Borrow's sweeping, uncorroborated assertions in *The Bible in Spain* (e.g. 'there is more hardness and less self-devotion in the disposition of the Spaniard' [*BIS* XII: 67]). Critic Dominic Head's survey of modernist short stories by James Joyce, Katherine Mansfield, and Virginia Woolf posits that these authors 'illuminate a certain aspect of character (and/or situation) in a single moment of insight'.[71] A reading strategy fuelled by an epistemic drive towards this 'insight', or the press to remove the patch that is the white drifter's identity, matters little to Lewis. His *Tramp* texts shift the weight of our attention from pursuing specificity to a space where cultural curiosity runs aground or hits an impasse. Against the familiar buzzwords of hegemonic aesthetic modernism (epiphanies, revelations, moments of rapture), Lewis withholds orienting moorings for comprehension. He stresses externalities ('large, dark eyes') that denote something at the limits of what we can decipher. Textual devices that once enabled 'faithful' representation of 'character' in a nineteenth-century naturalist-realist novel cannot bind or organise the unruly energy of Lewis's 'French vagabond'.

In the lengthy central digression of 'Le Père François', Lewis's narrator inspects the Borrovian vogue for nostalgic-romantic recreations of the literary vagabond:

> The part that [vagabonds] have played in life, now that they are out of life, and all its relations broken, they go on playing as though it were a theatrical *role.* Now that they are freest and least subject to restraint they dissemble more than ever, and their life is a constant characterisation. As [for] becoming *themselves,* stripped of all fanciful clothing, this would be the one thing that would make their unhappy life quite insupportable.[72]

Vagabonds are 'out of life' – as if they have traversed a threshold into a locus of nonbeing. Is this Lewis's attempt to signify the existential emptiness of those who try to subsist beyond the depredations of capital, stable 'relations', and obligations which invest 'human identity' with value? Here personhood becomes a panoply of brittle constructs,

71. Dominic Head, *The Modernist Short Story: A Study in Theory and Practice* (Cambridge: Cambridge University Press, 1992), 17–18.
72. Lewis, *The Complete Wild Body*, 281.

histrionic 'part[s]' or masks in a standup routine, to be donned or thrown aside depending on how each public interaction develops. In 'Le Père François', everyday habits seem to have no necessary substance outside the weird, alien, or peripheral social 'theatre' – Brittany or Galicia – that expresses them. Other contributors to *The Tramp* – like Arthur Ransome – depict Borrow's Romani pugilists and loafers as avatars of unqualified liberty and exceptional, if sometimes unlawful, mobility. For the Lewisian narrator, however, those who are 'least subject to restraint', beyond the reach of workhouses and rural labour camps, can dissolve into a rudderless psychic state ('broken', 'out of life') – tossed hither and thither amid the ill-defined confusions of advanced modernity. Sociologist Robert E. Park analysed this plight in his contribution to the seminal 1925 study *The City*. For Park, productive 'locomotion' is plotted, directed, and consolidates meaningful social ties. However, Park's vagabond, while he 'has gained his freedom', has 'lost his sense of direction'.[73] Lewis's notion of 'constant characterisation' – tomfoolery presumably distracts nomads from their own inner void – strikes a pathetic, even tragic note in this extract. The phrasing carries an echo of Jack London's conception of the vagrant who, residing at once everywhere and nowhere, and unsure how to savour fully the liberties derived from his placelessness, stands 'on the ragged edge of nonentity' in the 1897 essay 'The Road'.[74] Why does the Lewisian narrator shift from the generalised to the particular and circumstantial if it is not feasible to symbolise what is unfolding or construe the exclusions and precarity that have moulded a vagabond's 'unhappy' existence? It is notable that Borrow's irrepressibly inquisitive sensibility, diagnostic observations, and mimicry of others' verbal tics – the seal of 'a great writer' in Lewis's 1917 'Code of a Herdsman' – cannot guarantee, in this *Tramp* sketch, even partial access to the phenomenon of the Breton drifter. Perhaps it is Lewis's strategic principle to suggest that these protagonists in what Edward Thomas dubs Borrow's 'imaginative country' have become a litany of empty signs, forlorn 'bits' of character-drawing that neither cohere nor explicate. In the *Tramp* stories this is frequently the fate of such idlers and chancers, and it is that fate which warrants the nuance and effort of our critical scrutiny. Lewis's white nomads are either castaways and ciphers like Père François, or they

73. E. W. Burgess and Robert E. Park, eds, *The City* (Chicago: University of Chicago Press, 1925), 158.
74. Jack London, 'The Road', *Jack London Reports: War Correspondence, Sports Articles, and Miscellaneous Writings*, King Hendricks and Irving Shepard, eds (New York: Doubleday, 1970), 311–21.

seek sanctuary on the equivocal stage of the *pension*, having found it impossible to realise the promise of non-attachment, shaking oneself loose from a communal setting, unmoored from any society. This is why inns and boarding-houses – so diligently rendered in Borrow's *Wild Wales* such as the '*Tafarn Tywarch*' (Turf Tavern, Chapter XV) – feature prominently, indeed almost exclusively, in Lewis's early prose texts. Such venues, like the quick-witted rogues who haunt them, belong to no one, an aspect which Lewis explores further in the non-Breton story 'Unlucky for Pringle', which appeared a month before the final issue of *The Tramp*. The main difference between Borrow's narrator in *Wild Wales* and Lewisian boarding guests or *pensionnaires* is that through the former we register a palpable domain of crisply specified collective obligations and contracts. Borrow's narrator pays (sometimes liberally) for his bed and repast, is quick to glorify prompt service, witty discourse, and fine ale at Llangollen (Chapter LVI). However, Lewis's 'Pole', from an early story of the same name, is a scoundrel who will never have sufficient coin and even if he did would not remunerate his hosts. The generic Pole's social 'acts' are largely consequence-free, untethered from the economic actualities that *Wild Wales* crystallises through debates with various hoteliers, landlords, barmaids, and topers. The motley crowd of pubgoers and commercial travellers who make fleeting appearances in Borrow's text are, by and large, gregarious personalities who labour hard and relish sharing the latest news and views. Such georgic values and respect for precepts of solidarity and social relationship are crucial to D. H. Lawrence in his account of Brescian peasantry in his 1916 travelogue *Twilight in Italy*, which appeared a few years after Lewis's *Tramp* texts. However, communal zest is singularly lacking in Lewis's *Tramp* tales, as is any hint of genuine goodwill among the Breton kulaks, drunken freeloaders, and deracinated East Europeans. Even the innkeepers of Brest who house émigré artists exploit their young guests by accepting canvases in lieu of coin – works they can then sell for a handsome profit to metropolitan art connoisseurs. In a counterblast to the pre-industrial Celtic idylls of bestselling Borrovian romancer Robert W. Chambers, whose *The King in Yellow* (1895) conjures a serene 'Breton forest where sunlight filtered through spring foliage',[75] Lewis renders a torpid post-industrial enclave where visions of Gallic amity and organic plenitude are replaced by a mean-spirited, grubby parochialism. The lodging-houses and their environs are as threadbare and atomised as the Polish cities from which the *pensionnaire* has fled.

75. Robert W. Chambers, 'The Yellow Sign', *The King in Yellow* (London, 1895), 54.

Forty years later, in *Rude Assignment*, Lewis struck a Lawrentian note when revisiting the *Tramp* sketches: 'The "Wild Body" I envisaged as a piece of the wilderness. The characters I chose to celebrate—Bestre, the Cornac and his wife, Brotcotnaz, le père Francois—were all primitive creatures, immersed in life, as much as birds, or big, obsessed, sun-drunk insects'.[76] Lewis's lexis – 'immersed in life' that is Mediterranean, fecund, and Dionysiac – stands in stark contrast to what *The Tramp* sketches show us. Le père Francois is a creature 'out of life', disinherited and divorced from any sun-drenched pastoral paradise. Lewis re-visions the Borrovian beggar to appear more atavistic than primitivistic, locked into hollow rites of mask-wearing that barely conceal a numbing stasis. In truth, we are as far from Lawrence's blood-vitalism or Gaugin's territory here as we are from the genial wanderers who savour the wind on Borrow's heath in Maurice Hewlett's *Open Country*.

Shortly after *The Tramp* was wound up, Ford Madox Ford, from whose *English Review* Lewis had decamped to Goldring's (slightly better-paying) magazine, wrote a lengthy and carefully pondered article concerning the 'gorgeously English' Borrow for the weekly periodical *Outlook* to coincide with the 110th anniversary of Borrow's birth in 1913. This descriptor, coupled with the title of his earlier text *The Heart of the Country* (1906), implies that Ford had been swayed by the very Edwardian open-air clichés – the artist-tramp 'who loves the road for its own sake'[77] – that Conan Doyle and Lewis variously debunk. However, while Conan Doyle's story situates the author of *Lavengro* and *The Romany Rye* as a sadly diminished cultural phenomenon ripe for spoof, Ford was among those more formally ambitious cultural producers who burnished the 'singular' Borrow's posthumous popularity by looking beyond the facile tramping brand. Lewis admitted, in a letter to Ezra Pound after Ford's death in 1939, that he was no 'Fordie-fan'. However, Lewis would have appreciated, given the content and tenor of his own *Tramp* narratives, how Ford uses Borrow to unpick discourses about migration, non-attachment, corporeal mobility, and nationality. Ford's *Outlook* piece is particularly focused on the links and frictions between cosmopolitan indicators of modernity within specific nation-states and the shift of indigenous cultures as a result.[78]

> Mrs. Florence Gay [. . .] commits herself to the statement, 'Cosmopolitanism is the slayer of art.' [. . .] if Mrs. Gay will modify

76. Lewis, *Rude Assignment*, 118.
77. Ford, *The Heart of the Country*, 41.
78. Jeffrey Meyers, *The Enemy: A Biography of Wyndham Lewis* (London: Routledge, 1980), 29.

> her dictum to the extent of saying that many great artists have been in the highest sense the expressers of national ideals, I think I can agree with her. [. . .] And even for very national writers, their art is an extraordinarily international affair. Where, for instance, would Borrow have been without his Spanish travel, his Welsh, Irish, Norse, and gipsy studies [. . .] or his passion for the picturesque in the philology of fifty nations? Yet who was more gorgeously English than George Borrow?[79]

Ford, confessing that he has '*The Romany Rye* at this moment almost by heart', invites us to confront Borrow the paradox. The fiercely patriotic East Anglian who cleaves to local legacies, the traditional politics, laws and religious customs of his homeland, exists alongside a gifted internationalist with knowledge of 'the philology of fifty nations'. The craving for company and attention among foreign enclaves recounted in his books seems, to some observers, irreconcilable with his stated beliefs. Borrow's most extraordinary characteristic, Ford claims, is in how the petty provincialism of a self-avowed 'East Englishman' (*LSGP* XXXI: 221) and the amused tolerance of 'the Ulysses of the writing fraternity',[80] one who easily gains the trust of Spaniards, Jews, Romani, and Moors, accommodate one another. They do so in such a way that neither of these apparently conflicting traits loses one iota of its fervour. Borrow's occasionally blinkered and dourly conservative defence of 'national ideals' – we recall his bloviating on effete Englishmen who ape Gallic fashions in *The Romany Rye*'s Appendix ('On Foreign Nonsense') – is matched by an equally avid desire to play a citizen of the world, wandering among strangers in those remote corners of Western Europe that Lewis's *Tramp* tales portray. Ford's conclusion is this: Borrow is 'gorgeously English' because his 'gipsy studies' transcend Edwardian pastoral platitudes of 'the "good brown earth"' that Ford ascribes, in *Ancient Lights* (1911), to the literary influence of W. E. Henley.[81] If only Borrow could have exercised a principled cosmopolitanism in the company of equally fearless fellow travellers then he might have shed some of the

79. Ford Madox Ford, 'Literary Portraits – X.: Mr. Clement Shorter and *Borrow and His Circle*', *Outlook* (London) 32 (November 1913): 677–8. See also Helen Southworth, '"That Subtle and Difficult Thing: A National Spirit": Ford, Anglo-Saxondom and the "Gorgeously English" George Borrow', *Ford Madox Ford's Literary Contacts*, International Ford Madox Ford Studies 6, ed. Paul Skinner (Amsterdam: Rodopi, 2007), 25–39.
80. [Anon.], 'Literature', *Athenaeum* 3726 (25 March 1899): 361–2.
81. Ford Madox Hueffer, *Ancient Lights* (London: Chapman, 1911), 241–2.

bias of his native culture and assumed the mantle of 'a greater Defoe – a Defoe with a touch of poetry':

> So that there again we come to cosmopolitanism, since, given what these kingdoms are, cosmopolitanism is here almost the only practicable form of co-operation. English writers simply will not meet, mix, and from day-to-day exchange views about their jobs. It is impossible to bring them together. [. . .] So it was more or less with Borrow [. . .] imagine what might have happened to Borrow if he had come into weekly contact with the Goncourts, Flaubert, Maupassant [. . .] and even with Sainte-Beuve or Turguenieff.[82]

That Ford measures Borrow against the wayfaring 'Stevenson' in this article is telling. The latter's 1887 essay collection *Memories and Portraits* positions *The Bible in Spain* as one of those highly prized volumes that 'we re-read' and 'revisit' as 'we choose and revisit human friends'.[83] While John Buchan's 1895 obituary of Stevenson for the *Glasgow University Magazine* described its subject as at once scholar and gypsy, sage observer of Scottish mores and global adventurer, Ford construes Stevenson as an isolated pilgrim here.[84] Like Borrow, Stevenson's art would have benefited immeasurably from those cross-Channel literary interactions that Ford and Lewis cultivated throughout their own careers as novelists and cultural pundits.

Ford's 1913 article on cosmopolitanism for *Outlook* was not his last word on Borrow's oeuvre. Nearly a decade later, in *Thus to Revisit: Some Reminiscences* (1921), Ford returns to Borrow's complex status as a 'very national writer', and how it is indissolubly tied to questions of narration:

> I do not know how high the reader may be inclined to rate George Borrow. [. . .] rate him high or low, you cannot get away from the conviction that most of his facts are nonsense, whether in the *Bible in Spain* or in *Lavengro*—and that when they are not nonsense, they are mendacities. Yet these very nonsenses and mendacities give to his work such literary quality as it has—for [. . .] they make you intimate with the true George Borrow.

82. Ford Madox Hueffer [Ford Madox Ford], 'Ford, Literary Portraits – X.: Mr. Clement Shorter and *Borrow and His Circle*', *Outlook* (London) 32 (November 1913): 677–8.
83. Robert Louis Stevenson, 'A Gossip on a Novel of Dumas's', *Memories and Portraits* (New York: Scribner's, 1887), 228.
84. JB [John Buchan], 'Robert Louis Stevenson', *Glasgow University Magazine* 7 (9 January 1895): 141–3.

Ford contends that the 'true George Borrow' is an adroit fabricator who produces Bunyanesque 'similitudes'. This version of 'Borrow' bespeaks one who will not entirely 'draw up the curtain of his own eventful biography'[85] – a narrative strategy refined in *Thus to Revisit*. Rather than chiding Borrow, like the 1899 *Daily News*, as 'constitutionally careless in such matters [as] dates' – even culpable of a wilful counterfeit of personhood – Ford prioritises how *Lavengro* epitomises an experiment in life-writing that scumbles the textual frontier between 'dry as dust facts' and high-spirited 'nonsense' about the island nation and his place/lessness within it.[86] Ford learned the lessons of *Lavengro* well. In *Ancient Lights* (1911), for example, Ford's narrator proudly declares that '[t]his book' is 'full of inaccuracies as to facts, but its accuracy as to impressions is absolute'.[87] In *Ancient Lights* and *Thus to Revisit* Ford signifies that Borrow's narrative disruptions and professions of familiarity with places he had never visited undermine glib comparison with the most noteworthy (pseudo-)autobiographies, such as Thomas De Quincey's stylistically elaborate *Confessions of an English Opium Eater* (1821–2) or Carlyle's *Sartor Resartus*. These rival texts illustrate personalities whose rambles (in mind and body) are very different from those of Borrow's polyglot pugilist, blacksmith, and scribe. Thomas Seccombe claimed in 1902 that Borrow's 'surest source of inspiration was the unadorned truth'. However, Lewis's *Tramp* works and Ford's *Thus to Revisit* variously underscore that *Lavengro* and *The Romany Rye* pose persistently riddling questions about verisimilitude, spectatorship, and those deeper seams of fantasy, frustrated yearning, and myth activated by Leonard Bast's reaction to natural terrain in *Howards End*, for example.[88] What seemed scrappy, vain, and open for ridicule to early Anglo-American reviewers – Borrow's 'casual opening up and fading out of episodes and situations that we call Life'[89] – was for Ford a sign of 'literary quality'.

Lewis and Ford were not the only modernist novelists to address the truth-status and imagery of outsidership in *The Bible in Spain* and *Lavengro*. Debating Borrow's appealingly unorthodox texture of

85. [Anon.], '*The Bible in Spain*', *Edinburgh Review* 77:155 (February 1843): 113.
86. [Anon.], 'The Author of *The Bible in Spain*', *Daily News* 16525 (13 March 1899): 15; Ford Madox Ford, *Thus to Revisit: Some Reminiscences* (New York: E. P. Dutton, 1921), 190–1. See also John M. Robson, 'Review: Michael Collie, *George Borrow: Eccentric*', *Albion* 15:4 (Winter 1983): 366.
87. Ford, *Ancient Lights*, xv.
88. Thomas Seccombe, 'The Reader. George Borrow: His Homes and Haunts', *The Bookman* 21:125 (February 1902): 158.
89. Gerald Brenan, *The Literature of the Spanish People*, 2nd ed. (Cambridge: Cambridge University Press, 1953), 449.

thought in his mock memoirs was a family affair for Leslie Stephen and Virginia and Leonard Woolf. Like her husband and sister Vanessa Bell, Virginia Woolf admired Borrow's novelistic, anecdotal texts that cross genres between memoir and travelogue.[90] In what appears to be her first published response to Borrow's oeuvre, an astute 1905 piece concerning 'Journeys in Spain', Woolf scrutinises her literary antecedent's unusual 'faculty of seeing':

> Sterne, when he invented the title of *Sentimental Journey*, not only christened but called into existence a class of book which seems to grow more popular the more we travel and the more sentimental we become. It is their aim to include all that Baedeker ignores; but as their aim is more ambitious so is their success very rarely so complete. [. . .] Sterne succeeded and so did Borrow and Kinglake [. . .] They owe their success not to any strangeness in the things they saw or to any adventures they met with on the way, but to the faculty of seeing they had in them and of interpreting the sight to others. A book such as this is as much a guidebook to the mind of the man that wrote it as it is to any definite region of the earth's surface. [. . .] *The Bible in Spain*, for instance, gives a clear portrait of Borrow and of Spain, but it would be hard to say where Spain ends and Borrow begins.[91]

Here Woolf revels in what many of the 1850s Anglo-American professional critics bewailed: travel writing that downplays rigorous documentation of local landmarks, flora, and fauna in favour of painting a portrait of the artist as a young 'open-airist'.[92] As she does again later in her *Pointz Hall* typescript, Woolf situates Borrow alongside Alexander Kinglake and Sterne as purveyors of 'sentimental journeys'. These are not authors who will pique the interest of 'tourists', as her father Leslie Stephen defines them in his essay 'Vacation': 'notoriously a person who follows blindly a certain hackneyed round'.[93] As an antidote to the drab conventionalities of the Baedeker on which these tourists 'blindly' rely,

90. On Leonard Woolf's 'love of Borrow', see his article 'Coming to London – II', *The London Magazine* 2:10 (October 1955): 49–54; Leonard Woolf, 'The World of Books: George Borrow', *The Nation and the Athenaeum* 35:8 (24 May 1924): 262.
91. Virginia Woolf, 'Journeys in Spain' [1905], *The Essays of Virginia Woolf. Vol. I: 1904–1912* (London: Hogarth Press, 1986), 44–6. See also Gillian Fenwick, 'An Annotated Checklist of References to Borrow in Virginia Woolf's Writings', *George Borrow Bulletin* 4 (Autumn 1992): 13–17.
92. See [Anon], 'The Wind on the Heath', *Country Life* 34:862 (12 July 1913): 38.
93. Leslie Stephen, 'Vacation', *Men, Books, and Mountains: Essays by Leslie Stephen* (London: Hogarth Press, 1956), 174.

The Bible in Spain gives us, in Woolf's estimation, a deeply personal and – as she puts it in her 1919 *TLS* obituary on 'Lady Ritchie'[94] – 'queer country of the imagination'. Edward Thomas also affirms this feature through his 1912 account of Borrow's unofficial topographies in *George Borrow: The Man and His Books*. The title of Chapter 23 in Thomas's biography – 'Between the Acts' – reminds us of the late novel where Woolf undertakes her own sedulous excavation of an England 'of the imagination', one that resists the forces of fascist nationalism gathering overseas.

It is not just *The Bible in Spain* that snags Woolf's attention; in other reviews over the next decade, she identifies Borrow increasingly with literary figures whose neo-romantic credentials are underlined by their impressionistic mapping of the island nation's distinctive contours and communities. In her 1917 article on Edward Thomas's *A Literary Pilgrim in England*, Woolf proposes: 'When that "sense of England", as Mr Thomas calls it, comes over us driving us to seek a book that expresses it, we turn to the prose writers most probably – to Borrow, Hardy, the Brontës, Gilbert White.'[95] That 'sense of England' will reach its fullest articulation in Woolf's *Between the Acts*, though the text does not mention Borrow by name.[96] For Woolf in 1917, *Lavengro* renders 'to perfection' 'those portraits of queer people'.[97] Perfection because, as Woolf declared a year later concerning 'The "Movie" Novel' (1918): we 'can think' of 'Isopel [Berners]' or 'the Flaming Tinman' and 'how much of England is their background' even when 'we are no longer reading' *Lavengro* and *The Romany Rye* – such is the indelible imprint 'Borrow's central characters make on us'.[98] As Helen Southworth remarks, Woolf's admiring account demonstrates how Borrow's literary profile had risen considerably among a Bloomsbury clique keen to explore the historical complexity of the local regions, especially Wiltshire, Dorset, and Cornwall with their prehistoric tumuli, cromlechs, and downland escarpments. Such layered landscapes would dominate the visual and verbal texts of British neo-romantic artists leading up to the outbreak of World War II.

94. See Virginia Woolf, 'Lady Ritchie', *The Essays of Virginia Woolf, Volume III*, 14. Woolf assigns Borrow's 'absolute individuality' to the fact that he was 'so queerly adjusted to the world' that his vision 'reveals a new aspect of things'.
95. Virginia Woolf, 'Flumina Amem Silvasque', *The Essays of Virginia Woolf, Volume II 1912–1918*, ed. Andrew McNeillie (London: Hogarth Press, 1987), 163.
96. Borrow does make a fleeting appearance in Woolf's Pointz Hall typescript, however. In this draft, Isa Oliver enumerates the contents of the library: 'Borrow, *Bible in Spain*. Kinglake's Crimea'.
97. Virginia Woolf, *The Essays of Virginia Woolf, Volume II*, 111.
98. Virginia Woolf, 'The "Movie" Novel', *The Essays of Virginia Woolf, Volume II*, 290. See also Woolf, 'Men and Women', *The Essays of Virginia Woolf, Volume III 1919–1924*, ed. Andrew McNeillie (London: Hogarth Press, 1988), 194.

BORROW AND BRITISH NEO-ROMANTICISM

The Woolfs published subtle responses to new editions of Borrow's texts at precisely that time when a member of their friendship network, the journalist and literary editor Raymond Mortimer, was investigating a post-Cubist development in printmaking, the fine and decorative arts, photography, and theatre design. Mortimer's February 1928 'London Letter' for *The Dial* magazine situated Virginia Woolf as one with the sensibility of a 'romantic poet' – a writer alert to a cluster of intermingled aesthetic experiences that he labelled more precisely in a 1942 *New Statesman* review as 'neo-romanticism'.[99] Mortimer was conscious that deploying this unifying term was a risky endeavour given that this loose confederacy of artists had issued no mission statement. Nevertheless, Mortimer argued that such cultural producers are

> more capricious and less concerned with rationalizing the world of phenomena than most artists in the past have been: they are in revolt against the European tradition of humanism. The appeal of their art, I fancy, is to mystics and particularly to pantheists who feel a fraternity, or even a unity, with all living things, to those with the 'sense sublime of something far more deeply interfused.'[100]

At first glance, Mortimer's pointed allusion to Wordsworth's *Tintern Abbey* ('sense sublime') seems to chime with the attitudes, affectations, and habits of Borrovian weekend trampers like Leonard Bast who crave a fleeting pantheistic link 'with all living things' in *Howards End.* Closer scrutiny of Mortimer's article suggests a more serious effort to gauge the semiotics, institutional links, and public profile of a British avant-garde spearheaded by the landscape painters Paul Nash, John Piper, and Graham Sutherland. The Woolfs were aware of Nash's work as a war artist and professional journalist; his wood engravings feature in the 1925 *Chap Book (A Miscellany) no. 40*, alongside Leonard Woolf's short essay concerning 'obscurity' in 'ultra-modern literature'.[101]

For the young Nash, reading *Lavengro* proved decisive; it showed him Borrow's skill in recharging native geographical localities with

99. Raymond Mortimer, 'London Letter', *The Dial* (28 February 1928): 240.
100. Raymond Mortimer, 'Painting and Humanism', *New Statesman and Nation* 23:579 (28 March 1942): 208.
101. Harold Munro, ed., *The Chap Book (A Miscellany) no. 40* (London: Jonathan Cape, 1925), 7. For Nash's wood engravings see 56, 58.

sacramental suggestiveness.[102] When, in Chapter LX of *Lavengro*, Borrow's narrator proclaims, the 'spirit of Stonehenge was strong upon me!' (*LSGP* 319), we find a template for Nash's lifelong interest in rendering what he termed the '*genius loci*' ('spirit of a place'), an imprisoned force that reveals the 'reality of another aspect of the accepted' sensory, phenomenal milieu.[103] Nash finds in Borrow's portrayals of Stonehenge and other imperilled prehistoric residues a feature that Edward Thomas also pinpoints around the same time in *A Literary Pilgrim in England* (1917): Lavengro's 'business was not with forms, but with atmosphere'. It was, Thomas avers, 'what he saw *in it* [the material terrain]', not just 'what was there for the photographer, that mattered'.[104]

Borrow's novel – 'isn't *Lavengro* one of the finest books ever writ!' Nash excitedly declared to his friend, the poet and art collector

Figure 2 Paul Nash, 'Lavengro and Isopel in the Dingle' (1912–13). Item No. T01782 reproduced with kind permission from the Tate, London

102. The Nash of 1909–11 idealised 'Pan' and 'the hospitality of the woods and hedgerows' and read 'tramper poet' W. H. Davies (who was later to purchase two of Nash's watercolours, according to biographer Andrew Causey). See Causey, *Paul Nash* (Oxford: Oxford University Press, 1981), 18.
103. Paul Nash, *Paul Nash: Writings on Art*, ed. and intro. Andrew Causey (Oxford: Oxford University Press, 2000), 109.
104. Thomas, *A Literary Pilgrim in England*, 252–3.

Gordon Bottomley' in 1911 – inspired the subject of Nash's important early illustration: *Lavengro and Isopel in the Dingle* (1912–13).[105]

In his unfinished autobiography *Outline*, drafted in the mid-1930s, Nash recalled 'those strange beings, the roving scholar and that attractive enigma, Isopel Berners of Long Melford. The tentative relationship of these two, so dramatically met, thrown together and abandoned like shipwreck survivors on a deserted island, stirred my imagination.'[106] Nash's small drawing (ink, graphite, and gouache on paper) eventually appeared in the second number of the short-lived magazine *The Gypsy* (May 1916), and is currently housed in the Tate, London.[107] The illustration, designed in shallow space and at first blush tranquil, even contemplative in mood, portrays Borrow's tinker-narrator sitting with Isopel Berners, teaching her the rudiments of Armenian amid the deep, wooded valley which they share. Nash captures what is in the source text a moment of sad miscommunication and stymied mutual attraction. Borrow's eponymous protagonist cannot respond to Isopel's craving for simple tenderness because in place of her emotional maturity he has only toothless pedantry and a deep fear of his own instinctual promptings. The apparent intimacy of their campfire engagements (such as their tea-drinking ritual) exposes a tragic disconnect. All their verbal and non-verbal exchanges in *Lavengro* – neither romantic nor sexual – reveals a gulf that will never be bridged, thus triggering Isopel's sudden departure.

Borrow's staging of this encounter struck Nash as one that was rich in artistic possibility: 'Borrow, for I did not doubt that it represented himself, would never allow nature to take its course, as it were. Isopel might sigh and he might want her, but it was obvious he was tied up in one of his perverse knots and could only fall back on his usual habit of teaching or preaching something for which his audience had no ear.'[108] The 'real poetry' that Nash detects in Borrow's scene points to a common thread traceable through Nash's 'Lavengro' drawing as well as his other mystical works from this period, such as his 1911 watercolour 'The Wanderer', in which he evokes a Borrovian figure who, entering woodland, has left a trail etched through cornfields.[109]

105. Gordon Bottomley and Paul Nash, *Poet & Painter: Letters between Gordon Bottomley and Paul Nash 1910–1946*, intro. Andrew Causey (Bristol: Redcliffe, 1980), 27.
106. Paul Nash, *Outline*, 83–4.
107. *The Gypsy* journal only ran for two numbers (May 1915) and (May 1916).
108. Paul Nash, *Outline*, 83–4.
109. On Nash's fascination with Borrow's 'lush evocations of vagabond gypsy life', see James King, *Interior Landscapes: A Life of Paul Nash* (London: Weidenfeld and Nicolson, 1987), 99.

Figure 3 Paul Nash, 'The Wanderer' (1911). British Museum number 1958,0303.1. Reproduced with kind permission from the British Museum Company.

We see Nash here rethinking the visionary rural hinterlands associated with William Blake and Samuel Palmer by making the familiar trappings of the 'home/land' seem strange – a tactic that Borrow also employs in his reaction to the Standing Stones.[110] From beneath the familiar crust of outward appearances – the 'barrows and great walls of earth' (*LSGP* LX: 309) on Salisbury Plain, for example – Borrow hints at untapped animistic potencies.[111] Nash would label Borrow's alertness to the uncanny pulse of these gaunt derelictions as the 'living inanimate' in his interwar art criticism. This is why, in *Outline*, the 'vivid pictures of England' painted by the 'vigorous personality of Lavengro' are, to his mind, unique and unforgettable: 'I had found nothing like it. This was poetry of a new kind' – a poetry that repudiates the pastoral prettiness of Hewlett's *Open Country* to detail the undulating heathlands, burial mounds, Iron Age hillforts,

110. For a detailed account of these illustrations, see Causey, *Paul Nash*, 40–1.

111. Paul Nash, *Outline: An Autobiography*, ed. and intro. David Boyd Haycock (London: Lund Humphries, 2016), 60.

and blackened gorse of a deeper England, characterised by 'dread peculiarity'.[112]

In a March 1912 letter to Bottomley, Nash asks:

> How are you? it is so long since word came of or from you. I have been rather silent too being busy with a drawing of dire importance. 'Tis of Isobel [Isopel] & Lavengro in the dingle and I have thought of little else for weeks. First I looked cannily around for my models and lo! found first Isobel then Lavengro in real living friends [. . .] Of these I made two good drawings—at least they were good compared with any I have ever done afore, and then after thinking & walking & exploring & experimenting evolved a good dingle.[113]

For Nash, the 'Lavengro' sketch had become 'a drawing of dire importance' in terms of his aesthetic growth. It afforded an escape route from 'those little close rooms of Rossetti's', so enabling him to traverse 'open spaces' instead. 'Led by the voice of Lavengro I followed on to the heath.'[114] It was a drawing that Bottomley, near the close of World War I, judged as one of Nash's early 'masterpieces'. The reasoning behind Bottomley's high estimation is not difficult to fathom. That the work conveyed 'a singular and enchanting rapture', in Bottomley's words, is due to Nash's pursuit of the *genius loci* – the exacting, lifelong process of discovering the natural environment in a deeply personal manner for himself (as keenly felt sensation) rather than relying on the idealised 'tramp' fiction Nash had enjoyed as a young man, like W. J. Locke's *The Blessed Vagabond* (1906).[115] Whatever resonance the 'Lavengro and Isopel' encounter may have carried for Nash, the modest drawing retains a striking painterly signature, even more so when measured against the densely textured oils of gypsophile Augustus John or the mundane urban interiors rendered by Walter Sickert and the Camden Town Group. Nash's drawing is conceived and executed in such a way that it does not lend itself completely to a single interpretation. As Mortimer's definition of the neo-romantics implies ('less concerned with rationalizing the world of phenomena'), the 'poetry' of Nash's illustrative

112. Paul Nash, *Shell Guide to Dorset* (London: Architectural Press, 1936), 9–10.

113. Gordon Bottomley and Paul Nash, *Poet & Painter: Letters between Gordon Bottomley and Paul Nash 1910–1946*, intro. Andrew Causey (Bristol: Redcliffe, 1980), 30. Nash's model for Lavengro was the Slade student Rupert Lee. Nash's friend Mercia Oakley, whom he described as 'a gypsy-like girl', was the model for Isopel.

114. See Causey, *Paul Nash*, 43.

115. Gordon Bottomley and Paul Nash, *Poet & Painter: Letters between Gordon Bottomley and Paul Nash 1910–1946*, intro. Andrew Causey (Bristol: Redcliffe, 1980), 88.

technique resides in his refusal to let the interaction between Borrow's protagonists assume the glib human meanings and dimensions that the lingering trace of Pre-Raphaelitism in Nash's graphic style seems to promise. This is largely because of how Nash renders the backdrop, whose pyramidal shape is oddly replicated in the two figures, each of whom assumes a pyramidal form. For critic Andrew Causey, 'Lavengro makes one pyramid, and his legs alone a subsidiary one, Isopel makes a third, and the whole composition, figures and trees together, makes a fourth'. Nash's visual syntax and grammar points to an arcane lyrical language; it is related to, yet exists beyond, Mortimer's notion of a school of modern British landscape painting that reprogrammes eighteenth-century pantheistic romanticism. After World War I, Nash's canvases, collages, and photography map the bare solitudes of Wessex, the south-western tip of Pembrokeshire, as well as other Celtic shrines that Borrow surveys in *Wild Wales*. Taken together, Nash's visual texts comprise a remarkable 'retopographizing' of the British Isles, to employ David Mellor's coinage.[116]

A Second Borrow? Walter Starkie

By the time Paul Nash died in 1946, it appeared that his 'audience had no ear' for either neo-romantic cultural production or the figure who had inspired some his own early sketches and watercolours, George Borrow.[117] V. S. Pritchett also complained that 'we have suffered so much from our [. . .] flagon-thumpers' who 'have turned' the Borrovian 'wind on the heath into a monotonous literary draught'.[118] If 'the ghost of George Borrow'[119] no longer seemed to haunt the work of European vanguardists like Wyndham Lewis, his presence could still be felt in more crowd-pleasing literary genres. Permeating Lady Eleanor Smith's romantic interwar fiction – *Red Wagon* (1930), her first novel, which sold over fifty thousand copies, *Flamenco* (1931), *Tzigane* (1935), *Romany* (1935), *The Spanish House* (1938), *Caravan* (1943) – is a feeling that Borrow personifies, as she explains in her memoir *Life's a Circus* (1939), 'a younger, sweeter, half-forgotten England'.[120] Arguably the genre best

116. See Causey, *Paul Nash*, 40–3; David Mellor, *A Paradise Lost: The Neo-Romantic Imagination in Britain 1935–55* (London: Barbican, 1987), 34–5. See also Helen Southworth, 'Virginia Woolf's "Wild England": George Borrow, Autoethnography and *Between the Acts*', *Studies in the Novel* 39:2 (Summer 2007): 196–215.
117. Paul Nash, *Outline*, 83–4.
118. V. S. Pritchett, '*Raggle Taggle* by Walter Starkie', *Fortnightly Review* 133 (June 1933): 806.
119. Walter Starkie, *In Sara's Tents*, 182.
120. Eleanor Smith, *Life's a Circus*, 37.

equipped to illustrate 'half-forgotten' Romani lore and what Smith termed the 'decay of Borrow's England' was the popular travelogue, given its factual, documentary recording of routes interspersed with highly spiced anecdotes rather than diligent ethnographic appraisal.[121] Smith recalls, in *Life's a Circus*, a supper party at the Café Royal which she had attended with a 'gipsy girl' named Aurora:

> At the next table I saw Professor Starkie who was dining with his publisher, Mr Murray. I introduced Aurora to the gipsy professor, and we all went on to John Murray's publishing house. Here Aurora danced the *faruca* while Starkie played the fiddle. This party took place in the very room where 'Don Jorge' signed his first contract with the original John Murray, and I think the ghost of Borrow must have haunted our party.[122]

Here Smith portrays the folklorist Walter Starkie (1894–1976), who was appointed first Professor of Spanish at Trinity College Dublin in 1926 and President of the Gypsy Lore Society from 1962 to 1973.[123] Starkie's knowledge of Romani language, song, and the art of flamenco, documented in his *Spain: A Musician's Journey Through Time and Space* (1958), was as encyclopaedic as his style of conveying it was chatty and jocular. Across a prolific and decades-long publishing career, which included penning a preface to the 1960 Everyman's Library reissue of *Lavengro*, Starkie presented himself, in the words of the *Field* magazine, as 'A Second Borrow'.[124] Starkie's myriad travelogues were all released by Borrow's publisher John Murray, commencing with *Raggle-Taggle: Adventures with a Fiddle in Hungary and Romania* (1933) and continuing through to *Scholars and Gypsies* (1963), an autobiography that evokes both the subtitle of *Lavengro* and Matthew Arnold's poem published two years later in 1853.[125] Through all these works, and in a clear tribute to Borrow's storytelling panache, Starkie fuses multiple textual identities – the pilgrim, the obsessional traveller, the academic fieldworker and philologist, the mendicant, and, in the case of *Raggle-Taggle*, a wandering minstrel.

121. Eleanor Smith, *Life's a Circus*, 37.
122. Eleanor Smith, *Life's a Circus*, 209–10.
123. See also Kenneth Barrett, 'A Scholar and Gypsy about Gypsy Borrow – Walter Starkie's relationship to the Borrow Gypsy ideal', *George Borrow Bulletin* 40 (Spring 2010): 89–105.
124. [R. M.], 'New Books. A Second Borrow: Professor Starkie Takes the Road', *The Field* 167:4357 (27 June 1936): 1581.
125. See Starkie, *Raggle-Taggle* (1933), *Spanish Raggle-Taggle* (1934), *Don Gypsy* (1936), *The Waveless Plain* (1938), *In Sara's Tents* (1953), and *Scholars and Gypsies* (1963).

Dora Yates, de facto secretary of the Gypsy Lore Society, had argued in *My Gypsy Days* (1953) that Borrow had intentionally 'misled readers by mingling fiction with fact' when recording 'his own life'.[126] The same accusation could be levelled at the mercurial first-person narrator of *Raggle-Taggle* or the 'arrant sentimentalist' in *Don Gypsy*. Both texts recall Borrow's policy of 'slipping', as the 1936 *Observer* put it, 'whenever possible into a Romani skin'.[127] Starkie's protean narrator in *Raggle-Taggle* charts the 'grim realities of modern city life', its mechanical vulgarities, in pointedly sartorial terms. To embark on a trek through his own fantasies as a maverick maestro or mid-century Lazarillo de Tormes, the 'toga of respectability' – the oppressive raiment of a university don – must be cast aside.[128] So in Chapter II, a '*contadino* who worked in our garden gave me his rough costume and boots. It was very important not to be too well dressed if one wanted to follow the calling of a vagabond' and sidestep 'the appearance of an ordinary tourist'.[129] The narrator tries on for size a range of social poses to discern where he truly belongs, to locate his own centre. He is, by turns, a 'hardy, chronic tramp', 'not [. . .] a normal man', an Irish *flaneur*, a 'mad Englishman' with 'wild ideas', a footsore 'fiddler' living on the coin collected in his hat – echoing the episodic, 'headily hybrid' design of *Lavengro* and *The Romany Rye*.[130] This is most explicit in how *Raggle-Taggle* switches at intervals from first-person narrative to the layout of dialogue as featured in *The Bible in Spain*. The exchange between 'Demetrius Kármán' and 'Myself' in Chapter XXIII ('On the Road in Transylvania') is particularly Borrovian in its 'stagey' lexis and modulations.

The costume changes and tonal gear-shifts in Starkie's travelogues between 1933 and 1958 – features also felt even in his putatively 'straight histories' like *Grand Inquisitor* (1940) – are pervaded, as Jacqueline Hurtley rightly notes, by 'an atmosphere of carnival'.[131] That the narrator self-identifies as a 'fiddler' – at once dabbling in folk-music, social criticism, street performance, ethnographic fieldwork – also puns

126. Dora Yates, *My Gypsy Days: Recollections of a Romani Rawni* (London, 1953), 11.
127. See Walter Starkie, *Don Gypsy* (London: John Murray, 1936), 417; [R. A. G.], 'Spanish Raggle-Taggle', *Manchester Guardian* (14 November 1934): 5; [Anon.], 'Books and Authors', *The Observer* (31 May 1936): 6.
128. Starkie, *Raggle-Taggle*, 6.
129. Starkie, *Raggle-Taggle*, 7–8.
130. Jacqueline Hurtley, *Walter Starkie 1894–1976*, 123–4.
131. Jacqueline Hurtley, *Walter Starkie 1894–1976*, 123; Kenneth Barrett, 'A Scholar and Gypsy about Gypsy Borrow', 89–93; Walter Starkie, *Grand Inquisitor: Being an Account of Cardinal Ximenes de Cisneros and His Times* (London: Hodder and Stoughton, 1940).

on Starkie's attitude to truth-telling as well as travel-writing as *bricolage*. This implies a self-reflexive, strategic, and canny patchwork of citations, sources, and genres that strives for the spontaneity of utterance that Borrow attains in his Iberian narratives. Starkie 'stages' a verbal arabesque that mimics his virtuoso 'fiddling' near cafés or at street corners. His *Raggle-Taggle* persona improvises with whatever cultural shards are available, a pragmatic jotting down 'in spare moments' using 'odd scraps of paper'.[132] This admission chimes with Borrow's Preface to *The Zincali*, a similarly scrappy undertaking, stitched together (or embroidered) 'under very peculiar circumstances [. . .] *in moments* snatched from more important pursuits' (my emphasis).[133]

Appended to *Raggle-Taggle* is 'The Library of a Gypsy Lover: A Short Bibliography of Initiation'. Here Starkie's narrator describes how at school 'in England Borrow educated my vagabond personality, but the lesson he taught me was one of revolt against fifth-form classics and Eton jackets. Borrow appealed to the Irish in me.'[134] Perhaps recalling this same passage, Horace Horsnell, in a 1934 *Observer* review, presents Starkie as a Sancho Panza loyally serving Borrow's Don Quixote half a century after the knight-errant's demise.[135] Horsnell's notion is borne out by Starkie's admiring 'Wanderer's Library', the Appendix to *Spanish Raggle-Taggle* (1934). Here he acclaims *The Bible in Spain*, along with Borrow's ally Richard Ford's *Gatherings* and Gautier's *Voyage en Espagne*, as 'three books' which never 'grow old'. Such texts 'linger in the traveller's mind as a fragrant memory':

> *The Bible in Spain* still makes the greatest appeal to the true wanderer, who longs for hardship, provided that he can meet with adventure at every turn of the road. Anybody with pretensions to be a Romany rye will cast away all other books and pack George Borrow in his rucksack.[136]

As witty as the 'Sancho Panza' trope might be – and Starkie himself was emphatic regarding Borrow's status as a pioneer, 'ahead of his generation'[137] – the truth is rather more complicated. Starkie's travelogues

132. Starkie, 'Preface', *Raggle-Taggle*, xviii.
133. Borrow, 'Preface', *The Zincali*, vii.
134. Starkie, *Raggle-Taggle*, 326.
135. Horace Horsnell, 'A Spanish Adventure: Review of *Spanish Raggle-Taggle*', *The Observer* (4 November 1934): 8: Starkie 'comes, one might say, of such stock as produced Don Quixote and Sancho Panza, Laurence Sterne, George Borrow and – Paganini'.
136. Walter Starkie, *Spanish Raggle-Taggle, Adventures with a Fiddle in North Spain* (London: John Murray, 1934), 469.
137. See Francis Hindes Groome, *Gypsy Folk Tales*, Walter Starkie, foreword (London: Herbert Jenkins, 1963), 1.

and erudite contributions to the *Journal of the Gypsy Lore Society* in the decades after World War II also critically inspect Borrow's portrayal of nomadic subcultures.[138] Starkie achieves this on a formal level. The frontiers that previously separated traditional disciplines, literary codes, and genres – as well as nation-states and ethnic clusters – have been scrambled by the calamitous impact of two world wars. Starkie's bricoleurs or tinker(er)s, from *Raggle-Taggle* to the more historically oriented *The Road to Santiago* (1957), are not merely Edwardian summer vacation vagabonds who carry copies of *Lavengro* in their rucksacks. Starkie tries to empathise with those unhoused, internally displaced, or 'lonely pilgrims' who 'make the long journey guided solely by the myriads of wandering souls in the star-dust of the Milky Way'.[139] We are never made to forget that the patchwork 'threads' worn by these persecuted, needy, and 'wandering souls' – and Starkie's textual *fabric* with its jumble of intertextual resonances – mirror a south-western and central Europe repeatedly buffeted, falling into 'ruins', a 'waste country' strewn with postwar 'junk' and 'various miscellaneous objects'. This lends the narrator's fraught reaction to exiles, misfits, 'waifs and strays of humanity' an especial pungency (in every sense of the word).[140] For example, in Chapter IV of *Raggle-Taggle*, 'On the Road towards Budapest: Vagabonds and Vampires', Starkie documents the less than gracious treatment meted out to him by the 'sinister-looking' occupants of 'a few Gypsy tents' near the village of Tácz. In this chapter is a very different conception of the Magyars from that found in Starkie's 1937 article 'Hungarian Gypsy Fiddlers', which situates these people as 'the deftest flatterers on earth'.[141] The passage that follows provides ironic commentary on Borrow's remark in *Romano Lavo-Lil* (1874), one which Starkie repeats in *The Road to Santiago* (1957): "'Tis no use to go seeking after Gypsies. When you want to see them 'tis impossible to find one of them; but when you are thinking of other matters' you see 'plenty of them'.[142] In *Raggle-Taggle*, Starkie's uneasy narrator not only sees 'plenty': he is set upon and engulfed by a mob. Their behaviour unravels the taxonomy upon which his relatively privileged upbringing is founded: the hygienically structured versus the greasy, soiled, and unpalatable. He is alert to a deeper disturbance here. The manifold registers of brute force, physical and symbolic, to which 'the Gypsy' has been exposed across time are now

138. Walter Starkie, *Sara's Tents*, 57–8.
139. Starkie, *The Road to Santiago: Pilgrims of St James*, 63.
140. Starkie, *Raggle-Taggle*, 168, 298.
141. Walter Starkie, 'I. – Hungarian Gypsy Fiddlers', *Journal of the Gypsy Lore Society* 16:3 (1937): 98.
142. Walter Starkie, *The Road to Santiago: Pilgrims of St James*, 147–8.

suddenly turned on him, the 'prey'. The passage accentuates the appalling contrast between his sensory experience – trapped in an outlandish intimacy, literally shaken up and manhandled, devoured as a 'luscious object' – and the Borrovian ideal of the white male sovereign citizen who radiates a type of extroverted showmanship, who eagerly signs up for surprise on foreign paths, courts peril beyond insurance, while retaining his implacable self-belief and sway over the Romani other:

> As soon as I appeared there was a shout and from all sides there gathered a host of naked children, naked-breasted women, dogs, and villainous men. They did not understand the words of Romani I fired at them, but they thought that I was a luscious object to prey upon and they felt me all over, thrust their hands into my pockets, pushed me about and acted generally like a pack of mangy dogs smelling a juicy bone. I felt helpless. All the Borrow [. . .] I had read was of no use to me. [. . .] In George Borrow's adventures with Gypsies he was always the Romano rai and the noble patron who looked on the Gypsy with benevolent tolerance. He was always able to answer the Gypsy back in his own lingo and meet blow with blow and insult with insult.[143]

The phrasing 'there was a shout and from all sides', recalls *Lavengro*'s fifth chapter, in which the callow protagonist stumbles upon the camp of a Romani couple. In Borrow's scene of unauthorised trespass, 'the man looked up, and perceiving me, uttered a strange kind of cry, and the next moment both the woman and himself were on their feet and rushing out upon me' (*LSGP* V: 46). In *Lavengro*, the 'rushing' and seemingly enraged woman – 'her skin dark and swarthy, like that of a toad', 'her bosom [. . .] half concealed by a slight bodice' (*LSGP* V: 46) – becomes in Starkie's text an encounter imbued with menacing jeopardies and indecent exposures, such as a feral 'host' of 'naked-breasted women'. These 'women' perhaps remind him of something that once was familiar but has now gone – the tribes of hunter-gatherers scouring the earth for the next 'juicy bone'. His description – welding morbid fascination with visceral revulsion – of jostling, malodorous and ravening 'men' compels him to revise his earlier Borrovian whimsies of proud Romani resisters, with the regal 'Isopel Berners [towering] over all the heroines of the nineteenth century'.[144] The difference between the Petulengro clan depicted in his much-thumbed copy of *Lavengro* and

143. Starkie, *Raggle-Taggle*, 28–9; see also Barrett, 'A Scholar and Gypsy about Gypsy Borrow', 89–105.
144. Starkie, *Raggle-Taggle*, 326.

the grisly palpable actualities of this horde ('I could feel on my neck the soft flutter of countless bugs and lice that had forsaken the verminous [. . .] rags') makes him glad he is travelling solo: 'Suppose some friends had accompanied me on the quest of the raggle-taggle Gypsies and expected me to play the modern George Borrow'.[145] The discomfiting proportions of this assault on the senses – nauseating 'stench of their grimy bodies' – clashes with how reading Borrow's volumes lingers in a traveller's mind as a 'fragrant memory' (Starkie, *Spanish Raggle-Taggle*). This passage reveals Starkie's struggles to purge malign contemporary figurations of the '"Dirty" Gypsy', as the 1912 *Folk-Lore Gazette* put it: the Romani 'leper who never washes', a 'natural enemy of man, that is, *normal man*' (my emphasis).[146] Such imagery demonstrates, for Dominique Laporte, how 'civilisation despises odour and will oust it with increased ferocity as power strives to close the gap between itself and divine purity'.[147] Starkie's account is so arresting because it confirms Laporte's thesis of stench as 'the antinomy of order'; it delivers an olfactory shock to how Starkie's naïve narrator imagines entering the fray of the unknown, the 'life of *unwashed* freedom' (my emphasis) as a series of episodic jaunts. 'I have always found that smells are the leading motives' of nomadic trekking, he opines. Tangier, in *Don Gypsy*, for example, is a 'loud symphony of smells'.[148] The narrator's sceptical father-in-law, meanwhile, 'preferred to read of Gypsies in the literature of the mid-nineteenth century, but not to frequent and especially *not to smell them*' (my emphasis).[149]

Starkie could have staged this meeting in a more obviously slapstick manner, exploiting the comic possibilities of that 'mad inconsequential attitude towards life of the North Europeans who have always been incorrigible nomads'. There is, of course, an impish wit in how he measures his rattled, clumsy, and besieged *Gorgio* persona against the 'champion of the roads' Borrow, who is unflappable in the face of potentially fraught road-experiences that arrive unbidden. In the crisis of masculinity which besets Starkie's narrator, he becomes painfully conscious of his glaring deficiencies as a picaresque protagonist: 'If I had only been a boxer or wrestler, instead of a flabby-muscled musician'. He cannot help but compare his own physical frailties and helpless dread with the obstinately adventurous Borrow, 'a giant', a 'romantic hero'. When

145. Starkie, *Raggle-Taggle*, 28–9.
146. 'Editorial', *The Romantisshels' Didakais' and Folk-Lore Gazette* 1:2 (1912): 35.
147. Dominique Laporte, *The History of Shit* (Cambridge, MA: MIT Press, 2000), 83–4.
148. Starkie, *Don Gypsy*, 23.
149. Starkie, *Raggle-Taggle*, 7–8.

Borrow 'wandered' among itinerant tribes 'he described his exploits as feats of Gargantuan prowess', defiant courage and bullying power.[150] That this *Raggle-Taggle* episode unfolds in a more unsettling fashion shows how things can become precarious when one ushers meetings with the strange or alien – abjuring the familiar ways in which boundaries are patrolled 'in this humdrum world'.[151] Starkie also implies how the 'villainous men' operate according to tribal codes that have little in common with *Raggle-Taggle*'s early definition of the Hungarian term *mulatni* (to revel with gypsies so that 'all the cares of the world fall away from us').[152] These 'villainous' Hungarian Romani cannot be framed as hedonistic, glamorous outcasts or unspoiled peasantry, 'beloved' of artists' like D. H. Lawrence, 'and all those who seek for romance and mystery' overseas. The 'boisterous, animal spirits'[153] that Starkie's narrator locates in 'Gypsy girls' from Transylvanian towns like Huedin is here atavistic and animalistic. Fiercely protective of their time-honoured rites, the so-called 'villainous men' refuse to kowtow or 'assimilate' to dominant systems of thought and behaviour.[154] As this scene indicates, the abject, 'from its place of banishment [. . .] does not stop challenging its master'.[155] There is little hope that among this 'pack' Starkie's narrator will find what Borrow unearthed in the 'dialect, or jergo' (*WW* XXIV: 109) of despised outlaw tribes: the precious 'ruins' of European cultures widely scattered across time and space (ancient Greco-Roman lore, Charlemagne's Europe, Slavic, and Iberian mores). Here the 'pack' is typified by a defiant silence; apart from a 'shout', they 'did not understand the words of Romani I fired at them'. Rather than extend the hand of friendship to prying interlopers, this group 'thrust their *hands* into my pockets' and 'pushed me about'. In *Raggle-Taggle*'s unsparing account of the narrator's unhappy dealings with Hungarian gypsies, 'villainous men' seem to be 'lower' on the evolutionary scale than 'dogs' by virtue of their position in the sentence. Such derogatory lexis – hardly the 'absence of prejudice' or 'insular preconception'[156] that critic Horace Horsnell praised in these travelogues – is echoed later by the clergyman (Chapter XXVIII). He reviles gypsies as 'mangy, unclean dogs',

150. Starkie, *Raggle-Taggle*, 7, 28–9.
151. Walter Starkie, *Spanish Raggle-Taggle: Adventures with a Fiddle in North Spain* (London: John Murray, 1934), 124.
152. Starkie, *Raggle-Taggle*, 18.
153. Starkie, *Raggle-Taggle*, 160.
154. Starkie, *Raggle-Taggle*, 66.
155. Julia Kristeva, *The Powers of Horror* (New York: Columbia University Press, 1982), 2.
156. Horace Horsnell, 'A Spanish Adventure: Review of *Spanish Raggle-Taggle*', *The Observer* (4 November 1934): 8.

signifying a rapacious pack rather than a complex kinship network with venerable language and lore.

Starkie's narrative strategies are thrown into sharper relief when read alongside his later 1953 text *In Sara's Tents.* This travelogue probes the dimensions and cultural impact of Borrow's authorial self-placement as a boundlessly energetic trekker and student of picaresque fiction such as Jeronimo de Alcala's *Alonso de Muchos* (*Alonso of Many Masters*).[157] In contrast to Borrow's *Lavengro, In Sara's Tents* refines a less obviously 'virile' persona – that of 'the *juglar*', an itinerant songster, mime, or buffoon situated outside the social world and often remunerated in castoff clothing. The term *juglar,* Starkie's narrator explains, 'meant anyone whose profession it was to perform before an audience'. He 'was not necessarily a musician': he might be a 'hurdy-gurdy player' who regaled folk at inns, bathhouses, or weddings. If 'the troubadours were "high-brows", the *juglares* were certainly "low-brows"'.[158] The passage from *Raggle-Taggle* in which Starkie's narrator is assailed by wolfish Hungarian Romani suddenly makes more sense. As Starkie reminds us in a foreword to the 1963 reissue of Francis Hindes Groome's *Gypsy Folk Tales*, Borrow's narrator 'loved to pose and dramatize himself' as a troubadour.[159] Starkie's narrators, on the other hand, are embattled, relatively uncharismatic, and easily alarmed *juglares.* Starkie's 'lowbrow' song-and-dance man is not just exposed to the lawless caprice of an inimical crowd: he is reduced to the level of a 'juicy bone'.

That Starkie's sustained critical engagement with Borrow's oeuvre is more layered than idealising admiration or 'hero worship' is apparent in his introduction to the 1960s Everyman reissue of *Lavengro.* Starkie construes his literary precursor's mock memoir as a path-clearing endeavour. Borrow's achievement is to carve space for an off-kilter kind of text, an autobiografiction, one that queries the separation of knowledge into silos or categories.

> [Borrow] nerved himself to the task of creating a special *genre* of his own, an amalgam of autobiography, novel, poem, and tract which would draw together all the strands of his complex existence into one work of art, and still permit him to maintain his own Gypsy independence and roam through the world on his own secret errand.[160]

157. See Walter Starkie, *In Sara's Tents* (London: John Murray, 1953), 55.
158. Walter Starkie, *In Sara's Tents* (London: John Murray, 1953), 86–7.
159. Francis Hindes Groome, *Gypsy Folk Tales*, Walter Starkie, foreword (London: Herbert Jenkins, 1963), 1.
160. Starkie, 'Introduction', *Lavengro*, xi.

Here 'errand' suggests Borrow's 'errancy'. The latter term, in its original Latin form, carries a twofold resonance: to meander and to be incorrect or fallible, while the ancient Indo-European root word, *er*, signifies 'to go/move'. A 'historical tension', as Eluned Summers-Bremner remarks, is 'at the heart of errancy, between a freer, more general action of wandering without fixed direction and the later sense of the verb', denoting 'a "specific aberration" from a path'.[161] The invigorating complexity of *Lavengro*, for Starkie, resides in how it upholds that freer activity in its hybrid, apparently piecemeal textual design. It is, Starkie implies, the taking of wrong turns and the committed embrace of lostness that brings to light a route to the possibilities of new insights. Errancy leads to those unanticipated meetings, nimble improvisations, and happy accidents that prove so enriching, even transformative to Borrow's protagonist. Starkie's lexis ('special *genre*') also returns us to how Walter Benjamin's *Illuminations* traces important vistas for thinking about technically pioneering texts that 'transcend the norm' ('all great works found a genre or dissolve one – that they are, in other words, special cases').[162] It is the 'task' of future generations of readers, Starkie concludes, to pay forensic attention to the topographical and discursive errancies that make Borrow a special case.

161. Summers-Bremner, *Astray*, 17.
162. Walter Benjamin, 'The Image of Proust', *Illuminations*, trans. Harry Zohn (New York: Schocken Books, 2007), 201.

AFTERWORD: A GENRE OF HIS OWN?

For New Zealand author Janet Frame, in Volume I of her autobiography *To the Is-land* (1982), Borrow's *Lavengro* – 'the first book I had ever bought' – awakens sentiments, memories, and local attachments that will soon be 'buried' irreversibly beneath the rubble of a global conflict:

> I went to Jeffrey and Smith's and asked for my chosen book, *Lavengro* [. . .] because it combined many of my interests. Old Meg the gypsy, the Scholar Gipsy, it contained also the passage that I'd read often in our schoolbooks and that I longed to possess, to read again and again, especially now in 1939 in the midst of war: the passage [. . .] ending [. . .] 'There's sun, moon and stars, brother, all sweet things, there's likewise a wind on the heath. Who would wish to die?'[1]

The 'passage' that she recalls here was featured in countless British and Australasian schoolroom anthologies of nature writing at least until the early 1950s.[2] In some respects, Frame's plangent recollection evokes the motif of the 'snobbish Borrovians' at the start of this book – Edwardian cultists who cover our rural past in a glaze of false nostalgia according to Lewis's *BLAST I*. The year in which Frame's *To the Is-Land* appeared, 1982, was a vital one for experts of Borrow's oeuvre. Two intellectual biographies – David Williams's *A World of his Own: The Double Life of George Borrow* (1982) and Michael Collie's more exhaustive *George Borrow: Eccentric* (1982) – were published by prestigious academic presses. Both titles, released soon after the centenary of Borrow's death, aimed to stir renewed academic fascination with 'England's own Kerouac'.[3] In the eyes of some contemporary broadsheet reviewers, these volumes only succeeded in converting an unheeded author-traveller into a

1. Janet Frame, *To the Is-Land: An Autobiography* (New York: George Braziller, 1982), 223.
2. [Anon.], 'George Borrow: His Association with Ireland: To-Day's Anniversary', *Dublin Daily Express* (5 July 1913): 10.
3. Eric Korn, 'Shelf-travelling', *Times Literary Supplement* 4869 (2 July 1996): 36.

biographical curiosity. The poet Andrew Motion, in his *TLS* report on the 1981 Cheltenham Literature Festival, posed a question that also reverberates through Michael Collie's volume: why is it that the author of *Lavengro* and *The Romany Rye* has not secured a more conspicuous seat on the English 'rural bandwagon':

> Sometimes it is hard not to feel that the rural revivals of our own day have been made with an eye less to compatibility than to consolation. The recent and genuinely literary interest in the work of writers like Edward Thomas, Richard Jefferies and W.H. Hudson has been accompanied by a good deal of longing for their supposedly better days.
>
> [Given] the centenary of George Borrow's death, [. . .] there is good reason for celebrating him. But it is surprising that he has not found a more prominent place on the rural bandwagon before now. Much of his writing exhibits traces of the semi-mystical communion with nature which is fashionable these days, he was the subject of a biography by Edward Thomas.[4]

Motion's piece suggests, perhaps inadvertently, why Borrow was not swept up in the fad for 'rural revivals'. Unlike Jefferies, Hudson, and Thomas, Borrow is not strictly speaking a 'regional writer' who embraces Thomas Hardy's dictum, voiced in old age, that a novelist should know a 'little bit of the world remarkably well'.[5] Borrow drifts through regions and nation-states in a manner that indicates a geographically and stylistically borderless artist – one who has 'gone rogue'. There is, in the Borrow canon, no text which does for, say, East Anglia what Jefferies's spiritual autobiography *The Story of My Heart* (1883) does for Wiltshire – declaring deep, 'semi-mystical' ties to one's natal county. So without that 'prominent place' on the 'rural bandwagon', Borrow remains, as the September 1958 *TLS* bluntly put it, a 'freak', 'outside the stream of general development though highly contagious to the susceptible few'.[6] This is a pity given the burgeoning of scholarly interest in what Jason Cowley designated in 2008 as the 'lyrical pastoral tradition of the romantic wanderer', who reacts to species of spaces in more formally 'heterodox and experimental ways'.[7] A striking example is Paul

4. Andrew Motion, 'A Ramble with Borrow: George Borrow a Centenary Lecture, Cheltenham Festival of Literature', *Times Literary Supplement* (30 October 1981): 1266.
5. Quoted in Robin Hardy, 'Walking in Hardy Country', *New York Times* (10 June 1990): 8.
6. S. Norman, 'Vagabond and Polyglot', *Times Literary Supplement* (19 September 1958): 530.
7. Jason Cowley, *Granta 102: The New Nature Writing* (London, 2008), 10.

Farley's and Michael Symmons Roberts's *Edgelands: Journeys into England's True Wilderness* (2012). Such texts should have made Borrow and the chronicler of rural crafts and affairs George Sturt (1863–1927) – the latter sought to perfect 'a new art', 'proper to unrecorded and intangible beauties of the commonplace' – ripe for reappraisal.[8] Like Sturt, Borrow 'could draw more poetry from a wide-spreading marsh with its straggling rushes than from the most beautiful scenery'.[9] Sturt's tribute to his 'Uncle Jack' (10 June 1914) – 'His talk something like George Borrow's writing, but without Borrow's sourness'[10] – hints at the latter's fascination, especially pronounced in *Wild Wales*, with a textualised orality anchored in the spoken argot of the island nation and beyond.

It may be overstating the case to claim that there is still, among the global Victorian Studies community – departmental research centres, official networking clusters, and learned societies – a radio silence regarding Borrow. He features occasionally in a journal article or as a case study in essay collections such as *Victorian Fiction Beyond the Canon* (2016). However, we need to revisit and update the scholarly lexicon associated with Douglas Mao's and Rebecca Walkowitz's 2006 volume *Bad Modernisms*, whose contributors variously 'con/test' what and when we think 'Modernity', or 'Victorianism', to be. Mao and Walkowitz motivate us to undermine once clear distinctions between highbrow and popular art; to critique and scramble 'canons'; and to parse narratives by Borrow and those he inspired 'with fresh eyes and ears'. Borrow embodies, in Mao's phrasing, a 'troublesome', stubbornly strange, even 'bad' Victorian. His books indulge in creative and critical disruption, reordering the terms by which we tend to theorise mid-nineteenth-century fiction.[11] Troublesome also because his texts are 'marred and scarred and seamed [. . .] by passion and by prejudice', with narrators who play fast and loose with important 'dates and names'.[12] Borrow seems 'both a Celt and an East Anglian, flecked with Irish, Welsh and Gypsy traits' and was 'to a baffling degree made up of contradiction'.[13]

8. George Sturt, *The Journals of George Sturt, 1890–1927*, E. D. Mackerness, ed., 2 vols (Cambridge: Cambridge University Press, 1967), II, 335.
9. A. Egmont Hake, 'Recollections of George Borrow', *The Athenaeum* 2807 (13 August 1881): 209.
10. George Sturt, *The Journals of George Sturt, 1890–1927*, E. D. Mackerness, ed., 2 vols (Cambridge: Cambridge University Press, 1967), II, 698.
11. Douglas Mao and Rebecca Walkowitz, 'The New Modernist Studies', *PMLA* 123:3 (2008): 737–48.
12. [Augustine Birrell], 'George Borrow and His Works', *Quarterly Review* 189 (January/April 1899): 491; [Anon.] 'George Borrow', *London Evening Standard* (13 March 1899): 4.
13. Norman, 'Vagabond and Polyglot', *Times Literary Supplement* (19 September 1958): 530.

Nowhere is this contradiction more apparent than in his political affiliations (or lack thereof). In *The Bible in Spain*, the narrator refutes suggestions that he is 'of any political party or system' (*BIS* XIV: 204). It is true that labels such as 'Tory', 'Whig', or 'Radical' are often woefully inadequate when gauging his highly individualistic perceptions. His literary enterprise is propelled by a wider conception of 'Gypsy politics' (*BIS* XIV: 204) as the science of freedom. Borrow delineates how communities organise themselves in relation to other social models and ideologies. However, in the eyes of many early Anglo-American reviewers of *Lavengro*, Borrow's complex and evolving politics were of a piece with his general reluctance to play nicely or, as George Hyde remarks, to 'settle down into respectable Victorianism, either as a way of writing or as a way of life'.[14]

Hyde's wording alerts us to how Borrow's wandering fictions continually 'take liberties' (*LSGP* XXXVI: 215). *Lavengro* is not gesturing at a woolly political abstraction here. 'Liberties' are habits, privileges, and attitudes as well as enclosures, shortfalls, and exclusions. It encompasses the legal rights, liberty of movement, and vocational dignity that travelling clusters were, and are, routinely denied in territories that nevertheless trumpet the glories of free trade and market liberalism. 'Liberties' also signals bodily autonomy in the private and public domains – and, of course, the hermeneutic freedoms and incisive close readings that Borrow's texts warrant. As early as 1843, Richard Ford, in his glowing reaction to *The Bible in Spain* for the *Edinburgh Review*, pinpointed Borrow's incremental grasp of textual form: 'the single threads by which each particular is tied, are drawn up one after another, until, thickening into a rope, they raise a whole existence from the deep wells of memory'.[15] From these 'wells of memory' emerge notions of linguistic slippage, mis/translation, and going off-message. In *Lavengro* and *The-Romany Rye*, the narrator who documents palpable localities and landmarks is also obsessed by experiential subjectivity, fleeting moods, and uncanny interactions that 'spirit his reader at once away from mere reality'.[16] This in turn makes Borrow's mock memoirs, with their 'touches of the marvellous',[17] troublesome to place alongside the copious, mimetic descriptions of social worlds found in the 1850s fiction of Dickens, Elizabeth Gaskell, Anthony Trollope, and George Eliot.

14. Hyde, 'Why (Not) Read George Borrow', 35.
15. Humphrey S. Milford, ed., *Borrow: Selections* (Oxford: Clarendon Press, 1924), 19–26.
16. Humphrey S. Milford, 'Introduction', *Borrow: Selections. With Essays by Richard Ford, Leslie Stephen & George Saintsbury* (Oxford: Clarendon Press, 1924), 20.
17. [Anon.], 'Borrow's *Lavengro*', *Dublin University Magazine* 37:222 (June 1851): 711–20.

Borrow's portrayal of domestic, urban, and rustic enclaves reimagines the content, purpose, and affective parameters of mid-century British mimetic realism – broadly conceived as a generic expression of placid, unvarnished ordinariness.

If we are to kickstart a scholarly reappraisal of Borrow, one that lays bare fresh critical contexts in which his 'errant' narratives become rewardingly legible, then it will require something bolder than measuring his aesthetic against an 1850s Dickensian fictional template. One option is to interpret this troublesome, highly self-reflexive author's writings – and those of Borrow's most eloquent early biographer, Edward Thomas – as a harbinger of a class of unclassifiable book. This does not entail making overheated assertions about Borrow the puckish postmodernist innovator *avant la lettre*. Rather his representational strategies prompt comparison with that slippery, unsettled, and beguiling 'kind of writing' John Banville attributed to W. G. Sebald, 'another linguistic man from Norwich' whose 1995 text *The Rings of Saturn* charts an unnamed narrator's excursion, chiefly on foot, through the Borrow country of East Anglia.[18] Andrew Motion, in a 2007 *Guardian* review of Robert Macfarlane's *The Wild Places*, qualified Banville's estimation: 'in truth what felt new' in Sebald's intermedial narratives 'had as much to do with subtle adaptations of tradition as it did with pioneering a brand new kind of non-fiction'.[19] Motion contends that Borrovian mock memoirs and travelogues – from *The Bible in Spain* to Thomas's *The Icknield Way* (1913) – furnish an intriguing blueprint for Sebald's formally hybrid thought adventures. Motion's thesis is worth appraising, not least because *The Rings of Saturn* includes visits to 'the deserted estate of Boulge', where Borrow's friend and correspondent, Edward FitzGerald, 'grew up', as well as Dunwich, a 'place of pilgrimage' for Theodore Watts-Dunton, whose Minerva Library edition of *Lavengro* (1893) kept the name of 'the Great High Priest of the Ungenteel' alive at the fin de siècle.[20] In *Lavengro* and *The Romany Rye* – 'the all-time, all-comers' greatest road narrative [. . .] after the *Anabasis*', according to Eric Korn's 1996 *TLS* review[21] – Borrow's chronicle of exilic wandering,

18. John Banville, 'The Rubble Artist: Review of *Austerlitz*, trans. Anthea Bell', *The New Republic* (26 November 2001): 8; Miles Kington, 'Where does fiction begin and travel writing end?', *The Independent* (25 October 1999): 34–5.
19. Andrew Motion, 'Mapping Nature's Heartlands', *The Guardian* (25 August 2007): 16.
20. [Anon.], 'Literary and Art Gossip', *Leeds Mercury* (14 July 1884): 7; Sebald, *The Rings of Saturn*, 132, 142. For further discussion of the Sebald-Borrow link, see Phyllis Stanley, 'Borrow and his Family in Great Yarmouth: The George Borrow Society Weekend 12–14 May 2000', *George Borrow Bulletin* 20 (2000): 67–73; Dennis Burton, '*The Rings of Saturn* and George Borrow', *George Borrow Bulletin* 36 (Spring 2008): 63–71.
21. Eric Korn, 'Shelf-travelling', *Times Literary Supplement* 4869 (2 July 1996): 36.

traumatic loss, recovery, and remembrance is mediated through an intricate pattern of nested (and tall) tales. Similarly, in *The Rings of Saturn*, the narrator's search for an existential shelter becomes a framing device within which other cadences can be heard, if not always decoded.

In the second chapter of *The Rings of Saturn*, Sebald's narrator embarks on a trip 'to the coast in one of the old diesel trains' which 'ran from Norwich to Lowestoft at that time'. He visits a country house, Somerleyton Hall, then accessible to the paying public over the summer months. Tracing the myriad patrician families who had occupied the manor since the Middle Ages – the site is three miles north-east of Borrow's home estate at Oulton – Sebald's narrator identifies 1843 as a historical and cultural fault line. A brash railway contractor, who embodied in the eyes of the 1855 *Bentley's Miscellany*, an 'amount of wealth and an extent of influence that might stagger many a proud aristocrat', purchased the semi-derelict country castle.[22]

> In that year, Lord Sydney Godolphin Osborne [. . .] chose not to take up his inheritance and instead sold the entire property to Sir Morton Peto. Peto, who came of humble origins and who had worked his way up from bricklayer's labourer, was just thirty when he purchased Somerleyton, but was already among the foremost entrepreneurs and speculators of his time. [. . .] his financial interests in the railways being built in Canada, Australia, Africa, Argentina, Russia and Norway had made him a truly massive fortune in the shortest of times, so that he was now ready to crown his ascent into the highest social spheres by establishing a country residence.[23]

There are, to the best of my knowledge, no explicit references to Borrow's descriptive rambles through family, parish, national, and European history in the Sebald archives. This may be no surprise given that, by the time Sebald was publishing his major works, Borrow had 'sunk more or less into oblivion with the common reader'.[24] However, the portrayal of Sir Samuel Morton Peto (1809–1889) here, MP for Norwich between 1847 and 1854, places *The Rings of Saturn* in a fascinating intertextual relationship with *The Romany Rye*, a novel also engrossed by the modes in and through which personal and communal 'memory' is conveyed through 'the ages' (*RR* IX: 56). In Chapter VI of Borrow's

22. E. P. Rowsell, 'Samuel Morton Peto', *Bentley's Miscellany* 37 (January 1855): 186–90.
23. Sebald, *The Rings of Saturn*, 9.
24. George Hyde, 'Borrow and the Vanity of Dogmatising: *Lavengro* as Self-Portrait', *Cambridge Quarterly* 32:2 (2003): 161.

novel, the 'invention' of trains ('flying fiery vehicles') and 'the shoeing of England with iron' (*RR* VI: 45) will launch Peto and his associates into 'the highest social spheres', thus eroding the local legacies and cultural values that Borrow's narrator holds dear.[25] The Appendix to *The Romany Rye* decries Peto, who appears as the 'knavish millionaire' 'Mr. Flamson' (he is targeted no fewer than seven times in the addenda).[26] *The Romany Rye* measures the narrator's gracious 'gentlemanly' outlook against the swaggering pretension of Peto and his backers, who personify an excess of capital and a poverty of taste: 'cowardly miscreants, admirers of cowardly miscreants' (*RR* V: 281–2). Peto's development of the Lowestoft Railway and Harbour Company sliced through the middle of Borrow's cherished estate at Oulton Broad, just outside Lowestoft. This left Borrow, according to his 1899 biographer William Knapp, both 'inconsolable' and apoplectic at his flashy, free-spending neighbour.[27]

By the 1850s, Peto's Somerleyton estate had become, according to regional print outlets, a byword for lavish extravagance, especially after the abolition of the glass tax in 1845. Nothing signified Peto's vaulting ambition more than the mansion's majestic avenues and enormous winter gardens. A Renaissance-style cathedral of glass with an arched entrance, colonnaded corridors lined with sculptures, and collections of exotic plants, Peto's winter gardens embodied for the 1857 *Illustrated London News* a 'scene of enchantment' unmatched by anything of its type in England.[28] Sebald's reaction to Somerleyton contrasts Peto's 'palace' and its opulently fixtured spaces for public entertainment ('Not even Coleridge, in an opium dream, could have imagined a more magical scene for his Mongol overlord, Kubla Khan'), with its sorry condition in 1992:

> Somerleyton strikes the visitor of today no longer as an oriental palace in a fairy tale. The glass-covered walks and the palm house, whose lofty dome used once to light up the nights, were burnt out in 1913 after a gas explosion and subsequently demolished. The servants who kept all in good order, the butlers,

25. On Sebald, Borrow and the representation of Peto, see Dennis Burton, '*The Rings of Saturn* and George Borrow', *George Borrow Bulletin* 36 (Spring 2008): 63–71.
26. On how Peto is 'immortalised in *The Romany Rye*' as 'Mr. Flamson', see Herbert Jenkins, *The Life of George Borrow* (London: John Murray, 1912), 189; Adrian Vaughan, 'Samuel Morton Peto and his Impact on East Anglia', *George Borrow Bulletin* 10 (Autumn 1995): 47–50; Adrian Vaughan, *Samuel Morton Peto: A Victorian Entrepreneur* (Surrey: Ian Allan Publishing, 2009), 51–2.
27. William Knapp, *Life*, II, 52–3.
28. [Anon.], 'Somerleyton Hall', *Illustrated London News* (10 January 1857): 24; S. C. Hall, 'The Stately Homes of England', *The Art Journal* 11 (January 1872): 14.

> coachmen, chauffeurs, gardeners, cooks, sempstresses and chambermaids, have long since gone. The suites of rooms now make a somewhat disused, dispirited impression. The velvet curtains and crimson blinds are faded, the settees and armchairs sag, the stairways and corridors which the guided tour takes one through are full of bygone paraphernalia.[29]

Like Borrow before him – for example, his depiction of Pengwern Hall as a storehouse of social and religious history in *Wild Wales* (*WW* IX: 48) – the Sebaldian narrator is attuned to local landmarks as repositories of affect. His imaginative excavations uncover structures that are crusted with myriad ancestral signatures. Somerleyton is a survival of time; what has been passed on through generations since 'the Middle Ages' is not just tangible ('bygone paraphernalia') but is felt as a subliminal heritage. However, surveying the faded décor in the 1990s makes only a 'dispirited impression'. The lexis implies a 'de-spirited' venue whose furnishings are tenuous holdovers rather than physical heirlooms, no longer brushed by ghostly fingertips. Sebald's narrator hopes that the 'velvet curtains' and 'crimson blinds' will be storied curios or legible records of an august past. He discovers instead vestiges bleached of 'fairy tale' associations and incapable of transferring the climate of a lost locality. The very *fabric* of former patrician grandeur – rare tapestries, valuable miniatures and embroideries, silver-and-gilt mirrors, dark oak panelling – implies an architectural palimpsest whose once 'oriental' characters are effaced altogether. To cite Thomas Hardy's poem 'The Revisitation', 'Time's transforming chisel' has been unforgiving here.

For the disaffected narrator of *The Romany Rye*, the erasure of ancestral memory is nothing less than egregious cultural vandalism. This indictment he lays at the door of the contractor 'highwayman' Peto/Flamson – a case study in the corrupting temptations of power. In Borrow's Appendix, the railway magnate emerges as a brazen parvenu who believes decorative excess is tantamount to the finest style ('Mr. Flamson flaming in his coach with a million'). However, Borrow's narrator, whose dinner table is amply stocked with homegrown fare, and committed to a literary vision of picturesque poverty where Romani poachers roam a pre-industrial East Anglia, is so blinded by rage that he cannot grasp how the 'upstart' Peto/Flamson had, in fact, lifted many famished Norwich labourers and their dependents 'out of poverty'. Wishing to be the face of a more enlightened and enterprising capitalism, Peto paid for public drinking fountains and ensured his

29. Sebald, *The Rings of Saturn*, 12.

employees' dwellings had piped, clean running water. Sebald's narrator provides a more muted, low-key, yet unmistakably trenchant, critique: 'How uninviting Somerleyton must have been, I reflected, in the days of the industrial impresario Morton Peto, MP, when everything, from the cellar to the attic, from the cutlery to the waterclosets, was brand new, matching in every detail, and in unremittingly good taste.'[30] Though the two authors depict Peto using very different rhetoric – Borrow resorts to angry harangue while Sebald is studiously undemonstrative, anti-dramatic, and wistful – they both scrutinise how the zeal for the 'brand new', epitomised by the 'industrial impresario' Peto/Flamson, destroys the accumulated *patina* of regional lore linked with a once handsomely appointed estate.

'If his events are frequently as odd as a dream, they are always as perfectly commonplace and real for the moment as the events of a dream are.' This observation is not culled from one of the many favourable early reviews of Sebald's *Rings of Saturn*. The words are those of eminent late Victorian scholar George Saintsbury. For him, *Lavengro* and *The Romany Rye* comprised a 'succession of dissolving views which grow clear and distinct for a time and then fade off into vagueness before once more appearing distinctly'.[31] What Saintsbury discerns here – a complex literary impressionism (which Sebald develops) receptive to the oneiric, the spectral, the barely glimpsed – makes Borrow appear a Janus-faced author. The gypsy-gentleman who gazes back at his eighteenth-century literary heroes, conjuring in *Lavengro* the 'spirit of De Foe' (*LSGP* III: 28), also points towards topographical and imaginative edgelands that have been more rigorously charted by Sebald and those contemporary anglophone psychogeographers he inspired. On this compelling facet of Borrow's artistic vision more work needs to be done.

30. Sebald, *The Rings of Saturn*, 12.

31. Humphrey S. Milford, 'Introduction', *Borrow: Selections. With Essays by Richard Ford, Leslie Stephen & George Saintsbury* (Oxford: Clarendon Press, 1924), 20.

SELECT BIBLIOGRAPHY

Primary Sources

Borrow, George. *The Bible in Spain.* London: John Murray, 1843.
—. *Celtic Bards, Chiefs and Kings.* London: John Murray, 1928.
—. *Lavengro: The Scholar, The Gypsy, The Priest.* London: John Murray, 1851.
—. *The Romany Rye.* London: John Murray, 1857.
—. *Romano Lavo-Lil. Word-Book of the Romany or, English Gypsy Language.* London: John Murray, 1905.
—. *Wild Wales, Its People, Language, and Scenery.* London: John Murray, 1862.
—. *The Zincali, an Account of the Gypsies of Spain.* London: John Murray, 1841.

Secondary Sources

Aaron, Jane. *Welsh Gothic.* Cardiff: University of Wales Press, 2013.
Acton, Thomas. *Gypsy Politics and Social Change.* London: Routledge & Kegan Paul, 1974.
[Anon.] 'George Borrow', *National Observer* 15:378 (18 April 1896): 667–9.
—. 'Review of *Lavengro*, by George Borrow', *The Athenaeum* (8 February 1851): 159–60.
—. 'Review of *Lavengro*, by George Borrow', *The Athenaeum* (15 February 1851): 188–90.
—. 'Review of *Lavengro*, by George Borrow', *Dublin University Magazine* 37 (1851): 711–20.
—. 'Review of *Lavengro*, by George Borrow', *Eclectic Review* NS 1 (April 1851), 438–48.
—. 'Review of *Lavengro*, by George Borrow', *Gentleman's Magazine* 190 (March 1851): 292–3.
—. 'Review of *Lavengro*, by George Borrow', *Literary Gazette* (8 February 1851): 107–9.

—. 'Review of *The Romany Rye*, by George Borrow', *The Athenaeum* (23 May 1857): 653–5.

—. 'Review of *The Romany Rye*, by George Borrow', *Saturday Review* (23 May 1857): 480–1.

Anderson, Amanda. *The Powers of Distance: Cosmopolitanism and the Cultivation of Detachment*. Princeton: Princeton University Press, 2001.

Armstrong, Martin. *George Borrow*. London: Arthur Baker Ltd, 1950.

Armstrong, Nancy. *Desire and Domestic Fiction*. Oxford: Oxford University Press, 1995.

—. *Fiction in the Age of Photography: The Legacy of British Realism*. Cambridge: Harvard University Press, 1999.

Baucom, Ian. *Out of Place: Englishness, Empire and the Locations of Modernity*. Princeton: Princeton University Press, 1999.

Behlmer, George. 'The Gypsy Problem in Victorian England', *Victorian Studies* 28 (1985): 231–55.

Beier, A.L. *Masterless Men: The Vagrancy Problem in England 1560–1640*. London: Methuen, 1985.

Blair, Kirstie. 'Gypsies and Lesbian Desire: Vita Sackville-West, Violet Trefusis, and Virginia Woolf', *Twentieth-Century Literature* 50:2 (Summer 2004): 141–66.

Bonaparte, Felicia. *The Gypsy-Bachelor of Manchester: The Life of Mrs. Gaskell's Demon*. Charlottesville: University of Virginia Press, 1992.

Bowen, C. M. 'George Borrow', *Westminster Review* 173:3 (March 1910): 286–304.

Boynton, H. W. 'George Borrow', *Atlantic Monthly* 93 (January 1904): 244–53.

Burton, Dennis. '*The Rings of Saturn* and George Borrow', *George Borrow Bulletin* 36 (Spring 2008): 63–71.

Burwick, Frederick. 'Reviews: *George Borrow: Eccentric* by Michael Collie, and *A World of His Own: The Double Life of George Borrow*, by David Williams', *Nineteenth-Century Fiction* 39 (September 1984): 211–17.

Byrne, Aidan. '"He will bid me cross the border": George Borrow's *Wild Wales*, O.M. Edwards's *Cartrefi Cymru* and the Imagined Nation', *Studies in Travel Writing* 18: 2 (2014): 148–159.

Champagne, Michele. *'This Wild Gypsy Dream': The Gypsy in the Nineteenth-Century British Imagination*. Unpublished PhD dissertation: University of Michigan, 2002.

Charnon-Deutsch, Lou. *The Spanish Gypsy: The History of a European Obsession*. University Park: Penn State University Press, 2004.

Cohen, William A., and Ryan Johnson, eds. *Filth*. Minneapolis: University of Minnesota Press, 2005.

Collie, Michael. *George Borrow: Eccentric*. Cambridge: Cambridge University Press, 1982.

—, and Angus Fraser, *George Borrow, A Bibliographical Study*. Winchester: St Paul's Bibliographies, 1984.

Colton, Arthur. 'George Borrow', *Atlantic Monthly* 147 (May 1931): 601–7.

Conan Doyle, Arthur. *Danger! And Other Stories*. London: John Murray, 1918.

Cressy, David. *Gypsies: An English History*. Oxford: Oxford University Press, 2018.

Dearden, Seton. *The Gypsy Gentleman: A Study of George Borrow*. London, 1939.

[Dilke, Charles W.], 'Reviews: *Lavengro*', *The Athenaeum* 1215 (8 February 1851): 159–60.

[Donne, William Bodham], '*Lavengro*', *Tait's Edinburgh Magazine* 18 (1851): 270–6.

Duncan, Ian. '*The Moonstone*, the Victorian Novel, and Imperialist Panic', *Modern Language Quarterly* 55 (September 1994): 297–30.

—. *Modern Romance and Transformations of the Novel: The Gothic, Scott, Dickens*. Cambridge: Cambridge University Press, 1992.

—. 'Wild England: George Borrow's Nomadology', *Victorian Studies* 41 (Spring 1998): 381–403.

Dutt, William A. 'George Borrow and East Anglia', *Good Words* (January 1897): 318–23.

Ebbatson, Roger. *An Imaginary England: Nation, Landscape and Literature, 1840–1920*. London: Routledge, 2005.

—. 'Henchard and George Borrow', *The Thomas Hardy Journal* 19:3 (2003): 82.

—. *Landscape and Literature 1830–1914: Nature, Text, Aura*. London: Palgrave Macmillan, 2013.

Egmont Hake, A. 'George Borrow', *Macmillan's Magazine* 45:265 (November 1881): 56–63.

Elam, Samuel Milton. *George Borrow*. New York: Alfred A. Knopf, 1929.

Eliot, George. *Middlemarch: A Study of Provincial Life*, edited by Rosemary Ashton. London: Penguin, 1994; repr. 2003.

Elton, Oliver. *A Survey of English Literature, 1830–1880*. 2 vols. London, 1920.

F. E. P. 'Catholics and Intolerance', *The Nation* (24 July 1913): 75–6.

[F.G.O.], 'George Borrow', *The Academy* 2072 (January 1912): 88–9.

Findlater, Jane H. 'George Borrow', *Cornhill Magazine* 7:41 (November 1899): 596–603.

Fonseca, Isabel. *Bury Me Standing: The Gypsies and Their Journey*. New York: Vintage, 1995.

Ford, Ford Madox. *Thus to Revisit: Some Reminiscences*. New York: E. P. Dutton, 1921.

[—]. 'Ford, Literary Portraits – X.: Mr. Clement Shorter and *Borrow and His Circle*', *Outlook* (London) 32 (November 1913): 677–8.

Fraser, Angus. *A Rum Lot. 100 Years of Gypsy Studies*, edited by Matt T. Salo, Cheverly, MD: Gypsy Lore Society, 1990.
—. 'George Borrow's Birthplace and "Gypsy" Ancestry', *Journal of the Gypsy Lore Society* 51 (1972): 60–81.
—. *George Borrow's Tours of Galloway and the Borders 1866*. Warborough: The Lavengro Press, 2015.
—. 'John Murray's Colonial and Home Library', *The Papers of the Bibliographical Society of America* 91:3 (September 1997): 339–408.
Fraser, Angus and Ann M. Ridler, eds. *George Borrow in Cornwall 1853–1854. Notebooks and Correspondence*. Warborough: The Lavengro Press, 2014.
Frechet, Rene. *George Borrow (1803–1881), vagabond, polyglotte, agent biblique, écrivain*. Paris: Didier, 1956.
Free, Melissa. '"Dirty Linen": Legacies of Empire in Wilkie Collins's *The Moonstone*', *Texas Studies in Literature and Language* 48:4 (Winter 2006): 340–71.
Garrett, James. 'The Unaccountable Knot of Wordsworth's Gipsies', *Studies in English Literature* 40 (Autumn 2000): 603–20.
Gorman, Herbert S. 'George Borrow: Friend of Tinkers and Gypsies.' Review of *The Works of George Borrow*. Clement Shorter, ed.', *New York Times Book Review* (23 December 1923): 15.
Hancock, Ian. *The Pariah Syndrome: An Account of Gypsy Slavery and Persecution*. Ann Arbor: Karoma Publishers, 1987.
—. 'Romani Origins and Romani Identity: A Reassessment of the Arguments', *The Romani Archives and Documentation Center*. http://www.radoc.net:8080/RADOC-9-IDENT-1.htm. 8 October 2007.
—. *We Are the Romani People*. Hertfordshire: University of Hertfordshire Press, 2002.
Haworth-Booth, D.C. 'George Borrow: To the Editor of *The Saturday Review*', *Saturday Review* 87:2269 (22 April 1899): 497.
Hearn, Lafcadio. *Some Strange English Literary Figures of the Eighteenth and Nineteenth Centuries*. 1927; rpt. Freeport, New York: Books for Libraries, 1965.
Herbert, Christopher. *Culture and Anomie: Ethnographic Imagination in the Nineteenth Century*. Chicago: University of Chicago Press, 1991.
Herbert, Lucille. 'George Borrow and the Forms of Self-Reflection', *University of Toronto Quarterly* 40 (Winter 1971): 152–67.
Hooper, James. 'George Borrow', *National Review* 26:155 (January 1896): 670–84.
Howsam, Leslie. *Cheap Bibles: Nineteenth-Century Publishing and the British and Foreign Bible Society*. Cambridge: Cambridge University Press, 1991.

Hoyland, John. *A Historical Survey of Customs, Habits, and Present State of the Gypsies*. London: York, 1816.

Hyde, George. 'Borrow and the Vanity of Dogmatising: *Lavengro* as Self-Portrait', *The Cambridge Quarterly* 32:2 (2003): 161–73.

—. 'Travelling Across Cultures: George Borrow's *Wild Wales*', *The Cambridge Quarterly* 33:4 (2004): 331–43.

Jenkins, Herbert. *The Life of George Borrow*. [1912]. London, 1924.

Jessop, A. '*Lavengro*', *The Athenaeum* (8 July 1893): 65–6.

Jones, D. A. N. 'Gentleman Travellers', *London Review of Books* 5:17 (September 1983): 4–8.

Jones, Dora M. 'George Borrow', *London Quarterly Review* 2:1 (July 1899): 18–33.

Keighren, Innes M., Charles W. J. Withers, and Bill Bell. *Travels into Print: Exploration, Writing, and Publishing with John Murray, 1773–1859*. Chicago and London: University of Chicago Press, 2015.

Keith, W. J. *The Rural Tradition: William Cobbett, Gilbert White, and other non-fiction prose writers of the English countryside*. Toronto: University of Toronto Press, 1975.

Kenrick, Donald. *Gypsies: From India to the Mediterranean*. Paris: Gypsy Research Centre, 1993.

Kerrigan, Colm. *George Borrow's Journey through Cork in 1815*. Warborough: The Lavengro Press, 2015.

Knapp, William I. *Life, Writings, and Correspondence of George Borrow. Based on Official and Other Authentic Sources*. 2 vols. London: John Murray, 1899.

Kramp, Michael. 'The Woman, the Gypsies, and England: Harriet Smith's National Role', *College Literature* 31:1 (Winter 2004): 147–68.

Laurie, Kedrun and Norrette Moore. *George Borrow's Illustrators Part 1*. Warborough: The Lavengro Press, 2018.

Leland, Charles G. *The Gypsies*. 1882. Boston: Houghton Mifflin, 1924.

Lewy, Guenter. *The Nazi Persecution of the Gypsies*. Oxford: Oxford University Press, 2000.

Mancini, Michelle Marie. 'The Pursuit of Gypsiness in Nineteenth-century Britain'. Unpublished PhD: Berkeley, University of California, 2000.

Matthews, Jodie. 'Borrowing Welshness: *Wild Wales*, Affiliation and Identity', *North American Journal of Welsh Studies* 6:1 (2011): 53–61.

—. *The Gypsy Woman: Representations in Literature and Visual Culture*. London: I. B. Tauris, 2018.

—. 'Reading the Victorian Gypsy', Unpublished PhD dissertation: Cardiff University, 2008.

Mayall, David. *English Gypsies and State Policies*. Hatfield: University of Hertfordshire Press, 1995.

—. *Gypsy Identities 1500–2000: From Egipcyans and Moon-men to the Ethnic Romani*. London: Routledge, 2004.
—. *Gypsy-Travellers in Nineteenth-Century Society*. Cambridge: Cambridge University Press, 1988.
Meyers, Robert M. *George Borrow*. New York: Twayne Publishers, 1966.
Milford, Humphrey S., ed. *Borrow: Selections*. Oxford: Oxford University Press, 1928.
More, Paul Elmer. 'George Borrow', *The Nation* (27 June 1912): 633–6.
Nord, Deborah Epstein. *Gypsies and the British Imagination: 1807–1930*. New York: Columbia University Press, 2006.
—. '"Marks of Race": Gypsy Figures and Eccentric Femininity in Nineteenth-century Women's Writing', *Victorian Studies* 41 (Winter 1998): 189–210.
Okely, Judith. *The Traveller-Gypsies*. Cambridge: Cambridge University Press, 1983; rpt. 1998.
Oram, William A. 'Arnold's 'Scholar-Gipsy' and the Crisis of the 1852 Poems', *Modern Language Quarterly* 45 (June 1984): 144–62.
Parks, Edd Winfield. 'Portrait of Lavengro: A Biographical Essay on George Borrow', *Segments of Southern Thought*. Athens: University of Georgia Press, 1938.
['Parson Frank'], 'Reviews – *Lavengro*', *People's and Howitt's Journal* 4:N. S. (1851): 144–5.
Peppis, Paul. *Literature, Politics and the English Avant Garde: Nation and Empire, 1901–1918*. Cambridge: Cambridge University Press, 2000.
Quennell, Peter. 'The Real and the Imaginary in *Lavengro*', *New Statesman and Nation* (15 November 1941), n. p.
Ragussis, Michael. *Figures of Conversion: The Jewish Question & English National Identity*. Durham: Duke University Press, 1995.
Ralli, Augustus. 'George Borrow', *Fortnightly Review* 98:586 (October 1915): 711–24.
Robertson, Ian. *George Borrow in Portugal and North-West Spain*. Warborough: The Lavengro Press, 2018.
Robinson, Alistair. *Vagrancy in the Victorian Age: Representing the Wandering Poor in Nineteenth-Century Literature and Culture*. Cambridge: Cambridge University Press, 2021.
Rose, Lionel. *Rogues and Vagabonds: Vagrant Underworld in Britain 1815–1985*. London: Routledge, 1988.
Saintsbury, George. *A History of Nineteenth-Century Literature (1780–1895)*. London: Macmillan, 1906.
—. *The Collected Essays and Papers of George Saintsbury 1875–1920*. 1923; rpt. Freeport, New York: Books for Libraries Press, 1969.

—. 'George Borrow', *Macmillan's Magazine* 53:315 (January 1886): 170–83.
Sampson, John. *The Wind on the Heath: A Gypsy Anthology.* London, 1930.
Saul, Nicholas. 'Half a Gypsy: The Case of Ezra Jennings in Wilkie Collins's *The Moonstone* (1868)', *The Role of the Romanies: Images and Counter-images of Gypsies/Romanies in European Culture*, Nicholas Saul and Susan Tebbutt, eds. Liverpool: Liverpool University Press, 2004.
Seccombe, Thomas. 'Encore Borrow', *The Bookman* 42:247 (April 1912): 27–30.
—. 'Introduction to Everyman's *Lavengro*', by George Borrow. 1906; rpt. London: E. P. Dutton and Company, 1948.
—. 'The Reader. George Borrow: His Homes and Haunts', *The Bookman* 21:125 (February 1902): 156–62.
—. 'The Reader. George Borrow', *The Bookman* 45:265 (October 1913): 16.
Shorter, Clement K. *George Borrow and His Circle.* London: Hodder and Stoughton, 1913.
—. *The Life of George Borrow.* New York: E. P. Dutton, 1928.
Smith, Jos. *The New Nature Writing: Rethinking the Literature of Place.* London: Bloomsbury Academic, 2017.
Southworth, Helen. '"That Subtle and Difficult Thing: A National Spirit": Ford, Anglo-Saxondom and the "Gorgeously English" George Borrow', *Ford Madox Ford's Literary Contacts.* International Ford Madox Ford Studies 6, edited by Paul Skinner. Amsterdam: Rodopi, 2007. 25–39.
—. 'Virginia Woolf's "Wild England": George Borrow, Autoethnography and *Between the Acts*', *Studies in the Novel* 39:2 (Summer 2007): 196–215.
[Stirling, William], '*Lavengro* – "The Master of Words"', *Fraser's Magazine* 43:255 (March 1851): 272–83.
Summers-Bremner, Eluned. *Astray: A History of Wandering.* London: Reaktion Books, 2023.
Thomas, Edward. *George Borrow: The Man and his Books.* London: Chapman & Hall, 1912.
—. *The Pocket George Borrow: Passages chosen from the Works of Borrow by E. Thomas.* London: Chatto & Windus, 1912.
Tilford, Jr, J. E. 'Contemporary Criticism of *Lavengro*: A Re-examination', *Studies in Philology* 41:3 (July 1944): 442–56.
—. 'The Critical Approach to *Lavengro-Romany Rye*', *Studies in Philology* 46 (January 1949): 79–96.
—. 'The Formal Artistry of *Lavengro-Romany Rye*', *PMLA* 64 (June 1949): 369–84.

Towns, Jeff, ed. *Edward Thomas and Wales*. Cardigan: Parthian, 2018.

Trumpener, Katie. 'The Time of the Gypsies', *Critical Inquiry* 18 (Summer 1992): 843–84.

Turner, John. 'Purity and Danger in D. H. Lawrence's *The Virgin and the Gypsy*', *D. H. Lawrence: Centenary Essays*, edited by Mara Kalnins. Bristol: Bristol Classical Press, 1986: 139–71.

Vaughan, Adrian. *Samuel Morton Peto: A Victorian Entrepreneur.* Surrey: Ian Allan Publishing, 2009.

Vesey-Fitzgerald, Brian. *Gypsies of Britain*. London: Chapman and Hall, 1944.

Von Kaenel-Flatt, Jessica. *The Heath and the Drawing-Room: The Representation of Borrow's Gypsies in 'Lavengro' and 'The Romany Rye'.* Warborough: The Lavengro Press, 2017.

Walling, R. A. J. *George Borrow: The Man and His Work.* London: Cassell, 1908.

Watts-Dunton, Theodore. 'In Defence of George Borrow', prefixed to *The Romany Rye*, by George Borrow. London: Ward and Lock, 1900.

Williams, David. *A World of His Own: The Double Life of George Borrow.* Oxford: Oxford University Press, 1982.

Wise, Thomas J. *A Bibliography of the Writings in Prose and Verse of George Henry Borrow.* London: Richard Clay & Sons, 1914.

Wolf, Donald Alan. 'The Scholar Gypsy: Borrow as Lavengro.' Unpublished PhD dissertation: Columbia University, 1961.

Index

EU Authorised Representative:
Easy Access System Europe Mustamäe tee 50, 10621 Tallinn, Estonia
gpsr.requests@easproject.com

Printed and bound by CPI Group (UK) Ltd, Croydon, CR0 4YY
07/10/2026
02229138-0006